DEMOCRACY

THE

UNFINISHED

JOURNEY

508 BC to AD 1993

EDITED BY

JOHN DUNN

OXFORD UNIVERSITY PRESS

OXFORD
UNIVERSITY PRESS

Great Clarendon Street, Oxford OX2 6DP

Oxford University Press is a department of the University of Oxford.
It furthers the University's objective of excellence in research, scholarship,
and education by publishing worldwide in

Oxford New York

Auckland Bangkok Buenos Aires Cape Town Chennai
Dar es Salaam Delhi Hong Kong Istanbul Karachi Kolkata
Kuala Lumpur Madrid Melbourne Mexico City Mumbai Nairobi
São Paulo Shanghai Taipei Tokyo Toronto

Oxford is a registered trade mark of Oxford University Press
in the UK and in certain other countries

Published in the United States
by Oxford University Press Inc., New York

© Oxford University Press 1992

First published 1992
First issued in paperback (with corrections) 1993
Reprinted 1994, 1995, 2000, 2001, 2002, 2004, 2005

British Library Cataloguing in Publication Data

Data available

Library of Congress Cataloging in Publication Data

Democracy: the unfinished journey, 508 BC to AD 1993
edited by John Dunn.
Includes bibliographical references.
1. Democracy—History.   I. Dunn, John, 1940- .
JC421.D4637 1992   321.8'09—dc20   92-8526

ISBN 0-19-827934-5

9 10

Printed in Great Britain by
Biddles Ltd, King's Lynn
www.biddles.co.uk

Preface

THIS is a book about the history and significance of an old but vigorous idea: that in human political communities it ought to be ordinary people (the adult citizens) and not extra-ordinary people who rule. This is not a very plausible description of how things are in the world in which we live. But it has become the reigning conception today across that world of how they ought to be. The idea itself is devastatingly obvious, but also tantalizingly strange and implausible. In this book we try to grasp both of these aspects, and to judge what the relation between the two really means for human beings today and in the future. We tell the story of its invention, suppression, propagation, and reinterpretation, showing how it has changed human societies at intervals throughout its history, and how the realities of these societies have in turn repeatedly changed it.

Two thousand five hundred years ago the small Greek city-state of Athens made a series of adjustments to its domestic political arrangements. The reforms of Kleisthenes were a severely local response to protracted local difficulties, not an attempt to implement a coherently thought-out general conception of the political and social good for human beings (or even just for Greeks). No contemporary of Kleisthenes could possibly have imagined that his reforms might pioneer a form of regime that would come to serve as a virtually unchallenged standard for political legitimacy for all the peoples of the world.

Democracy is a very simple idea: simple in its appeal and power, and simple, too, in its severe and ineliminable limitations. What we hope to do in this book is to describe and explain its extraordinary political career. To do so, we try first to convey what those initial democratic institutions of the Greek *polis* really were: how they came to be invented, how they worked, and how and why they changed over time. We explore how the Greeks came to understand their strengths and defects, and how these same strengths and defects, in turn, helped to shape the dynamism and insight of Greek thinking in many other fields—logic, ethics, psychology, political theory, epistemology, biology. We try, too, to assess why it should have proved politically so easy to crush this powerful and appealing idea a mere two centuries after its inception, and why the idea of democracy could be eliminated not just from the history of Greece itself, but from virtually any other civilized society for by far the greater part of the two thousand and more years that have followed. We consider why this thoroughly suppressed (and extensively vilified) political conception should nevertheless have resurfaced recurrently and in a wide variety of settings, and why in the last two and a half centuries it should have done so with increasing energy and peremptoriness. Above all, we try to grasp why its recent triumph should have been so sudden, and why, in some respects, it should now seem so overwhelming—so close to being complete. But we also attempt to capture why that overwhelming triumph should still in many ways appear so hollow, should somehow always turn out to be so devastatingly distant from the power, simplicity, and charm of the idea itself.

Seen over 2,500 years, the history of democracy has been intensely dramatic, by turns exhilarating and chilling. But viewed less exuberantly and more parochially, its keynote is above all its determined ordinariness, its will (and in some degree even its capacity) to domesticate the life of a human community, and to do so all the way through. The power and appeal of the idea come from its promise to render the life of a community something willed and chosen—to turn the social and political existences that human beings share into a texture of consciously intended common action. In a democracy, the people (the *demos*), its human members, decide what is to be done, and in so deciding they take their destiny firmly into their own hands. The power and appeal of democracy comes from the idea of autonomy—of choosing freely for oneself.

In the ancient Greek case, this simple idea can be taken as a reasonably accurate (if selective) description of the reality of political life. Most modern states, however inauthentically, take a far more expansive view of the membership of the *demos* than Athens did, dispensing with the institution of slavery and graciously incorporating, for example, the female gender. But in no modern state do its members, male or female, decide what is in fact done, or hold their destiny in their own hands. They do not, because they cannot.

In the forms in which it is practically relevant to us democracy is a far less simple idea; and it is also distinctly less appealing; less clear, less honest, and incomparably less seductive. But it has been this more practical and less engaging version of it, the representative democracy of the modern constitutional state, which has enjoyed such a sudden and striking recent triumph. The practical power of modern democratic institutions today comes from their very ordinariness, and especially from their peculiar aptness to the economic world in which we now live. (Once the flattering comparison with the socialist command economy has been decisively removed, this aptness is likely to come into increasingly painful question.) As in the past, the future prospects of these institutions will depend on many other facts. But if we are to understand the hazards and opportunities of modern democratic life, we still need to grasp the odd and paradoxical past of this simple idea, the sources of its continuing force, and the reasons for the sense of disappointment and distrust which has haunted it ever since it began. In the end, that disappointment and distrust is aimed at human freedom itself—at the formidable impediments to its realization, and the threats and dangers that it will always pose— dangers that can only be precluded by restricting it or removing it entirely. It is merely stupid not to regard the freedom of any human beings (very much including oneself) with some apprehension. But human communities have to act. In face of the obscure and extravagantly complicated challenges of the human future, our most urgent common need at present is to learn how to act together more effectively. An ingenuous attitude towards democracy is a discredit to any modern citizen. But a settled hostility towards it will always involve, under careful inspection, a substantial measure of ingenuousness towards some other human grouping, and one which will necessarily over time prove at least equally deserving of distrust. All action carries risks. But those risks are as nothing in comparison with the risk ensured by paralysis.

I should like to express my thanks to Eleni Cubitt for her kind initial prompting to undertake this book, to Michael Kustow for two invigorating and exacting conversations, to Ruth Muessig for her kind help at Yale, to Kim Scott Walwyn, Tim Barton, and others at Oxford University Press for much encouragement and efficiency throughout, and to the contributors for their forbearance.

J.D.

Yale University
December 1991

Contents

CONTENTS

Contributors

NEAL ASCHERSON was born in Edinburgh in 1932. He has worked as a journalist for—especially—the *Observer* and the *Scotsman*, and is now columnist on the *Independent on Sunday*. Most of his attention has been upon East-Central Europe, especially Poland and Germany, and upon Scotland. Among his books are *The Polish August* (1981), *The Struggles for Poland* (1987), and a collection of short pieces: *Games with Shadows* (1988).

JOHN DUNN is a Fellow of King's College, Cambridge, and Professor of Political Theory, University of Cambridge. His books include *Western Political Theory in the Face of the Future* (CUP, 1979), *Modern Revolutions* (CUP, 2nd edn.: 1989), *The Politics of Socialism* (CUP, 1984), *The Political Thought of John Locke* (CUP, 1969), *Locke* (OUP, 1984), *Political Obligation in its Historical Context* (CUP, 1980), and *Interpreting Political Responsibility* (Polity Press and Princeton UP, 1990).

CYNTHIA FARRAR has been a Research Fellow of Christ's College, Cambridge. She is now Project Director, Special Commission on Infant Health, at the New Haven Foundation. She is the author of *The Origins of Democratic Thinking* (CUP, 1988).

BIANCAMARIA FONTANA has been a Research Fellow of King's College, Cambridge, and a Jean Monnet Fellow at the European University Institute at San Domenico di Fiesole. She is now Professor of the History of Political Doctrines at the University of Lausanne. Her books include *Rethinking the Politics of Commercial Society: Political Economy and the Edinburgh Review* (CUP, 1985) and *Benjamin Constant and the Post-Revolutionary Mind* (Yale UP, 1991). She is the editor and translator of the first English edition of Constant's *Political Writings* (CUP, 1988).

NEIL HARDING is Professor and Head of the Department of Political Theory and Government at the University of Wales, Swansea. His books include *Lenin's Political Thought*, 2 vols. (Macmillan, 1977 and 1981), *Marxism in Russia* (CUP, 1983), and *The State in Socialist Society* (State University of New York Press, Albany, 1984).

SIMON HORNBLOWER is a Fellow of Oriel College, Oxford, and University Lecturer in Ancient History, University of Oxford. His books include *The Greek*

World, 479–323 BC (Routledge, rev. edn.: 1991), *Thucydides* (Duckworth, 1987), and *Commentary on Thucydides*, i. *Books I–III* (OUP, 1991).

SUNIL KHILNANI has been a Research Fellow of Christ's College, Cambridge. He is now Lecturer in Politics at Birkbeck College in the University of London. His book *The French Left: An Intellectual History, 1945–1989* will be published shortly by Yale University Press.

G. E. R. LLOYD is Master of Darwin College, Cambridge, and Professor of Ancient Philosophy and Science, University of Cambridge. His recent books include *Magic, Reason and Experience* (CUP, 1979), *The Revolutions of Wisdom* (University of California Press, 1987), *Demystifying Mentalities* (CUP, 1990), and *Methods and Problems in Greek Science* (CUP, 1991).

CHARLES S. MAIER is Krupp Foundation Professor of European Studies at Harvard University. He is the author of *Recasting Bourgeois Europe* (Princeton University Press, 1975), *The Unmasterable Past* (Harvard University Press, 1988), and *In Search of Stability* (CUP, 1987) and editor of *Changing Boundaries of the Political* (CUP, 1987).

SUSAN MENDUS is Senior Lecturer in Politics at the University of York. Her books include *Women in Western Political Philosophy* edited with Ellen Kennedy (Harvester, 1987), *Sexuality and Subordination: Interdisciplinary Studies of Gender in the Nineteenth Century*, edited with Jane Rendall (Routledge, 1989), and *Toleration and the Limits of Liberalism* (Macmillan, 1989).

QUENTIN SKINNER is a Fellow of Christ's College, Cambridge, and Professor of Political Science, University of Cambridge. His books include *The Foundations of Modern Political Thought*, 2 vols. (CUP, 1978), *Machiavelli* (OUP, 1981), and *Meaning and Context: Quentin Skinner and his Critics*, ed. James Tully (Polity Press and Princeton UP, 1988).

GORDON S. WOOD is University Professor of History, Brown University, Providence. He is the author of *The Creation of the American Republic, 1776–1787* (University of North Carolina Press, 1969) and *The Radicalism of the American Revolution* (Knopf, 1992).

DAVID WOOTTON holds the Lansdowne Chair in the Humanities and is Director of the Centre for the Humanities, University of Victoria, British Columbia. He is the author of *Paolo Sarpi: Between Renaissance and Enlightenment* (CUP, 1983) and editor of *Divine Right and Democracy* (Penguin, 1986), *Locke on Politics* (Penguin, 1992), and (with Michael Hunter) *Atheism from the Reformation to the Enlightenment* (OUP, 1991).

CHAPTER 1

Creation and Development of Democratic Institutions in Ancient Greece

SIMON HORNBLOWER

HISTORY

THE history of European democracy begins, arguably, not in Athens but in Sparta. This is a paradox because Sparta has usually been seen as the opposite of the 'Open Society' which Periclean Athens is taken, by a simplification, to represent. But youthful Sparta was different from the totalitarian monster she grew up to be. A constitutional document, whose date and interpretation are one of the fiercest battlegrounds of ancient Greek history, stipulates that a Spartan popular assembly should meet at regular intervals (Plutarch, *Life of Lycurgus*, ch. 6). Even on the most audaciously late of the possible datings—about 600 BC—this stipulation puts Sparta well ahead of Athens, where there was no provision for *regular* assembly meetings until the time of Kleisthenes in 508/507 BC. The same document appears to provide for some kind of *probouleutic* council, to chew things over before submitting them to a more general decision. This invention of *probouleusis* has been hailed as the 'Spartan contribution to government'; it certainly has implications for popular sovereignty, and such sovereignty may be explicitly asserted in one sentence of the document. Much is, however, obscure about early Sparta, whose precocious early political development was in any case blighted by social and economic factors which do not here concern us. So what really matters for us is Athens, where almost equally early political innovation was developed much further than in Sparta, and in an orderly and amazingly rapid sequence of reforms. What resulted was a system of participatory democracy which combined a complexity and sophistication of political detail on the one hand (including a very severe attitude to individual accountability), with the principle of almost total amateurism on the other, in a marriage which remains unprecedented to this day.

But before we move on to Athens, we should ask whether *European* and specifically Greek democracy really was the first democracy of all. The recent reaction against 'Hellenocentricity', 'privileging the Greeks', and so on, may be more than mere fashionable reaction against the European-mindedness (and anti-Semitism) of the past two centuries of classical scholarship: there are serious grounds (Bernal 1987, 1991) for giving the Phoenicians some of the credit traditionally given to the Greeks. The Phoenicians, in western Asia, had something comparable to the self-regulating city-state or *polis* of archaic and classical Greece. Since it is now agreed that the Greeks took their alphabet and their methods of colonization, perhaps even the city-state concept itself, from the Phoenicians, we should be similarly prepared for the possibility of Phoenician origins for some of the Greek political arrangements we most admire. Scientific study in this area has, however, hardly begun: as with the Spartans, we can do no more than mention the Phoenicians and move on.

Even if we concede priority to the Greeks, we still need to ask, without much hope of an answer, what was special about them. Why democracy *there*? One interesting approach (Sallares 1991: 181 ff.) is in terms of age-classes, that is, the system, familiar to anthropologists, whereby political privilege is strictly doled out according to age. Stratification of society on these lines is often military in origin, and the structure of the early Greek (and indeed Roman) state was essentially military and remained so. Early tyranny was the stage of political development which succeeded the hereditary aristocracies of early Greece. Tyranny sometimes happened when individuals, often young men of brilliant athletic or military prestige and so with (in their own view) a claim on privilege beyond the level to which their age restricted them, made good that claim by force. Once the idea spread that the age-class could be transcended in this or some other way, it was (the theory goes) a short move to the more general idea that privilege should be distributed without respect to age.

Other ancient societies, where privilege was allotted only to absolute rulers, or to aristocratic and priestly élites, had no weak point where the democratic 'thin end of the wedge' could be inserted. This is an attractive general theory; it would be positively compelling if there were evidence that age-classes were really crucial in Athens, the cradle of democracy. The 'why Greece?' question has to remain unanswered, except by unfashionable reference to national character.

The further question, 'why Athens?' is harder to answer with a theoretical formula. We need to look at the concrete realities of the early sixth-century Athens and Attica for which the first great European reformer, Solon, legislated in 594 BC. (Attica was the name of the territory surrounding Athens, but the *polis* of Athens comprised both Athens city and Attica.)

The precondition for the beginning of democracy at Athens was a kind of 'emancipation of the serfs'. About 600 BC the condition of the agricultural labouring population of Attica was dire. An arrangement, of disputed origins and antiquity, but possibly voluntary rather than representing a sort of involuntary debt, had long required 'the many' to hand over to 'the few' one-sixth of the produce of the land. This arrangement was peculiar to Athens. It had evidently been tolerable once; but it had recently ceased to be so, perhaps because of the disparities in wealth caused by the great new phenomenon of the eighth and seventh centuries: overseas colonization. Colonization put luxuries within the grasp of the 'few' and so helped to widen gaps in economic and social status. Literal enslavement could be a consequence of inability, in this harsher world, to pay your 'sixth part'. Solon 'freed the black earth', as his most famous poem puts it, by abolishing such slavery-producing 'loans' made on the security of the person.

This abolitionist act was called the 'shaking-off of burdens'; it is Solon's chief economic reform. Tidy-minded scholars tend to treat the economic reforms of Solon separately from the political. But the economic reform was basic to everything else: it produced the mentality of an exclusive 'citizen élite'. As democracy grew, so too would exclusiveness: the barriers to the acquisition of citizenship by outsiders were raised higher as the history of classical Athens went on.

How did this concept of a citizen élite come into being? To 'free the earth' is a metaphor. If we cash the metaphor and ask, what now happened to the free black earth (for instance, who now owned it?) the answer must be, the former payers of the sixth part now owned the land they had previously tilled for someone else. Solon, in fact, created an

3

Attica of smallholders. These men were not just a citizen élite but a self-confident military force which knew that the defence of the territory of Attica was on its shoulders. From the military point of view they were the 'hoplites' or heavy-armed soldiers: hoplite warfare was an innovation of the seventh century and implied a new degree of cohesive fighting. Indeed, one possible explanation of the Solonian 'economic' crisis is not economic at all, but has to do with self-respect and group solidarity. By Solon's time the hoplites may have felt that the payment of a sixth part was demeaning, even if the quantum handed over was not actually oppressive in all cases. Were they themselves not the (military) masters now?

There is a further point: after Solon, somebody had to do the work which had previously been done by the sixth-parters: enter chattel slavery. This is relevant to the history of democracy in two ways. First, by creating the stratum of slave labour in Athens and Attica, Solon surely 'raised the consciousness' of the citizen élite in an emphatic and visible way: here were *things* (as the Greeks thought of slaves) doing the work which the citizens themselves or their ancestors had previously done. Psychologically, smallholders now had more in common with their former masters than with the work-force by which they themselves had been replaced. This was a powerful extra inducement to the growth of a fortress attitude towards citizenship and also of a notion of equal distribution within the privileged peer group. Second, possession of slaves made active political life, and so eventually democracy, easier (it would be too strong to say that it made it possible), by giving the citizen élite the leisure for political discussion and office-holding. (The effects of this would not, however, be fully felt until the fifth and fourth centuries.)

The widening of eligibility for such office-holding was the first of the strictly political reforms of Solon. The archaic Athenian state before Solon was an aristocracy: you could hold political office as for instance an archon or magistrate, only if you belonged to one of certain well-born families. Solon replaced this rule or convention by a principle of eligibility by wealth, determined by four fixed census-ratings of which the third was the hoplite class (called *zeugites*). The fourth and bottom was the class of *thetes* who in the classical period manned the fleet.

This is a far cry from democracy: later theorists would call it 'timocracy', after the word for census-ratings, *timai*. But it was an opening-up. It is hard (but no more than that) to change the economic category into which you are born: it is a logical impossibility to change your natural family.

Secondly, Solon introduced a Council of 400 members, presumably to prepare business for the popular assembly (*ekklesia*; the English word will be used in this chapter). *What* popular assembly? The answer is that we do not know. There were popular assemblies in Homer, before which took place rhetorical duels between leaders like Achilles and Agamemnon. A speaker in the *Iliad* defines a leader as a speaker of words and a doer of deeds, in that order (9. 443). (Passages like that tend, incidentally, to weaken modern suggestions that it was only after the development of competitive rhetorical skills in the fifth century that democracy could emerge. Rhetoric was *further* developed in the fifth century, certainly; but it was not created then.) In the world of the epic poems, however, the flow of rhetoric was in one social direction only: the common man, personified by Thersites, is silenced by Odysseus, to general merriment. It is unlikely that the Athenian assembly in 600 BC was much more socially representative, or more participatory, than those described in the *Iliad*.

The details of Solon's new council, as given by the ancient sources, are largely made up, but that is not a reason for doubting that he introduced such a council at all. It was probably elected. Kleisthenes at the end of the century replaced it, as we shall see, by a Council of Five Hundred, about which we know a good deal: in the tradition about Solon, the functions of this later council have simply been retrojected on to the earlier. The Council of Four Hundred was not the only Athenian council even in Solon's time: well before 600 BC there was a Council of Elders called the Areopagus, which continued in existence down to and beyond the end of democracy in the late 320s, soon after the death of Alexander the Great. But at this date the Areopagus was a force for preserving, not undermining aristocratic privilege. The importance of the new Council of Four Hundred, whatever its exact relationship to the assembly, consists in the probability that it had a relationship *of some sort*. That is, the assembly now had an institutionalized existence: its meetings would not happen on the say-so of an Agamemnon but would occur in formal relation to, and presumably in the control or under the presidency of, a smaller elected body which did not have a vested interest in perpetuating aristocratic rule. This, admittedly, is vague and unsatisfactory language, but it is preferable to the two interpretative extremes: outright denial that such a council existed; or misleading fullness of detail about what the Council of Four Hundred actually did. The council's importance is nevertheless colossal: its institution is the first conscious, definite, and datable political innovation in European history. It is the first concrete attempt to create what has been called a 'third force' (the first and second being the intellectual few and the masses): a circle of men for whom the interests of the *polis* became a paramount concern. From now on, 'step by step, broad sections of the community were set new objectives, until in the end they acquired decisive power in the community' (Meier 1990: 215). Finally, we should note that Kleisthenes' far more sophisticated and democratically significant council had a precursor in Solon's, which is important for that reason alone.

Thirdly, Solon established a popular lawcourt, the *heliaia*, to which there was a right of appeal from unjust decisions of magistrates, who (the fourth reform) were made *accountable*. In the fourth century BC, the age of systematic political analysis, this right of appeal was given high praise as one of the most democratic things Solon did. But its importance was merely potential before the introduction of pay for juries in the 460s. And in the sixth century BC it would be a brave man who would stand up and personally (there were no barristers and as yet no speech-writers) denounce a greedy, oppressive aristocrat—especially since the *heliaia* could increase the penalty rather than reducing it.

Did sovereignty henceforth lie in the hands of the assembly? That is the traditional view. Or of the lawcourts? That is the radical alternative trenchantly argued for by M. H. Hansen in the 1970s and 1980s (see Further Reading). I postpone until the section on 'Structure' an attempt to answer this question, in so far as it is a meaningful question: 'sovereignty' is not a word with an obvious Greek equivalent, nor did the Athenians see the issue as a problem.

Solon's economic and social reforms do not exhaust what he did. His social measures, which cannot be fully analysed here, tended to move the emphasis away from the household or family and towards the *polis* or community. That is the point of, for example, his limitation on ostentatious funerals (occasions for aristocratic display) and his granting of the right to bequeath property away from the family. Here were more seeds of the democracy which had, however, not yet appeared above the surface of Solon's 'black earth'.

After Solon, there was a period of anarchy, followed (546–510) by a family tyranny, that of the Pisistratids. This was not a period of complete political freeze: magistrates continued to be elected. (We have a stone inscription, found in the 1930s by the American excavators of the Athenian civic centre. It lists archons from the 520s, one of whom is the future democratic reformer Kleisthenes, thoroughly compromised, on this evidence, with the tyrannical regime.) More positively, the Pisistratids anticipated Kleisthenes' reforms in certain ways. Above all they brought the constituent villages or *demes* of Attica, an exceptionally large territory by Greek city-state standards, into an active relation with Athens city. They did this by building roads and by appointing '*deme* judges' to travel round Attica and dispense uniform justice; perhaps also by a propagandist and centralizing use of religion, though the artistic evidence for this is controversial. All this was important because it prepared the citizens of Attica for the not-distant notions of participation and representation. Ancient states were agricultural, and this created a political problem: how to prevent the city assemblies from being dominated by the urban population. Kleisthenes' solution was subtle and complex, but the tyrants deserve credit for facing the rural/urban problem first.

It was, however, Kleisthenes who, as Herodotus put it (6. 131), 'created the tribes and the democracy', in that order. 'Tribes' are subdivisions of the citizen-body. Kleisthenes replaced the old four by a new ten, based on residence, not just birth. The new tribes were themselves made up of fixed numbers of *demes* (of which there were 140), and the *demes* supplied councillors to a new Council of 500. Councillors could serve only twice in a lifetime, for a year at a time. That is the essence of Kleisthenes' reform; we shall return to his council shortly.

Herodotus elsewhere (5. 66) treats Kleisthenes' championing of the popular cause as an accident: he took the people into partnership because he was doing badly in the struggle for aristocratic power after the fall of the tyrants. Modern scholarship has amplified this accusation of self-seeking, by arguments which try to show that Kleisthenes' own family, the Alkmaionids, were intended to benefit unduly from his changes, which involved nothing less than a comprehensive reorganization of Attica. But one motive does not always exclude another, and Kleisthenes could have wanted short-term gains but still have been a genuine and idealistic reformer as well. In any case, some of the evidence for 'Kleisthenes the fixer' is Hellenistic (inscribed lists of councillors, which may show that some tribes, *demes*, and families were unfairly well represented); but it has recently been claimed that Kleisthenes' system was radically shaken up in 403, at the end of the Peloponnesian War. If this is right, the inscribed lists are not evidence for Kleisthenes' intentions at all.

It has also been argued recently that the essence of Kleisthenes' reforms was not political but military: his organization of Attica was intended to make mobilization easy. This is a valuable insight, worked out with ingenuity. But again, it does not reduce Kleisthenes' claim to be the creator of democracy, especially if we recall that for Greeks and Romans political and military categorization were always close. (Women did not fight,

7

which helps to explain the automatic ancient assumption that they should not vote either.)

Kleisthenes' new tribes, unlike their purely heredity-based predecessors, were artificial constructs. Each was built up of three elements, called *trittyes*, which were defined by geography: the city, the inland, and the coast. These *trittyes* were even more artificial than the tribes, which had at least a military identity in that members of the same tribe fought and trained together; however, there is some evidence that *trittyes* mattered in the organization of the fleet. The ten tribes each sent fifty councillors to the new council, and these councillors were drawn from the *demes* in accordance with their population. This is the key to Kleisthenes' reforms: the Council of Five Hundred was a way of involving all of Attica in decision-making, not just the city population which found it easiest to attend political meetings. The words for the regional equality thus produced was *isegoria* or 'equality of speaking' (in the council, that is). That word, and perhaps *demokratia* (quite literally, 'people-power'), are the only slogans we can associate with Kleisthenes himself, although it has been—too confidently—said that he used *isonomia*, 'equality of political rights'. In any case, it has been pointed out (Myres 1932: 666) that *demokratia* may at this date have been a word of abuse: 'rule by country cousins' (*demes*-men).

Kleisthenes may also have defined the assembly, reckoning its paper total at 30,000. Certainly this figure is used by Herodotus as the notional total of Athenians; and both 6,000, and the fraction of one-fifth, feature in rules about quorum attendance and so forth, suggesting Kleisthenes was doing some fairly obvious mathematics. This precision is important enough—Solon had merely taken an assembly of some sort for granted in his legislation—but even more important was the provision made for what were probably (at this stage) monthly meetings of the assembly; in the next century and a half the number would increase to three or four a month.

The council was given definite *probouleutic* functions in relation to this large body. It prepared business for it. One of the ten tribes, that is one-tenth of the Council of Five Hundred, summoned and presided over the council and assembly for one month or *prytany* of the year. The council also had functions of its own, which we shall consider later.

The Kleisthenic constitution was in many ways not particularly democratic at all, compared with what was to come in the next century. The Areopagus retained important legal functions. There was as yet no pay for serving on juries, on the council, or in the assembly. This means that decision-making was in the hands of the better-off. Solon's 'timocratic' rules still determined eligibility to the archonship. And the archons were elected, not appointed by lot (the change to 'sortition' was made in 487 BC). The ten generals or *strategoi* were also elected; this new panel was created half a dozen years after Kleisthenes, on a tribal basis. The *strategoi* went on being elected right through classical Athenian history; they are the main exception to the principle of amateurism so evident elsewhere in Athenian arrangements. (But the principle was anyway eroded after 403: see below.) What is more, the *strategoi* could, very unusually for Athenian magistrates, be re-elected without limitation. But ostracism (a picturesque system, involving inscribed potsherds, for getting rid of prominent men for ten years) provided a check on individual ambition. It is uncertain whether it was Kleisthenes' invention or was introduced in the early fifth century.

But though much of this looks cautious or negative (ostracism showing that even without the tyrants, the big man was still frighteningly in mind), nevertheless in important positive ways democracy *had* arrived. Kleisthenes' complex Council of 500 members, with its rotating membership and restrictions on re-election, succeeded in extending political participation in an organized way across the entire geographical sweep of Attica. Herodotus was right to put the new 'tribes' first when summing up Kleisthenes' achievement. A new Kleisthenic tribe was not a bunch of docile voters in the pocket of a great family; instead, it was a chimera, made up of bits from the three regional parts of Attica, and so much harder to bribe or coerce. Its members trained as soldiers together, they might act together as a pressure group in the lawcourts, and they served together as 'tribe in *prytany*' for an annual month of presidency over the assembly. The bonds cementing 'tribesmen' were artificial but were deliberately cemented by religion: each tribe had a 'tribal hero', an object of cult.

Athens' political development might have stuck there but for events which Solon and Kleisthenes cannot possibly have foreseen. The Persian Wars (490–479) made Athens an imperial power, specifically a tributary maritime empire. This had five main effects which concern the historian of democracy. The first is simple but too seldom recognized: The council and assembly *now had more, and more important, matters to discuss and decide on a regular basis.* Self-esteem was surely enhanced. Secondly, tribute from the empire provided the cash for the introduction of political pay (initially pay for juries and for councillors) in the 460s, so radicalizing the democracy further. This link between radical democracy and imperialism is uncomfortable but undeniable. Thirdly, Athens' imperial position gave her the muscle to export democracy round the Aegean Sea. We must be careful about this: tiny communities could not realistically be told to set up a Council of Five Hundred with the same restrictions as were in force at Athens—they would run out of councillors in no time. Athens (as inscriptions show) was in fact flexible and did much through support of personnel rather than by ideology; and there is undeniable evidence for toleration of oligarchies ('rule by the [wealthy] few') inside the empire. Fourthly, empire and its incidental economic gains made Athenians still more aware of themselves as a political élite: the citizenship rules were tightened in 451, so that you now needed citizen descent *on both sides*. As a result, Athens acquired a large, perhaps five-figure, population of disfranchised non-citizen residents ('metics'). But it has been pointed out that modern 'democracies' like Germany have similarly numerous *Gastarbeiter* without political rights. Fifthly, the flow of tribute (which helped to pay for the fleet), and the possibilities for individual self-enrichment, softened the resentments of the wealthy at Athens, who might otherwise have hankered for oligarchy sooner than they did. (When after the disastrous Sicilian Expedition of 415–413 the total economic burden of the fleet looked like falling on the rich, democracy was indeed briefly overthrown.) But Athens' remarkable freedom from *stasis* or civil strife, which was the curse of so many Greek states, is largely to be explained by the material gains to be made, by all classes, from the empire—until 415.

But in the mid-century, imperial democracy was a winning ticket. The third main reformer after Solon and Kleisthenes was called Ephialtes, and he (with his younger colleague Pericles) did his work in the late 460s. The central feature was a downward adjustment of the role of the Areopagus. Its powers were redistributed between the Council of Five Hundred and the jury-courts. Both the council and courts were now paid (as we have seen); the council stayed the same size but it was probably now that the rules for appointment were changed: sortition not election. The juries were now much increased in size, and henceforth had full authority to hear cases at what lawyers call 'first instance', that is, not just on appeal from magistrates. Ephialtes extended the principle of accountability of magistrates much further. This process was called *euthuna*. Finally, a reform of 457, which opened the archonship to *zeugites* and *thetes*, thus ending the restriction to the top two or cavalry-owning classes, should be seen as the final instalment of the Ephialtic package.

That is the end of the named sequence of reformers. The half-century which followed was eventful but not marked by formal and lasting constitutional change. It is the period of Pericles' ascendancy (down to his death in 429) and the political vicissitudes of the Peloponnesian War, including two oligarchic revolutions, in 411 and again in 404 after Athens' defeat in the war and the loss of the empire. Following a cue in the ancient sources, particularly Thucydides 2. 65, modern research has tried to identify a moment when 'new politicians' (the 'demagogues', originally a neutral word for popular leaders) began to try out brasher methods of persuasion, appealing direct to the people and repudiating old ties of kinship. More positive claims are also made: Athenian public affairs (the argument goes) were so complex that somebody backstage must have done the hard work and the sums. The demagogues were the indispensable experts who kept the system going. The moment of their emergence is usually taken to be Pericles' death; the archetypal demagogue is taken to be the 'classless' Kleon. Actually, Pericles had a good deal of the demagogue in him, and the slowness of ancient technological change makes it unlikely that Athenian political methods changed overnight; contrast the way Lyndon Johnson, running for the Senate in 1948, exploited new techniques (opinion polls; a helicopter for cross-state canvassing) to produce genuinely 'New Politics' (Caro 1990: xxxii, 403, and part 2 generally). Athenian politicians, from Kleisthenes through Pericles and Kleon to Demosthenes (the fourth-century opponent of Philip of Macedon), tended to be rich and well-born, and used rhetoric just as Agamemnon had: 'deferential voting' was a feature of Athens as of other democracies. They also used the power of their wealth, often through so-called *liturgies*, a tax system which enabled you not just to pay but ostentatiously to over-pay your debts to the state. Such wealth brought the prestige which enabled Alcibiades to claim the command against Sicily not because he was an experienced general or was an expert on western Greece—but because his chariots had won at the Olympic Games. There was no real change in 429; it is merely that Thucydides disliked Pericles' successors.

But there was, arguably, one other moment of deliberate change: in 403, when democracy was restored after the war. At this time Athens' laws were codified; restrictions were put on the assembly's power to legislate; and Kleisthenes' system of *deme* representation in the council was perhaps overhauled. Pay was introduced for attendance in the assembly. Generally, fourth-century Athens permitted more specialization in finance and military affairs, and *elected* managers of funds acquired great power. The democracy became more efficient—but less democratic. The last notable event before the outright suppression of the democracy by Macedon in 322 was the so-called Social War of the mid 350s, fought by

Athens against secessionist allies who sought to escape from a 'Second Athenian Confederacy' set up in 377—a scaled-down version of the fifth-century empire. The Social War was important because it ended Athens' capacity to export democracy; the will to export it had in any case been growing weaker, and Athens was (as we have seen) never doctrinaire about it even in the fifth century.

STRUCTURE

All the main institutions of Athenian democracy have now been mentioned. Some of them, like the archonships, the Areopagus, and the Assembly, predated the democracy: they were there before Solon, let alone Kleisthenes or Ephialtes, and other Greek states had comparable institutions. What the Athenian reformers did was make special rules about them. Other institutions, like the enormous juries and the complicated *deme*-based Council of Five Hundred, were indeed inventions of the Athenian democracy. But even here there are surprises: oligarchic Rhodes and Ptolemaic (monarchic) Alexandria, at the end of the fifth and fourth centuries respectively, copied the Athenian *deme* system. And it now seems possible that the Kleisthenic *trittyes* system was borrowed from oligarchic Corinth; certainly, tribal changes not unlike those of Kleisthenes happened at Rome and Cyrene in North Africa at roughly the same time as at Athens, but without producing anything much like Athenian democracy. Even sortition was used at Rome, but merely to settle competing claims of aristocrats or oligarchs (*sortitio provinciarum*), not for radical democratic purposes; though we ought to notice in passing that the tendency in recent work on the Roman republic has been to stress its more democratic features and to challenge the long prevalent insistence on clientship and family ties. To return to Athens: what matters is not so much the institutions as the way they interact, and the rules and definitions governing them. To all this we may now briefly and finally turn.

Severe rules governed the definition of the citizen élite itself. The Athenian democracy was one of the most participatory of all time—if one focuses on the powers and privileges of those who were included in its operations. But the total of those *excluded* was large. We have met most of them already: slaves, women, subject-allies in the two periods of naval hegemony, metics. There were degrees of exclusion, and exceptions were made for occasional privileged groups. But a quorum of 6,000 voters in the assembly was needed for citizenship to be conferred on an individual, and there were very heavy penalties for usurpation of citizenship.

The assembly met, sitting down, on a hill called the Pnyx, on which in the classical period only 6,000 people (slightly, but only slightly, more in the fourth century) could sit. This finding is the result of meticulous archaeological research. It and other evidence suggest that only at most one-fifth of Kleisthenes' notional 30,000, and a considerably smaller fraction of the 43,000 adult males attested by Thucydides for the year 431, normally attended at any one time. As a percentage of the enfranchised population, this is nevertheless awesomely large by modern standards. The assembly met at most forty times a year. The significance of this will become clear when we turn to the council, which met far more often. A normal meeting began at sunrise and stopped at noon, so taking no more than a bite out of the working day. Votes were counted only rarely; more usually they were estimated in an approximate way. There is some evidence that the supporters of a particular politician would sit round him. Careful work on the inscriptions and speeches of the orators has shown that in the fourth century the number of Athenians who might propose a motion or mount a political prosecution at any one period might run into hundreds—again, an impressive total—but the 'professional' or semi-professional *rhetores* (a *rhetor* is just a 'speaker') would not number more than perhaps twenty.

The word 'professional' needs comment: *rhetores*, as such, did not get salaries (unlike generals, who were paid on campaign) but there were other perks politicians could hope for. Puzzlingly, it seems that magistrates were paid in the fifth century but not in the fourth. Juries and the council were paid in the fifth and fourth centuries, the assembly only in the fourth. Not all these changes can be simply explained by the availability or otherwise of public money: the introduction of assembly pay actually coincides with the *loss* of the tributary empire. It was a device to boost attendance.

The people's court has in the last two decades been promoted to the centre of academic argument. The strongest claim on its behalf is that it, rather than the assembly, was 'sovereign'. Certainly, there is no reliable, categorical ancient statement of the assembly's sovereignty; and the role of the people's court in vetting or quashing legislation was important at all periods, and has been insufficiently acknowledged in the textbooks. But there is no evidence for the kind of clashes which, for instance, caused the American Supreme Court to strike down elements of F. D. Roosevelt's New Deal. The membership of the assembly and of the large popular courts overlapped too closely for that kind of thing to happen. But the courts were central to the democracy: our sources insist, not without a touch of pride, on the almost incomprehensibly elaborate provisions for the impartial choosing of jurors. Again, there is no doubting the control exercised by the courts over the activities of politicians: candidates for magistracies had their qualifications checked in the court, which also handled their *euthuna* or accounting process. After the middle of the fourth century, when the system was changed, it was in the court rather than in the assembly that a politician's career might be destroyed by an *eisangelia* or denunciation for a serious offence like treason.

Magistrates themselves were numerous: perhaps 600 of them, in addition to the 500 members of the council, who should really be regarded as a panel of magistrates. The minimum age was 30. This produces a pool of some 20,000 eligible persons to provide about 1,100 magistrates a year: a high level of participation. Sortition played a large part in the selection of all but the generals and (in the fourth century) ninety or so other officers, mostly financial. The accountability (not just financial) of all magistrates was severely enforced. In military contexts this might have been expected to result in undue caution, but you could not win, because you could be prosecuted for *failing* to take an initiative: Thucydides' narrative provides some examples. Thucydides also speaks, from time to time, as if generals in the field had unfettered powers of decision-making; a good example is 3.51, 'Nikias wanted . . .' to achieve a certain military result—with no mention of the assembly from which ultimately he took his orders and to which (or the courts) he might eventually have to explain himself. Thucydides may be nearer the truth than the handbooks, ancient and modern. The truth may simply be that success, even if unconstitutional, would not be punished, unless you were unlucky and had made an enemy of an unusually proficient *sykophant* or malicious prosecutor (nobody has ever explained satisfactorily how that word got its different modern meaning).

The Council of Five Hundred was an important but to us shadowy body. Of dozens of surviving speeches only one (Demosthenes 51) was delivered before the council. Thucydides hardly mentions it, perhaps for literary reasons: like Homer, he was concerned with highlighting his heroes or villains and with the power of the great collectives, 'the Athenians', 'the Spartans', and so on. The social composition of the council is an interesting problem. The council met on something like 275 days of the 354-day Athenian year—far more often than the assembly. The sacrifice of time this entailed would—one would have thought—

tend to produce a better-off membership for the council (pay for council attendance admittedly improved things but it was not princely). On the other hand, social pressures, it has been claimed, would militate against too easy refusal to offer one's name for the ballot as a councillor. And there is little specific evidence for different, that is more upper-class, social attitudes on the part of the council compared to the assembly—if anything the opposite (Lysias 30. 22). The functions of the council were extensive and detailed, particularly in the financial and diplomatic spheres. But the occasional evidence of, for example, secret diplomacy by the council does not add up to a serious erosion of the assembly's powers. The council was an essential administrative motor but no more—and no less: we have seen that Kleisthenes' introduction of a complex representative system for this central institution was the single most powerful push towards the concept of participation in the history of Athenian democracy.

It is totally unclear how far-reaching were the intentions of Solon or Kleisthenes, the ostensible founding fathers of democracy. (The reformers of the 460s and of 403 have a better claim to be thought of as conscious architects of democracy, but Ephialtes is personally obscure and the men of 403 are more or less anonymous.) But it is certain that the citizens of classical Athens regarded their own constitution with pride and even reverence. Pericles' Funeral Oration in Thucydides has too often been over-interpreted (the section specifically on democracy is short, embarrassed, and defensive, an answer to critics who said that the democracy was not good at exploiting outstanding individual talent); Pericles does, however, say that Athens' political arrangements generally, and her way of life, were an example to the rest of Greece. But for the real positive attitudes we need to go elsewhere: there was a cult of *Demokratia* in the fourth century and sacrifices were made on behalf of Democracy in the fifth; more than one trireme (warship) was called *Demokratia* (it has been amusingly noted that there was by contrast no trireme called *Isonomia*; see above p. 8 for the significance of this). Despite Pericles' diffidence about democracy as such, two and a half thousand years have shown that though particular Athenian institutions have been surprisingly little copied (contrast Roman), the Athenian ideal of participatory democracy has been an example to far more than just one small set of bickering ancient communities in the eastern Mediterranean.

REFERENCES

Bernal, Martin (1987, 1991), *Black Athena: The Afro-Asiatic Roots of Greek Civilisation*, 2 vols. (London).

Caro, Robert (1990), *Means of Ascent: The Years of Lyndon Johnson* (London).

Demosthenes, *Speeches*, trans. J. H. Vince, A. T. Murray, and others in the Loeb Classical Library, 7 vols. (Cambridge, Mass., 1956 and later reprints).

Herodotus, *Histories*, trans. David Grene (Chicago, 1987).

Homer, *Iliad*, trans. E. V. Rieu, Penguin Classics (Harmondsworth, Middx., 1950; often reprinted); there is also, in the same series, a more faithful translation by Martin Hammond (1987).

Lysias, *Speeches*, trans. W. R. M. Lamb, Loeb Classical Library (Cambridge, Mass., 1930).

Meier, Christian (1990), *The Greek Discovery of Politics* (Cambridge, Mass.).

Myres, J. L. (1932) 'Cleisthenes in Herodotus', in *Mélanges Glotz* ii (Paris), 657 ff.

Plutarch, *The Parallel Lives*, trans. B. Perrin, Loeb Classical Library, 12 vols (Cambridge, Mass., 1919 and reprints).

Sallares, R. (1991), *The Ecology of the Ancient Greek World* (London).

Thucydides, *History of the Peloponnesian War*, trans. R. Warner, Penguin Classics with introduction and notes by M. I. Finley, (Harmondsworth, Middx., 1972); or trans. B. Jowett, revised by S. Hornblower, with introduction and notes, World's Classics series (Oxford, forthcoming).

CHAPTER 2

Ancient Greek Political Theory as a Response to Democracy

CYNTHIA FARRAR

I N Book 2 of Plato's *Republic*, Glaucon challenges Socrates to answer questions that reach to the heart of the Athenian political experience. Glaucon maintains that men in general do not see a connection between the requirements of political life and the fulfilment of their own needs. They do not equate happiness with justice. Men regard justice as 'tiresome and disagreeable' and 'accept it as a compromise' only because they lack the power to fulfil their own desires with impunity (*Rep.* 2. 358–9). In posing and responding to this cynical view of political order, Plato goes to great lengths to show that the ordering power of the *polis* is essential to the happiness of each individual, whatever his conditions of life may be. Glaucon insists that Socrates offer an argument for justice that will apply even to Gyges, who possesses a ring that renders him invisible. The man with the ring of Gyges may fulfil his every desire with impunity. Why should he act justly?

The shape of the argument of the *Republic* reflects the power of the ancient Athenian belief that the *polis* exists to express and secure the good of its citizens. Justice is called into question if it conflicts with the attainment of personal desires. Justice is legitimated if it is shown to be essential to personal well-being. Athenian political life raised the possibility of maintaining a bracing tension between personal and civic identity. The need to neutralize the corrosive potential of this uneasy union motivated the great anti-political theories of Plato and Aristotle (and Aristotle's invention of political science). Aristotle sought to show that 'man is by nature a *polis* animal', but he, like Plato, honours the *polis* in the breach. As I shall indicate below, both theorists short-circuit the challenge posed by political (and particularly democratic) existence. By building the order required at the level of the *polis* directly into the individual, they banish the ghost of Gyges, which thrives in the spaces created by politics.

The need to come to terms with the intimate but unnatural connection between polity and individual spawned political theory. This connection was born with the *polis* and exacerbated by the development of democracy. The story of the evolution of political thinking suggests that—and why—man's civic and personal self-understanding are bound to come apart and to stay together. This story has modern significance. Like Plato and Aristotle, we short-circuit the political challenge, but by magnifying rather than collapsing the distance between the individual and the polity. There is room enough for Gyges, who may function invisibly as a 'private citizen'. The development of ancient political ideas in response to democracy suggests that this naïve hope is an illusion.

The space that both Plato and Aristotle eliminated, the space occupied by politics, was created by the ancient Greeks in the archaic period. (Here I shall speak exclusively of the Athenians, since they left the most evidence and had the most influence on the development of democracy and political theory.) The *polis* was a boundary. The word itself derives from a root meaning 'wall'. This boundary was not merely a mark of security from external coercion, a warning to potential invaders that the residents of a particular enclave shared a determination to defend its integrity. Indeed, at Athens the creation of the boundary was directed inward, spurred by the need to institutionalize an intention not to practise or be subject to coercion. The ancient *polis* created a space between slavery and tyranny. This was not, as Plato's Glaucon suggests, a cynical compromise, but a glorious achievement.

The boundary that distinguished citizen (*polites*) from non-citizen marked out a realm of personal efficacy, order, and relative equality. Slavery and tyranny were genuine threats. Citizenship in the *polis* offered tangible benefits: freedom, the security to pursue one's own good, the opportunity to win honour by guiding and defending the community. The *polis* was an instrument of justice; the rule of law was meant to ensure that each man received his due. Politics was the expression of the freedom to participate in ordering one's own life, a freedom denied to women or slaves and unavailable to indentured peasants. The *polis* was quite literally the guarantor and the boundary of this freedom.

By its very nature, then, citizenship in the *polis* was both intimately connected to personal well-being and discontinuous with personal characteristics. Political status abstracted from personal attributes, including one's place in a social or economic hierarchy. The citizen occupied a place formally set off from the household world of production and reproduction inhabited by slaves and women. In Athens as elsewhere, political status formally transcended social status: peasants and shopkeepers were included as citizens when the boundaries of the *polis* were articulated by Solon in the early sixth century BC. The new *polis* boundary distinguished Athenian from alien and free man from slave. Solon forbade the making of loans on the security of a person, and thereby guaranteed the Athenian citizen freedom from enslavement by his neighbours.

Within the public space of the *polis* (often called *to meson*, the middle place), each individual acquired a civic identity. Solon's reforms made explicit the citizen's political privileges and responsibilities. All citizens, whatever their social or economic status, had an assigned role, although the role varied according to the amount of property they possessed. By law, any citizen who failed to take sides in a factional dispute would lose his membership in the *polis*. The preservation of a just order was implicitly defined as the responsibility of every citizen.

The potential for conflict between the individual's personal and his civic identity was built into the foundations of the *polis*. As Glaucon's account of human motivation suggests (in an extreme form), the citizen's personal attributes and desires are bound to irrupt into the political arena. Citizens are also individual men, with personal affiliations, histories, and motivations, including slavish and tyrannical desires. *Stasis*, the factional strife that pitted one group of aristocrats against another or the rich against the poor was, as M. I. Finley asserts, 'avowedly a clash of interests' (Finley 1983: 134). Yet participation in *stasis* was also, as Solon's law forbidding neutrality indicates, a mark of commitment to preserving an order that met the needs of all of its citizens. The word *demos* (and hence the word *democracy*) embodies this ambiguity: it can mean either the entire citizen body, or the poor masses. Altering the shape of the political order through violence or external coercion was always a real option, frequently exercised in city-states throughout Greece and attempted more or less successfully in Athens several times during the fifth century. This fact does not suggest that self-interest vitiated the importance of maintaining the integrity of the *polis* boundary. On the contrary: precisely because the *polis* was valued for its ability to secure the good of its members through the preservation of freedom and order, the citizens continually reassessed its capacity to perform this function.

The ability to accommodate this dual identity was the hallmark of the political and particularly the democratic achievement of the Athenians. In Athens as elsewhere, the implicit tension between freedom and order was muted in the early years of the *polis* by general acquiescence in the political as well as religious authority of the traditional rulers, the nobles. The shift to democracy, initiated by Kleisthenes and accelerated in the first half of the fifth century, heightened the intimacy and the awkwardness of the civic experience. Questioning of the status of the traditional hierarchy, and uncertainty about the criteria and meaning of citizenship were fostered by the rule of the Pisistratid tyrants (546–510 BC). Kleisthenes affirmed the purely political source of both freedom and order. His reforms re-emphasized the power of the political boundary to cut across traditional affiliations. He accorded status to all free residents of the region through purely political means, and contrived to undermine the local domination of aristocratic families and connect every Athenian politically to the wider community.

The social and personal qualities traditionally associated with power and order were no longer politically decisive. Political power came to rest with an assembly of men who were not themselves, as individuals, powerful; individual members might well be inexperienced, uneducated, and unused to responsibility. Unity was no longer to be secured by respect for traditional authority. In drama and political argument, the Athenians sought to come to terms with the vastly broadened scope of the *polis*: its claim to achieve order from the unordered, and to express the power of the powerless. Neither the workings of the democratic *polis* nor the attempts to understand its implications ever dissolved these contradictions. For to dissolve them—as Plato and Aristotle did—was to end politics.

The emergence of tragic drama coincided with the period of political upheaval that gave birth to Athenian democracy. The tragedians explored the questions raised by democratic politics and looked to democracy itself for the answers. Concern about democracy, about reconciling man's civic status and responsibilities with his personal characteristics and aims, arose from two adjacent angles. Why should one think that the consequence of assembling the views of individuals freed at least formally from a traditional hierarchy and traditional values will in fact be order? And would a political order of this kind be genuinely compatible with the expression of personal aims? In the *Suppliants* (produced *c.*465–459 BC) and the *Oresteia* (produced in 458), Aeschylus suggests in different ways that democratic politics may be able to integrate political claims with those which are personal or kinship-related. *Autonomos* man literally makes the forces of order (*nomos*) his own. The constraints associated with the old aristocratic order are now conceived as self-imposed. Democratic man is part of a political élite. Because of his political status, and despite persisting social and economic inequalities, he is capable of instantiating the personal qualities associated with the aristocracy and essential to communal order—bravery, excellence, reverence, justice, capacity to contribute to the community.

In the *Suppliants*, King Pelasgus of Argos insists on a political response to the barbarian women's request for political protection from their Egyptian cousins. The ultimate decision rests with the *demos*, which votes to extend protection to the suppliants. In his portrayal of the king's encounter with the Egyptian herald near the end of the *Suppliants*, Aeschylus interweaves references to being female (emblematic of the non-political) and to the behaviour of barbarians and despots, to underscore the themes of the play. Pelasgus declares that the Egyptians' claim to have restored order and displayed manhood through subduing the women is hollow. The Argives, who govern by political authority, based on persuasion and consent, are the true men (*Suppl.* 951). Authority is not defined solely by particular laws, but also in terms of a more general standard: reciprocity of respect and the rejection of coercion. It is adherence to this standard which underlies the Athenian democracy's claim, as represented in this play, to express personal aims in political actions. The resolute commitment to a political expression of individual views is embodied in the Argive decree that those members of the *polis* who refuse to be bound by the deliberate decision of the *demos* in assembly are to lose their citizen status (*Suppl.* 61 ff.).

A few years later, Aeschylus analysed Athenian politics in rather different terms. The *Oresteia* trilogy was produced after the murder of Ephialtes, who had led a successful effort to reduce the powers of the aristocratic Areopagus. At the time, some Athenians were prepared to betray the city to Sparta. The trilogy reflects Aeschylus' concern that the thrust toward full democracy at the expense of traditional authority could result in anarchy. Significantly, this concern is articulated not in terms of a struggle between democracy and oligarchy, but in terms of a more basic conflict between the claims of the *polis* and the family. The trilogy recounts the cycle of vengeance that follows King Agamemnon's sacrifice of his daughter Iphigeneia in order to secure divine sanction for his campaign against Troy. As in the *Suppliants*, the female element—Queen Clytemnestra, who murders her husband, Agamemnon; her effeminate lover, Aegisthus; and the Furies, who stalk Clytemnestra's son Orestes after he kills his mother—represents disorder, rebellion against authority, and personal grievance, as well as the commitment to ties of blood above the claims of political order or authority. Apollo, protector of Orestes, speaks for the male principle. Each side appeals to a powerful, divinely sanctioned set of values, both of which have force for political order within Athens.

Like Pelasgus, the goddess Athena refers the case to the representatives of the *polis*. Aeschylus' choice and portrayal of the Areopagus as the political arbiter evokes both the claims of traditional authority and the explicitly political structure of power. While the decision of the Argives was unanimous, the Athenians who constitute the Areopagus are divided. This division of opinion exposes the implications of a purely political basis for order founded on a decision-making procedure, which can decide but not resolve a deep and tragic conflict between legitimate claims. The political community must therefore absorb and domesticate conflict, and express the various demands to which men take themselves to be subject. Athena casts the deciding vote in favour of the male, political principle, but she uses her political skills to persuade the Furies not to withdraw from Athens. She succeeds in politicizing their traditional function and rooting political order in the personal motivations and attachments they represent. The incorporation of the Furies ensures that each citizen is constrained by fear of inevitable punishment.

In the figurative and allusive way characteristic of drama, these two plays evoke, respectively, the belief that the democratic *polis* enables the free, collective determination of civic aims, thereby combining unity with respect for the autonomy of the citizens; and the belief that if the exercise of autonomy by all citizens is indeed to produce harmony, then individuals must exhibit respect for traditional, socially embedded norms of behaviour.

The sophist Protagoras sought to demonstrate what Aeschylus dramatized: that political interactionl constitutes both the exericse of power through collective self-expression and the achievement of order through collective self-restraint. Protagoras was not an Athenian citizen. He was a contemporary of Aeschylus, resident and professionaly active in Athens in the 460s and 450s. In the *Protagoras*, our major source of evidence about the sophist's political theory, Plato uses Protagorean doctrine as a foil to suggest that the ability to assess their own interests and to help guide the affairs of the *polis* cannot be ascribed to men simply by virtue of their citizen status. But as can be seen from the integrity of certain parts of the dialogue, their compatibility with independently attested fragments, and their incompatibility with the Platonic framework, the historical Protagoras did formulate a coherent political theory. Unlike Plato, he did not see the need to construct a political psychology. Like Aeschylus, he sought to show that social, economic, and personal differences could be politicized, by being both expressed and transformed.

In response to the question of democratic legitimacy, Protagoras argues that the interaction of the citizenry and leadership characteristic of the *polis* fosters good judgement on the part of the decision-making *demos* and ensures the best possible leadership flourishes. The *polis* can ascribe judgement and the capacity to contribute to political order to the citizen *qua* citizen, because it requires and fosters these qualities. Political interaction promotes both universal competence (man is the measure; all citizens are capable of contributing to political order) and individual excellence (some men are better measures than others; some are better able to contribute to political order). In his political theory, Protagoras offered an account of socialization and leadership and the relationship between the two. This account embodies Protagoras' own superior understanding of the fundamental characteristics of human experience, and invited men to test it against their personal experience.

The Protagorean story (*muthos*) and argument (*logos*) recounted by Plato in the *Protagoras* is designed to show that man needs the *polis* and to indicate how the *polis* itself makes possible political efficacy and communal order. The *muthos* describes the gods' attempt to equip newly created and defenceless man for survival. Prometheus gives every man technical wisdom and fire, which enable him to invent speech, fabricate houses and clothes, and secure nourishment. However, men remain vulnerable. They are unsuccessful in their attempts to forge larger, more secure communities until they are given *aidos* (respect, reverence) and *dike* (justice) by Zeus. Possession by all men of the most basic technical skills and political qualities is essential to the survival of the species.

While the *muthos* illuminates man's nature and his needs, the *logos* indicates how he acquires the qualities required to fulfil this nature and meet these needs. In the *polis*, everyone teaches or transmits the essential social virtues and skills, such as obedience to law, language, and the capacity to use fire, so that everyone achieves competence. Above this basic level, the social and the technical diverge. Or rather, they diverge in the

democratic *polis*. In the oligarchic *polis*, the best men teach political qualities only to their own sons or peers, just as (in all *poleis*) the best craftsmen
transmit their skills to their sons. In the democratic *polis*, however, political ability is thought to be essential to the continuation and effectiveness
of the political order. Thus the most skilled and virtuous citizens teach
everyone, through interaction in the assembly and on the council. As a
result, all those who are naturally gifted—not merely the sons of the
gifted—attain excellence. The political order takes over and extends the
aristocratic commitment to excellence.

In an affirmation of democracy's radical extension of political power to
all citizens, Protagoras argues that the highest form of self-realization—for
demos and élite alike—was to be achieved by means of the constant interaction of men of all classes, since men of great natural ability were to be
found outside as well as within the élite of the wealthy and well-born.
For Protagoras, in contrast to Glaucon, political society is not merely an
instrumental good, but essential to human well-being. The *polis* secures
more than human survival. Politics makes possible man's development as
a creature capable of genuine autonomy, freedom, and excellence. The
very process that enables every citizen to be a citizen (and hence fully a
man) enables him to be the best citizen and man he can possibly be. All
men—*demos* and traditional élite—can be expected to appreciate that the
workings of the democratic *polis* serve their own best interests.

Protagoras' theory was offered as a contribution to the socialization
and enlightenment to be achieved through political interaction. Yet the
theory was an argument prompted by contemporary questioning of the
political order. In the years after Protagoras offered his analysis of the *polis*
and its relation to human needs and human awareness, and in part
because of the increased reflectiveness engendered by the theory and the
developments it was meant to address, the Athenians came to regard the
political practice itself as external. The Athenians inhabited a realm of
formal equality which in its democratic form sought to transcend the
reality of persisting personal and social inequalities. The experience of
accommodating this tension itself sparked awareness of the distinction
between man as man and as citizen. It became increasingly tempting to
regard *nomos* as the subjective expression of the interests of some portion
of the citizen-body, imposed by them on others whose interests it did not
represent. Experience of policy-making in the assembly and the administration of justice by popular juries prompted the reflection that the decisions of the *demos* might be both arbitrary and coercive. The *demos* could
be whimsical, their decisions founded on nothing but individual belief.

Because of uneven enforcement of the law, and the disproportionate power and influence of a few men or of the majority, binding decisions might well not be expressive of the collective good.

Contemporary drama provides evidence that a view of the political order as arbitrary, coercive, and manipulative was at least widely mooted. Compare Aeschylus' *Suppliants* to Euripides' treatment, some forty years later, of the same theme: while Aeschylus' king leaves the decision to the *demos*, which must determine for itself what risks it is willing to incur, Euripides' king asserts that the people will follow his lead, but that by involving them he will increase their loyalty to the cause.

Euripides' *Hecuba*, produced in 425/424, vividly portrays this subtle change in outlook. The Trojan queen has been enslaved by the conquering Greeks. A slave and a woman, excluded from the political structure, Hecuba (like the Furies before her and Antigone after her) embodies traditional aristocratic values. She appeals to the leader of the Greek army, King Agamemnon, to punish the outrageous murder of her son by a guest-friend to whom she had entrusted him. Agamemnon refuses to apply *nomos* to protect the weak because he fears the reaction of the Greek army, even though he believes Hecuba's cause to be just. Hecuba responds in terms which point beyond the dramatic context to the condition of the contemporary *polis*: 'Alas, among mortals is there no free man? To money or to fortune man is slave; the city's rabble or the provisions of the law constrain him to turn to actions that violate his judgement' (*Hec.* 864–7). Political interaction does not secure order based on the common good, nor does it express freedom. Persuasion and rhetoric are seen not as means to express and secure common values, but rather as ways to manipulate others in pursuit of one's own private aims.

The writings of the sophist Gorgias present Euripides' reflections on the character of political persuasion as an argument. In the *Defence of Helen*, Gorgias maintains that persuasion, traditionally the antithesis of force and compulsion, reduces others to slaves. Men are compelled to act in certain ways by the irresistible power of argument. Gorgias argues in the *Palamedes* they are coerced even by their own belief that to act in certain ways will benefit them. Men are coerced from within, by forces which bear no necessary relationship to the achievement of their own well-being.

As in Glaucon's account, the *polis* order is seen as purely instrumental. The *polis* appears unable to integrate the citizen's political pursuit of his own interests with the achievement of general well-being. Contemporary discussions and arguments place no emphasis on a common good or a shared vulnerability. Compare Glaucon to Protagoras: the relative equality of men is treated as a contingent, not a necessary, feature of the human condition. Gyges is presented as a real threat. Here is the legacy of Athenian imperial power, power in a realm whose members are not, unlike men, relatively equal. The Athenian empire offered a vivid example of the possibility of violating or even escaping social constraints through sheer strength.

Both the pursuit of individual good and adherence to communal values are reconstrued in non-political terms. In the *Antigone*, the term *autonomia*, meaning political self-determination both within the *polis* and in relation to other *poleis*, is applied to the situation of a citizen who is defying the political order. Internal relations have come to be seen as if they were as distanced as external ones. Antigone's *autonomia* is no longer political, but marks a resolute adherence to values which politics, portrayed as narrow and partisan, is deemed to have neglected. A comparison of two tragedies on the same theme, one by Aeschylus the other by Euripides, illustrates in a striking way the shift from a political to a personal conception of the sources of human action, and the difficulty of harmonizing different communal and personal claims. In the *Oresteia*, the conflicting demands on Orestes are expressed through a political process. The corresponding claims on human motivation are eventually accommodated within the *polis*. Euripides' Orestes, by contrast, is driven mad by these conflicting claims. Orestes has internalized the conflict, and politics is irrelevant.

In a world in which politics is perceived as irrelevant or antithetical to individual well-being, and the indulgence of individual motivation and desire leads to chaos and conflict, how is order to be secured? Antiphon the Sophist, writing in the late fifth/early fourth century, offered a clear but restricted answer: the demands of nature (*phusis*), stringent and inescapable, express man's autonomy and his interests, while *nomos* is both contingent and coercive. Because they are based on agreement and seek to promote collective security, the laws are too loosely fitted to individual interests, too general and external, to achieve their ostensible aim. Antiphon, like Glaucon, ascribes to the laws the limited goal of ensuring that men who do no wrong suffer none. The *polis* (as Protagoras said) is a transformer: it induces men to adopt habits of justice and to act as if their interests are social. According to Antiphon, the *polis* thereby endangers rather than enhances the well-being of individual men. Wrongs are not always righted, and citizens are required to place themselves at risk when their own interests are not directly involved, for example by testifying against a fellow citizen. Antiphon's theory of the good for man (self-preservation and prudent pleasures) is primitive and—from the point of view of social order—purely negative. The grip of the theory is therefore very strong and universal, its scope very narrow.

Even the most direct and participatory democracy the world has known was vulnerable to the criticism that by treating individuals as citizens, democracy undermines its own goal of securing the well-being of all of its members. Thinkers as different from each other as Socrates and Callicles share Antiphon's belief that the *polis* distorts man's understanding of his real interests and prevents him from realizing them. By invoking the most basic and uncontentious human good, self-preservation, Antiphon evades the question of how conflicting views of the good, either among individuals or within them (witness Orestes), are to be reconciled. Although their theories invoke more complex human goods, Socrates and Callicles also evade this essentially political question. They seek a personal basis for social order. There is no need for political reconciliation of conflict because their teleological theories privilege one aspect of the conflicted self and the conflicted society at the expense of the other. Both physically and socially, there is no need for self-control, only self-realization.

In the *Protagoras*, Socrates claims that most men 'look at knowledge as a slave who gets dragged about by all the rest', that is, by passion, pleasure, or pain. This portrayal of motivation also evokes the experience of democracy as the expression of raw desire. Democracy has subverted its own aims by assuming that extant motivation defines real interests. At stake is the achievement of genuine autonomy. According to Socrates, the only interests whose expression can be said to reflect man's freedom are his real interests as defined by reason. Desire has no independent force: his own good is all that a man can be said genuinely to desire. Thus in the *Gorgias*, Socrates asserts that he may be the only Athenian who 'undertakes the real political craft and practises politics' (521d6) because he does not seek to gratify his fellow citizens but to help them understand how to achieve the good (521a3, 521e1) through the reasoned sifting of their beliefs.

If for Socrates real interests (as defined by reason) are the only genuinely motivating ones, for Callicles motivating interests (as defined by desire) are the only genuinely real ones. Callicles argues that order is only legitimate if it expresses man's instinctive understanding of his good. He characterized human agency in terms of the capacity to fulfil one's desires. Reason has no independent force. It is reasonable to want as much as one desires. Nature now dictates not mere survival, but domination. Existing *nomoi* must be shattered, for they do not represent the collective interest, but merely the interest of the weak in restraining the lust for power. According to Callicles, the dominion of the strong is naturally just.

All three theorists—Antiphon, Socrates, and Callicles—reject the notion that the political order has any role to play in securing individual well-being. (The commitment to obedience to the laws articulated by Socrates in Plato's *Crito* defines a purely external order.) They characterize the good in terms of one aspect of human nature, and assign to the individual the task of realizing that good. These theories eliminate the potential for conflict between reason and desire, real and perceived interests, personal and civic identity, social order and individual freedom. The individual need not be concerned about social conventions or expectations. All that is required is that he pursue his own best interests, and that is unambiguous. For Callicles, the result may be a clash between weak and strong. But none of these theorists leaves room for conflict at the level of beliefs or motivations. Self-preservation, reason, desire—each is universal and univocal.

The fifth-century critics of the *polis* believed that the creation of a social order that sought to accommodate every citizen's understanding of his good had resulted in the subversion of individual well-being. Moreover, by seeking to transform man into civic man, the *polis* had corrupted his understanding of his own good. Yet Antiphon, Callicles, and Socrates did not argue that it was necessary to reform the *polis* directly, only to strip away its pretensions and to open men's eyes.

In response to critiques of this kind, and to contemporary developments which heightened and revealed the tensions inherent in the functioning of a democratic *polis*, the three most penetrating analysts of the Athenian *polis*, Plato, Aristotle, and Thucydides, insisted on the importance of the *polis* to human well-being, for good or ill. Unlike Protagoras, they acknowledged that the political order could not be assumed to connect up with the individual's real interests, but must be made to do so. The citizen's understanding of these interests might be obscured by visceral desires or aggressive self-assertion. Was it indeed possible for the *polis* to contribute something to man's ability to realize his good, and at the same time to express each citizen's understanding of that good?

Plato and Aristotle did seek to answer this democratic question, and to answer it affirmatively. Their theories can be seen as attempts to change the world so as to make it safe for democratic principles. They answered the question by reducing it to a tautology: there could be no conflict between the *polis*'s capacity to transform and to express, because the political order must be structured so as to reflect the real and transparent interests of each of its members. Social status was no guarantee that reason would rule over unreason. Nor could the political boundary succeed in banishing the primitive, the chaotic, the visceral (the slavish and womanish) from civic life. The rule of reason had to be built in to the individual and the political order. In Plato's theory, the *polis* structure orders the human soul; in Aristotle's, man's character orders the *polis*. Only Thucydides offers a political theory, one which (like the *polis*) seeks to accommodate the potential conflict between the civic and the personal and among different construals of the good, and to do so through the interaction of different and autonomous individuals.

Ober (1989) has argued that by the early fourth century the Athenian *demos* had resolved the potential conflict between egalitarian principles and the need for political leadership by exercising control of political ideology. Élite leaders were continually required to demonstrate both rhetorically and materially that they deserved the approval of the people. Public rhetoric obviated the need for political theory, Ober suggests. Indeed, the development of political theory may have been motivated by the desire of members of the élite to explain their own failure to control political life. Yet the anti-political theories of Plato and Aristotle raise troubling issues about political interaction. The evidence of tragedy suggests that citizens in the fifth century were worried by the implications of democracy. Fourth-century Athenians may not have been troubled: the system was entrenched and it worked. But the existence of a mass ideology is no guarantee that the ideology is likely to secure individual or collective well-being, nor that it is not itself corrupt and corrupting. The *demos* could of course alter its interpretation of its own interests from one assembly or court case to the next. But on what grounds did citizens assess leaders or proposals? Plato and Aristotle argued that the good for man could only be achieved by dissolving politics. Thucydides, writing in and about the late fifth century, offered a perspective on the good which was intended to be relevant to citizens of the democratic polis.

Plato wrote the *Republic* in the 380s or 370s. He had lived through the protracted political upheaval that afflicted Athens in the final decade of the Peloponnesian War and its aftermath. At the age of 29, he had witnessed the prosecution and execution of Socrates. He regarded the public life of his own *polis* as lethal to sound human development, understanding, or political order. Not only was the political order corrupt, but the human psyches shaped by this order offered no basis for the restoration of individual or communal well-being. Plato insists against Protagoras that ordinary man, who must rely on judgement founded on experience, cannot measure the good. Those who care about justice and the good must begin *de novo* to investigate 'what, exactly, a man is' (*Theaet.* 174b).

Plato's argument in the *Republic*, his most elaborate and mature analysis of justice, takes the form of a claim about the understanding of his own interest that each man would attain if he lived in a *polis* that promoted optimal fulfilment of and harmony among his desires. Because men by nature differ dramatically in their individual capacity to understand and comply with the dictates of the good, it is not in the interests of most men to determine their own fate. Plato offers a powerful critique of a system which simply designates individuals as free, equal, and autonomous and assumes that the consequences of interaction will be the full development and expression of the individual's capacity for order, efficacy, and well-being. The existing *polis* is incapable of creating order from the unordered; political interaction is not ennobling, but degrading.

The just city is designed to secure the good of all citizens individually, and to permit them as much critical freedom as their natures permit (see Reeve 1988). The ordered *polis* supplies what they need in order to realize their good. Human beings (including the philosopher, who would prefer not to return to the cave) are not self-sufficient and can reliably achieve individual happiness only in a stably happy *polis*. Justice and happiness are to be attained by both individual and *polis* through the rule of reason over appetite both psychologically and politically. Unlike the real *polis*, Plato's republic does not ask more of men than he can be confident they are psychically and cognitively able to provide. They must all be enabled to attain the highest possible level of cognitive development; they must not be required to act as if they can be, or contribute, more than their psychic structure (nurtured under optimal conditions) permits.

Also unlike the real *polis*, Plato does not ask more of the *polis* than it is able to provide. The just *polis* does not transform the capacities of the individual, but embeds those capacities in a political order structured psychologically. Plato argues that the political order must nurture the healthy development of the human psyche, and that it does so by embodying the appropriate relationship between reason and appetite. As in the existing *polis*, the relationship between individual and social order in the just *polis* is intimate. Indeed, it is so intimate that there is no room for awkwardness. There is no politics, no interaction among autonomous individuals to achieve order. The world described by Plato is not a merely adequate world, but a perfect one, which exactly mirrors and secures the real interests and the innate potential of each individual. All conflict between reason and desire, real and perceived interests, is eliminated. The just *polis* instantiates in an extreme form the connection between individual and collectivity which the *polis* sought to maintain, and eliminates the necessity of doing so politically.

In a *reductio ad absurdum* of the *polis* ideal, Plato sapped the *polis* of its political structure by extending its claims to the innermost reaches of the psyche, and to all inhabitants, whatever their status in the community, and however disparate their resources, capacities, and experience. The individual's freedom and well-being are not in any significant sense his own achievements. To be free is not to rule oneself, but to be ruled by reason. Because all men are subject to the rule of reason, all citizens are essentially alike, and friends (*philoi*). Even the slave, Plato insists, flouting all convention, is *philos*. Slaves have apparently been incorporated into the *polis*. Women certainly have. Just like men, they contribute according to their psychic capacities. The *polis* boundary, and particularly the boundary established by the democratic *polis*, implied that some differences among individuals (being free, being male) are decisive, while others (being uneducated, being a labourer) are irrelevant. For Plato, the decisive differences among individuals are those which determine their capacity to live according to the rule of reason and realize the good. No person is capable of political freedom alone; all achieve their full potential as members of the just *polis*.

Plato surpasses the goals of the *polis*, articulated most forcefully in the democratic *polis*, by substituting psychic for political structure. The just *polis* expresses individual interests, transforms man's understanding of his interests through his membership in the *polis*, and achieves order from the unordered—from the aggregation of any and all human beings, not just those who are male and free.

By the time he came to write the *Laws*, Plato no longer believed that the form of the good could so permeate a soul as to render it incorruptible. No psyche could be relied upon to rule the *polis* according to reason. Instead of transforming any and every man's capacity for order by placing him within a psychic structure, Plato used political categories to accommodate existing inequalities. In the *Laws*, no slave can ever be a *philos*. The elaborate rules and regulations stipulated in the *Laws* are based on principles of proportional equality. Plato's *Laws*, like the *Republic*, enforces an abrogation of individual autonomy: in one case by the philosopher-kings, embodying the good; in the other by Plato the philosopher, legislating it.

31

Aristotle agreed with Plato that men differ enormously in their capacity to understand and realize the good. What men in general, in existing *poleis*, take to be in their interests does not represent the realization of human potential. Unlike Plato, however, Aristotle does not believe that the gulf between those motivated by base desires and those ready to order their lives according to reason can be spanned by the ordering force of the *polis*. Aristotle argued that Plato's theory violated human nature by making the *polis* as much of a unity as the individual. But if the *polis* is essentially a plurality, how can it possibly embody the good for man? While Plato adapted the central democratic tenet that the *polis* can transform ordinary men into citizens capable of promoting the common good, Aristotle insisted on another democratic premiss, namely the importance of individual autonomy. The only *polis* capable of expressing the views and character of its citizens and also embodying an order which secures the well-being of all citizens is the perfect *polis*, a *polis* consisting solely of virtuous men. For Aristotle as for Plato, the political order matches the order in individuals.

Like Plato, Aristotle vitiated the *polis* boundary in the process of affirming its aims. Plato resolved the tension inherent in the *polis* by incorporating all men and all aspects of men into one order; Aristotle resolved it by banishing most men and most aspects of man. Aristotle's ideal *polis* preserves the characteristics of Athenian democracy for an élite. The citizens are not formal but actual equals. Aristotle makes no attempt to bridge the gap between social and political status. In the best form of *polis*, a share in civic administration is allotted 'according to virtue and merit' and 'no man can practise excellence and virtue who is living the life of a craftsman or labourer' (*Pol.* 1278a19). Aristotle declares that 'we cannot consider all those to be citizens who are necessary to the existence of the polis' (*Pol.* 1277b35).

Aristotle's exclusion of the 'necessary and the useful' from the life of the best *polis* or the best man is both a reflection of fourth-century developments in the condition of the city-state and a rejection of the implications of those developments. It was becoming increasingly obvious that some of the men now indispensable to the *polis*—not just slaves, but wealthy aliens who often functioned as merchants and bankers, and mercenaries—were not part of it politically. The *polis* no longer incorporates the 'useful' (those who feed and protect the *polis*) into a political identity; the citizenry is simply a privileged subset of the larger society. Aristotle addresses the increasingly apparent arbitrariness of the *polis* boundary by shrinking the *polis* even further. He restricts the *polis* proper to those who are by nature capable of exhibiting virtue and excellence. The arbitrariness disappears, because the *polis* boundary simply corresponds to the landscape of human nature.

In Aristotle's theory, the human form takes the place of the Platonic form of the good. It is man's nature that is decisive for relations among men. For Plato, the good is available to all men. For Aristotle, 'nature' marks the apex of human development, which only a few men will ever attain. Among non-human creatures and substances, the form characterizes virtually all members of the class. Man is unique in his capacity to block the realization of his own potential. Therefore the claim that 'man is by nature a *polis* animal' is highly paradoxical. Most men are not capable of virtue; they pursue the useful, not the good. Aristotle observes that the *polis* 'originates in the bare needs of life and continues in existence for the sake of a good life' (*Pol.* 1252b27–30). Yet most states do not exist for virtue. They correspond more closely to a mere alliance, which ensures 'security from injustice' and makes possible 'exchange and mutual intercourse' (*Pol.* 1280a35).

In discussing politics, Aristotle offers both a teleology and a biology. He divides his attention between the achievement of virtue, on the one hand, and effectiveness as a citizen, on the other. Most men do not live in states where virtuousness as a man and as a citizen coincide. Most constitutions are 'bad' constitutions. They reflect the narrowly partisan desires of those to whom they allocate power. *Ethics* and *Politics* have come apart. So have normative political theory and political science. Issues of political causality—how to secure a given aim—are pursued independently of the question of how the good for man might be embodied in a polity. Good citizens are men who promote the stability of the constitution under which they happen to live. Aristotle recognized that men are naturally keen to fulfil their own desires and secure their own interests, on their own behalf, and according to their own understanding, which is shaped by class and fortune. The *Politics* therefore addresses 'not only what form of government is best, but also what is possible and what is easily attainable by all. There are some who would have none but the most perfect; for this many natural advantages are required' (*Pol.* 1288b37–40).

Aristotle analysed at length how constitutions and political norms can best be adapted to the character and aims of the citizens. He classified democracy as the best of the bad constitutions, because collectively the poor judge reasonably well and have the greatest stake in the *polis*. Aristotle argues that the best form of democracy is one which is the least democratic, that is, does not embody the defining characteristics of democracy: most of the people are not poor, the poor do not govern, and they do not act as equals. He ranks democracies in terms of the 'natural classification of their inhabitants' (*Pol.* 1318b8).

In his insistence that political forms, whether real or ideal, express and reflect but do not transform the nature of the citizen body, Aristotle rejects the essential premise of the democratic *polis*. His separation of the normative from the empirical itself constitutes an implicit rejection of politics. The *polis*, and particularly the democratic *polis*, was intentionally un-natural. The *polis* was designed to enable order to emerge from the un-ordered, to make it possible for men to be more than their conditions or resources would suggest they are capable of being.

Plato and Aristotle abandoned the notion that the good of the individual could be attained through politics. Writing in and about the period before democracy became entrenched at Athens, Thucydides the historian formulated a theory which, unlike those of the great anti-political theorists of the next generation, valued the tension that structured *polis* life. Thucydides' *History*, an account of the Peloponnesian War, displays his deep awareness of the dynamic interplay between human character and the charater of the social world. He recognized that the *polis* cannot simply put to one side man's visceral and anarchic aspect, and in fact may exacerbate it. In the face of a stark contrast between what the *polis* in principle contributes to human well-being and human capacities, and the realities of political life, Thucydides did not flinch. He accepted the possibility of conflict, of disorder, of the triumph of desire over reason, in order to preserve the slender chance that a *polis* could realize its full potential to both express and transform the beliefs and capacities of its citizens.

Thucydides presented his analysis of human interests and the power of politics in the form of a history because only history offered a perspective from which real individuals, within real *poleis*, could assess the connection between their own good and their behaviour as citizens and determine how to act on that understanding. Thucydides believed that human nature and the good for man can be known only historically. There are no static truths about men, only experience of them and understanding of particular situations. Indeed, Thucydides offers a historical analysis to show why it had become true that only history could now serve as a reliable guide. The *History* portrays the effects of social and ethical disintegration. Thucydides records the advent, in conditions of insecurity and conflict, of constant suspicious calculations of advantage, which led to greater insecurity and more damaging conflict. Under such conditions, a political construal of man's interests of the kind offered by Protagoras must give way to a construal of the interests of men as individuals in particular circumstances. The teleological theories of man as essentially a rational soul (Socrates) or natural instinct (Callicles) cannot meet this need. They increase man's reflective distance from experience and thus further undermine his capacity to act prudently to secure his real interests.

Thucydides' historical construal of man's nature and his interests acknowledges that men are now, irrevocably, reflective judges of their own well-being and suspicious of social constraints. His *History* shows that under such circumstances well-being can be secured only in a political context and only by deploying principles of historical understanding. The speeches of Pericles and Thucydides' historical analysis suggest that self-control can be fortified through understanding of the character and powers of reason, including its vulnerability to chance and passion. The reader or listener is invited to participate imaginatively in a set of interpreted experiences which guide assessment of what is appropriate (prudent) under various circumstances and of how men tend to behave, so that he may learn how to judge for himself.

Both Thucydides' own *History*, and the historically-minded leadership embodied by Pericles, constitute arguments: they not only show that history is the proper way to think about (and in) politics, but also justify a particular set of actions in the world shaped by historical and psychological forces. Judgement rests on historical analysis, the capacity to perceive how the present has been brought about by the past, what it is actually like and how it is to be understood. In the section of the *History* known as the Archaeology, Thucydides analyses the consolidation and accumulation of power in early Greece. The human qualities that propelled this process—particularly the constant search for more—are characteristic of the Athenians. The ultimate result of this process is polarization, and an inevitable conflict which will cause precisely the unsettled conditions and civic strife overcome by Greece in her accession to strength and power. The consolidation and articulation of political power eventually bring it about that the principle which has fuelled the development—namely that for the powerful, promoting their own interests means subjugating others, in their own and other communities—is the principle which strangles it. The two aspects of gain—greed (*pleonexia*) and safety (*asphaleia*) are no longer complementary, but antagonistic. Passions and instincts—fear, daring, ambition, desire for security—must now be controlled by reason if the entire structure of mutually advantageous relations (within and among *poleis*) is not to collapse. In such a world, the attempt to secure additional power for one's own exclusive benefit—by a tyrant, be he individual ruler or city—can only result in further polarization, antagonism, and eventual defeat. A Gyges who needs the cloak of invisibility, whose interests are at odds with those of his fellow citizens or cities, is all too visible. Thucydides acknowledges the power of the passions that drove Gyges, and even their utility, but shows that there is no longer any room for the free exercise of such ambitions.

The level at which self-control was possible and at which the disintegration of Hellenic power could, perhaps, be halted, is the level of the political community. Within the *polis*, men could be brought to reinterpret their circumstances and to reorient their understanding of their interests, and to exercise self-control. Thucydides emphasizes the importance of leadership, directed not just outwards, to the preservation of power, but inwards, to the control of the desire to act and expand. The leader acts as mediator between the citizens and the entity they collectively constitute, by making possible reflective unity. The contextual understanding of the behaviour of political communities which lacked judgement was intended to show that (and to show why) Periclean Athens was superior, both to post-Periclean Athens and to Sparta.

These contrasts indicate the dangers—and the potential strength and greatness—of democracy. Under the guidance of a leader—Pericles—capable of offering and promoting historical understanding, the Athenians could secure both autonomy and order. The reflective agent is guided by political interaction, but a form of interaction responsive to and expressive of the agent's own reflection on his experience, his interests, and his nature. In post-Periclean Athens, there was no leader who could or would mediate the purely personal desires of the Athenians. Indeed, the leaders participated in the indulgence of crude self-interest and fell victim to the polarized atmosphere they helped create. As a result, the city responded irrationally to experience, thereby further exacerbating antagonism within the *polis* and the imprudent pursuit of exclusive interests.

In contrast to the Spartans, the Athenians exhibited self-reliance, energy, resourcefulness, and the spirit of enterprise generated by a system which sought to express the collective interest. They could also be rash and undisciplined. Under the historical circumstances created by those attributes characteristic of the Athenians, the challenge was to control Athenian desires and unify and stabilize her policies without smothering the energy, intelligence, and capacity to respond creatively to experience which had built Athenian power and remained her greatest resource.

The contrast between the two aspects of the *polis*—as a collectivity and as an entity—is starkest for the Athenians. Democracy repeatedly and urgently poses the question of whether a political order can simultaneously express and transform the views of its citizens so as to forge a reflectively stable civic identity. When he says that Athens 'though in name a *demokratia* was in fact becoming rule by the foremost man' (2. 65. 9–10), Thucydides is not praising monarchy, but rather a singular kind of aristocracy whose force is not institutional but psychological. (He commended the moderate blending embodied in the constitution of the Five Thousand, perhaps because it offered an institutional approximation of this ordering force.) Institutional answers (like the Spartan social system) risked blunting the self-reliance of the citizens and their adaptability. Reliance on judgement was the only way to maintain the capacity to respond to changing circumstances. The more a *polis* resembles a collectivity, the harder it is for it to display prudence. Yet if a genuine collectivity succeeds in acting as an entity, through leadership, then it may achieve both prudence and greatness.

Robert Dahl expressed the view of many modern political theorists when he criticized ancient thinkers for the belief that freedom could be achieved only within the *polis* (Dahl 1989: 21–3). Modern liberalism is founded on the belief that freedom attaches to men (and women) as such, from birth. The character of the polity in which we are born may in fact make an enormous difference to our life chances. But the political boundary is not meant to make a difference to our rights or our potential as human beings. Conversely, the character of the political order is not meant to be affected by what we happen to be like: our social status or personal capacities. Autonomy is construed not as an achievement but as an attribute, and political order not as a vehicle for expressing and realizing our nature but as the price for pursuing our own private aims.

Just after the triumph of the American Revolution, Thomas Pownall explained why the ancient intimacy between polity and individual posed a threat to personal freedom. In his view, the 'ancient Legislators and Institutors of Republics' saw the need for

an exact conformity between the Constitution of the State and the Species of Individuals, the form of the community and [the] nature of the basis on which such [a] State must be founded. No such Basis was there in Nature; they therefore tried a thousand different projects to form such in Art . . . Not finding the natural situation of men to be what it was necessary to the System of their Polity it should be, they endeavoured to make it what it never could be, but under force and violence done to nature. They destroyed or perverted all Personal

Liberty, in order to force into establishment Political Freedom. (Pownall, *A Memorial Addressed to the Sovereigns of America* (London, 1783), 67–8; cited by Rahe 1984: 288)

For Pownall, personal liberty—the opportunity to pursue one's own natural inclinations—is the overriding value. The polity must not abstract from or attempt to transform man's personal qualities.

Plato and Aristotle sought the 'exact conformity' criticized by Pownall. The order required at the level of the *polis* had to be built into the human soul and reinforced by the political structure. Yet they insisted on this identity because they, like Pownall, believed that men in general were not capable of political freedom.

The ancient advocates of political freedom did seek to shape human nature. However, they, unlike Plato and Aristotle, acknowledged the significance of the *polis* boundary. The *polis*, and particularly the democratic *polis*, neither completely abstracted from, nor redefined or remade, the personal characteristics of its citizens. Politics was an attempt to enable men of different classes and attributes to become capable of citizenship, to express and transform their understanding of the good through political interaction. Politics demanded much of individuals, yet this was not a violation but rather an affirmation of their capacity for autonomy.

Thus Dahl's stricture, like Pownall's, misses the essential point. Ancient democracy was itself an attempt to extend genuine freedom, the ability to shape their own destinies, to men whose background or skills suggested that they were incapable of autonomy. Although the Athenians did exclude women and slaves, the shape of the ancient democratic achievement is not in itself hostile to the idea of inclusiveness. On the contrary. Yet greater inclusiveness did not, for the ancients, mean a dilution of the meaning of citizenship. In fact, a more demanding political order was required to ensure that an assortment of different individuals could indeed preserve their own freedom and fulfil their potential. An order of this kind cannot eliminate the possibility of Gyges, of man unbound. But in an order founded on political freedom, the citizen's self-understanding and sense of personal efficacy are tied to public sources of meaning through politics. The citizen of ancient Athens was visible and continuous: Gyges without a magic ring, but within a magic boundary.

REFERENCES

Aristotle, *The Politics*, trans. H. Rackham (London, 1977).

Dahl, R. (1989), *Democracy and its Critics* (New Haven, Conn.).

Finley, M. I. (1983), *Politics in the Ancient World* (Cambridge).

Ober, J. (1989), *Mass and Elite in Democratic Athens: Rhetoric, Ideology and the Power of the People* (Princeton, NJ).

Plato, *Gorgias*, in Plato, *Lysis, Symposium and Gorgias*, trans. W. R. M. Lamb (London, 1925).

——*Protagoras* in Plato, *Laches, Protagoras, Meno, and Euthydemus*, trans. W. R. M. Lamb (London, 1924).

——*Theaetetus*, in Plato, *Theaetetus and Sophist*, trans. H. N. Fowler (London, 1921).

Rahe, P. (1984), 'The Primacy of Politics in Classical Greece', *American Historical Review*, 89: 265–93.

Reeve, C. D. C. (1988), *Philosopher-Kings: The Argument of Plato's Republic* (Princeton, NJ).

CHAPTER 3

Democracy, Philosophy, and Science in Ancient Greece

G. E. R. LLOYD

D ID democracy influence other areas of Greek thought, and, if so, how? At first sight those questions have a certain air of incongruity. Clearly there is nothing at all surprising in the claim that democratic institutions and practices had some impact on ancient Greek *political* theories, just as, conversely, those theories had a certain, limited, effect on political practice in ancient Greece. But to claim any connection between democracy and, say, mathematics or astronomy or zoology might seem bizarre in the extreme.

Two fundamental distinctions are needed at the outset. First, we should be careful to distinguish between theory and practice in politics. Evidently the actual institutions and practices of states that called themselves democracies are one thing: but what any given political theorist, let alone an advocate of democracy, associated with that concept is another. As we shall see, the influences of democracy are as much a matter of its ideology and of its self-image as they are of the historical realities of democratic institutions.

The second distinction is that between influences attributable to democracy in particular, on the one hand, and those that may be associated more generally with Greek city-state politics, on the other. My argument will be that while both the idea and the practice of democracy

41

itself were significant influences on several domains of thought in ancient Greece, some important characteristics of Greek intellectual enquiry owe as much to the essential structures of the city-state as to the specific form those structures took in their democratic realization.

We may begin with that last point in order, first, to identify the key ancient Greek political institutions. From at least the mid-fifth century BC onwards a standard contrast was drawn between three basic constitutional types: democracy, oligarchy, monarchy (though of course some more complex classifications were proposed). These three were often characterized, as a first step, as the rule of many, the rule of few, and the rule of one person. But it was not just a matter of the *numbers* of those who (in some sense) ruled, but also one of how they achieved or legitimated their power and in whose interest it was used. Just as there was, in principle, a distinction between a hereditary monarch and a tyrant who seized power by force, so there were possible contrasts between more, and less, accountable versions of democracy and oligarchy, and between those that served the narrow interests of a particular group and those with at least some pretensions to operate for the benefit of the state as a whole.

More important, who counted as the 'few', and how the 'many' are to be defined, were intensely disputed questions. As Aristotle recognized, the 'few' were often equated with the wealthy, and in the view of many anti-democratic writers the rule of the 'many' meant rule by the poor. Conversely, while, at the limit, for the democrats the 'many' could mean the entire citizen-body, that still left wide open the crucial question of who was entitled to citizen status. Even the broadest ancient democracy was, of course, limited to citizens, and that by definition excluded all women and resident aliens, as well as a considerable slave population.

Ancient Greek democracies differ radically from modern ones in being participatory, not representative. The citizens of Athens did not elect some of their number to represent them in the assembly: they attended the assembly themselves. And the assembly, in the fifth century BC, was plenipotentiary. Its business was prepared by a council (itself chosen by lot, so that *any* citizen might find himself serving) but it was the assembly itself that took all the important decisions, not just whether to go to war or make peace (for instance) but even on strategy and tactics.

The involvement of all citizens in the political process could in principle be, and often in practice was, intense. True, in a state the size of Athens city-dwellers were far more likely to be able to attend the assembly than those who lived in outlying parts of Attica. Yet the basic point remains: ancient Greek citizens had, for the most part, far greater direct experience of politics than all but a handful of individuals in modern states. Moreover, if that point is especially true of ancient democracies, even in the oligarchies too there was political discussion and debate, although the proportion of the total population which participated was less.

Similarly the legal institutions of Athens and other democracies gave a large number of citizens some direct experience of the processes of law. If they were engaged in litigation themselves—and many seem to have been—they conducted their own cases, whether as prosecutors or defence, though from the mid-fifth century there were professional speech-writers who wrote speeches for others to deliver. But far more strikingly the large size of ancient 'dicasteries' meant that sooner or later any citizen would find himself serving in them. These 'dicasts', conventionally translated 'jurors', combined the roles of both judge and jury. They decided points of fact and of law, matters of guilt and innocence, and they delivered sentences as well as verdicts. The dicasts were chosen by lot—a key democratic institution that ensured the wide diffusion of responsibility and experience, in political as well as legal matters. And a further important development, introduced in Athens in the fifth century, and hailed by friends and foes of democracy alike as a move that had radical repercussions, was the institution of pay for service on the dicasteries. Since there could be as many as 5,001 dicasts serving in a single court, participation was widespread. Once pay was introduced the poor were certainly not disadvantaged—and some held they were positively encouraged to serve their turn.

These basic data concerning ancient Greek political and legal institutions in general and those of the democracies in particular are well known, but it is against their background that we now have to try to diagnose and evaluate influences. This is not and cannot be a matter of the direct and immediate effect of certain political reforms on any given ancient Greek philosopher or scientist. It is not as if the constitutional changes introduced by a Solon or a Kleisthenes at Athens found a direct echo in the work of contemporary intellectuals. But if we investigate broader possible influences, some positive suggestions can be made. It would, no doubt, be foolhardy to represent the influences or connections that may be suggested as *the*, or even as *among* the determining causes that gave Greek philosophy and science the particular characteristics they possess. However, some of those characteristics appear, not unnaturally, to reflect the social and political situation in which the philosophers and scientists worked, and it is these broader connections that we may try to identify as precisely as possible.

Five lines of enquiry appear particularly promising. We may consider, first, some aspects of the concept and use of evidence; secondly, the polemical or adversarial manner in which much intellectual (as well as political) discussion was cast; thirdly, the development of theories of both rhetoric and demonstrative argument; fourthly the privileging, in certain circumstances, of the abstract analysis of concrete situations; fifthly we may consider what the notion of radical revisability in philosophy or science may owe to the institutions of democracy. In conclusion I shall attempt briefly to test some of the hypotheses proposed concerning the ancient Greeks by means of a comparison and contrast with ancient China, which offers certain striking similarities and differences both in the political situation and in the aims and styles of philosophical and scientific enquiry.

It has often been pointed out that politics and the law provide much of the general vocabulary that Greek philosophers and scientists used for evidence and for the testing of ideas or theories. Of the general terms used in Greek for 'evidence', *marturion* is directly derived from the word for witness, *martus*. Two others, *tekmērion* and *sēmeion*, while not legal in origin, were extensively used in that context. Of the terms used for testing, *elenchos* and *elenchein* have, as their primary senses, the examining of witnesses or of an opponent's case. *Basanos* and *basanizein*, used primarily of testing gold by the touchstone, were regular terms for the torture to which slave witnesses were subject when called in evidence. *Dokimasia, dokimazein*, are used primarily of testing a candidate's eligibility for office, then more generally for other modes of evaluation. One of the most common expressions used in philosophical or scientific demands for an explanation is *logon didonai*, literally 'give an account', and that too had a particular technical use in relation to rendering a financial account or audit.

There might seem to be no more to all of this than a mere parallelism, the deployment of a general vocabulary in two types of domain, the political and legal on the one hand, the philosophical and scientific on the other. However, the ways in which evidence was cited in Greek philosophy and science may reflect the legal use in two more specific, but contrasting, respects. On the one hand the *ideal*, in legal matters as elsewhere, was to establish the truth. Witnesses should, after all, tell the truth, and neither lie nor inadvertently mislead. In principle the witnesses' own feelings should be discounted: the only thing that counted was the facts to which they were able to testify. The notion that there are objective matters of fact in suits brought before the courts may well thus

44

have served as a source of positive models for the development of the powerful idea of a truth that is both objective and investigable in philosophy and science.

On the other hand, ideals are one thing, actual practice another. It is clear that in actual Greek legal practice witnesses were generally assumed to be anything but impartial. They were marshalled on either side of a case mainly for the purposes of expressing solidarity and as direct support. Whether that aspect of witnessing also finds its echo in such other areas of enquiry as philosophy and science poses an interesting question. Of course in the investigation of nature the principal evidence is not that of human witnesses. That *all* the evidence relevant to a problem should be collected and evaluated is a principle to which many philosophers and scientists adhered and some made considerable efforts to implement it in practice. Yet the actual performance of many Greek speculative theorists in this regard still often fell far short of the ideal that most professed. The phenomenon of an anything but entirely open-minded review of the known, accepted, or assumed, data is common in all areas of Greek science, from astronomy to medicine, and at all periods. This reflects, in part, the adversarial nature of much Greek intellectual debate that I shall be discussing shortly. However, it is particularly striking that on many of the occasions when deliberate and explicit testing procedures are invoked, the aim was not so much to devise an experimental set-up that could be seen to be neutral between antecedently equally balanced alternatives, but rather to provide further supporting argument in favour of a particular theory. It is remarkable that even in what are some of the best prepared and most systematic experiments carried out in Greek antiquity, the quantitative investigations of the amounts of refraction between various pairs of media (air to water, air to glass, and water to glass) reported in Ptolemy's *Optics*, the results have clearly been adjusted to suit his general theory, since they all fit it exactly.

Now one might comment that a tendency to favour the evidence that supports the conclusion one wishes to arrive at is not just an ancient Greek, but rather a universal human characteristic, and it is certainly one that can be extensively exemplified in science at later periods, including in the twentieth century. Yet in judging why it is so prominent a characteristic in ancient Greek science it should be borne in mind that *witnessing* as a whole was there a part of *advocacy*.

This takes me to my second, more fundamental, theme, the well-known adversarial or agonistic traits that extend well beyond the strictly legal or political domain into many other areas of enquiry. Evidently in the law-courts and the political assemblies each speaker made every effort to establish his own position and to undermine that of his opponents. Destructive arguments designed for the latter task often provided the main means of recommending a positive position. Clearly in a lawsuit the opposition between prosecution and defence ensured the direct confrontation between a pair of antithetical positions. While in the political arena a more complex range of options might often be in play, the issue was still one of which, or whose, policy was to carry the day, and victory for one was often to be had only at the price of the defeat of all its rivals.

The extent to which Greek philosophical and scientific debates were cast in a similarly adversarial mode is remarkable. To begin with, the range of antithetical positions that were seriously entertained, in physics, in cosmology, in medicine, in epistemology, is extraordinary. Already in the pre-Socratic period we find both the view that change is constant (Heraclitus) and the opposite extreme, the flat denial that change exists (Parmenides). Against those who argued that the cosmos is eternal, many held that it is created. Some maintained that there is a single cosmos, others that there is a plurality, even an infinite number, of worlds, separated either in time or in space. Against those who argued that time, space, and matter are infinitely divisible continua, were ranged the atomists who held that all three are constituted by fundamental indivisibles. While many insisted that knowledge of underlying reality is possible, there were sceptics who challenged that belief, some denying that possibility, others claiming that on that, as on all other speculative questions, judgement should be withheld. Even in medical theory the variety of positions held stretches from the view that all diseases come from a single cause to the opposite extreme, the belief that every instance of disease is unique.

In part this extraordinary proliferation of theories on almost every type of problem can be seen as reflecting the rivalry among those who sought to make a name for themselves in one or other domain of philosophy or science. Certainly Greek theorists exhibit considerable ingenuity in propounding new solutions to existing problems and indeed in identifying new problems to be resolved. However, while in offering new explanations it was not necessary to proceed via a destructive critique of other, earlier or contemporary, theories, that was often one of the principal techniques used. Aristotle regularly begins his discussion of a problem with a review—generally a highly critical review—of earlier views or common opinions, both to identify the difficulties that had to be resolved and to suggest where earlier theories can be used or need correction. Of course there is no need to see this as a *direct* influence that derives from the types of debate held in the legal and political fields. Yet Aristotle himself acknowledges, at one point, how even philosophical discussion might take the form of adversarial debate. 'We are all in the habit of relating an enquiry not to the subject-matter but to our opponent in argument,' he says in *On the Heavens* (294b7 ff.), where the point at issue, in this cosmological treatise, is whether the earth is at rest and if so what keeps it from moving. How far arguing both sides of a case is appropriate in philosophy or medicine itself becomes a much debated issue. Plutarch, for instance, complains that Chrysippus did so to such an extent that it was difficult to say what his own position was (*On Stoic Self-Contradictions*, ch. 10) and it was a favourite tactic with those who sought to undermine *both* sides of an argument equally in support of a sceptical conclusion.

No doubt writers and audiences alike were well aware of the differences between the actual situation in a court of law and the polemical contexts of intellectual exchange. But perhaps the widespread experience of the former both encouraged that style of presentation of intellectual debates and provides a relevant background for their interpretation. It may be that just as in the lawcourts the dicasts learned to discount some of the rhetorical exaggerations of prosecution or defence, so too in the contexts of the exhibition speeches given by such sophists as Gorgias, and both mentioned and exemplified in some of the extant medical treatises from the fifth and fourth centuries, some of the more outlandish claims made would similarly have been discounted. The fundamental point remains, however, that much Greek philosophy and science presupposes an audience that prides itself on its ability in the evaluation of evidence and arguments; and if we ask where that ability came from, then the experience in lawcourts and political assemblies provides at least part of the likely answer.

My third theme relates to the separate but connected developments of rhetoric and of demonstrative argument. The explicit analysis of techniques of argument goes back to the composition of works called *Arts* by such writers as Corax and Tisias in the mid-fifth century BC. Thereafter we hear of a wide variety of writers who developed the subject, including Gorgias, Thrasymachus, Theodorus, Polus, and Alcidamas. Plato himself had much to say on the subject, notably in the *Gorgias* and *Phaedrus*, and Aristotle produced a systematic treatise covering all three main types of rhetoric—forensic, deliberative, and epideictic—and analysing both those techniques of persuasion that depend on the speaker or the audience, and those that have to do with the nature of the arguments used.

We cannot say that the development of the *practice* of rhetoric—associated with the development of the political and legal institutions in which it was primarily deployed—*inevitably* led to the self-conscious analysis of that practice. Yet clearly the fact that rhetoric was both so widely used and so important in so many contexts stimulated its study. The claim made by those who wrote about, or taught, the art was that they could help to ensure success in persuasion; and that was evidently a most desirable goal, even though many had their doubts as to how well-founded the claims in question were.

Of course those claims were greeted with a scandalized reaction from the likes of Aristophanes and Plato. The charge they and others levelled at rhetoric and the new learning as a whole was that its proponents taught people how to make the 'worse' causes appear the 'better'—where 'worse' and 'better' spanned both moral and non-moral evaluations. The new learning was held to undermine traditional morality. 'Sophist' came to be used, by Plato and others, in a pejorative sense, of those who—he would have said—made largely fraudulent claims to wisdom. But it is important to be aware of the polemical motives for that usage. Plato in particular was keen to distance his own and Socrates' teaching from that of those he criticized. Yet, as is well known, Socrates himself was used by Aristophanes as a representative of the new learning. Apart from their apparent success as lecturers and teachers, some of the most famous sophists, Protagoras, Gorgias, and Hippias, would seem to have been highly respected, at least in some quarters: thus the last two both acted as ambassadors for their home states on missions abroad.

Rhetoric as a self-conscious art was developed primarily for the sake of its use in politics and litigation—where, as we said, the opportunities for its use were extensive. However, its eventual repercussions, including in philosophy and science, were widespread. When Gorgias refers to the powers of persuasion through speech in his exhibition piece, the *Defence of Helen*, he mentions three examples. These correspond, roughly, to philosophy, to physics, and to legal contests. It would be a mistake to underestimate the extent to which Gorgias himself and others whom Plato names as sophists (Hippias, Prodicus, Antiphon) engaged in enquiry into physics, mathematics, music, astronomy, and medicine. But too little of their own work survives for us to be able to judge their styles of argument.

We have, however, ample direct evidence of the impact of rhetoric on the last of those fields, medicine. Of course the particular modalities of persuasion that a doctor would need to use in his contacts either with potential patients or with his own colleagues are, from some points of view, specific to medicine, though it is as well to bear in mind that the gap between 'professional' and 'lay' person was much less marked than we are used to today. There can be no doubt, though, that many early and later Greek medical theorists were highly self-conscious in their efforts to *be* persuasive. Some of the extant medical treatises from the fifth and fourth centuries BC themselves take the form of exhibition speeches. Again one other work, *On Diseases*, I, provides advice on how to deal with the veritable cross-examination the doctor might have to face, from patients, their friends, and other doctors, at the bedside. Doctors from the literate élite, it seems, might well be called upon to justify their diagnoses or their treatments, and quick-wittedness and fluency in argument were useful qualities. In his dialogue the *Gorgias* (456b ff.) Plato makes Gorgias claim that he would be more successful in persuasion than his own brother (a medical man) whether when dealing with particular patients (to win them round to accept treatment) or in presenting himself as a candidate for appointment as public doctor—when the decision as to whom to appoint was sometimes taken by the assembly. No doubt Plato means his readers to register this as an exaggerated claim, typical of the pretences of the sophists. Yet remembering that anyone could set themselves up as a doctor, for which no legal qualification was necessary nor available, we may say that what Gorgias is made to claim, in Plato, is far from incredible.

While no Hippocratic text we have goes so far as to recommend that a medical practitioner should study rhetoric, the work *Decorum* certainly provides tips on such matters as how to react to stubborn respondents, or to silent ones, and presents as an ideal that the doctor should be able to set forth 'clearly and gracefully' what he has demonstrated. Again *On Diseases*, I, explains how to ask questions and to answer them correctly, indeed how to carry on a veritable debate, and not merely on such general topics as the nature of the medical art, but also on the specific points at issue in particular cases. Yet another Hippocratic treatise *Precepts* issues warnings against descending to such tactics as the learned citation of poetry, or even the cultivation of an ostentatious appearance (luxurious headgear and the wearing of exotic perfume). To be sure, such practices are here condemned, but that would hardly have been necessary if the temptation to use them did not exist. We may conclude that just as, in Aristotle's *Rhetoric*, the cultivation of an appropriate image is part of the tactics of persuasion—for the speaker must present himself as someone worthy of credence—so in practice in medical contexts some explicit attention was given to this point.

The cultivation of the techniques of persuasion in medicine is readily understandable in so far as medical treatment depends on the consent of those treated. But it was not just in medical practice, but also in theoretical discussions of all kinds that rhetorical skills came to be deployed with greater or less self-consciousness. A Hippocratic treatise *On the Nature of Man* refers to those who held public debates on the topic of the constitution of the human body. To us it may well seem surprising that an apparently technical subject, such as element theory, should be the topic of debates in which first a number of speakers each presented a thesis, and then the result—who had won the argument—was decided by the audience itself. In part the aim of the speakers themselves may have been publicity: they used such occasions to make a name for themselves, often with the idea of attracting fee-paying pupils. Certainly we hear of lectures and debates held at venues such as the Panhellenic Games, when maximum publicity could be expected. But when acting as adjudicators at such discussions, the audience was doing no more than it was expected to do in the lawcourts and assemblies. Indeed the Greeks themselves noted the parallelism between these different types of debate, even while some commentators at least insisted on the difference in the degree of seriousness of the subjects debated. In Thucydides (3. 37 ff.) Kleon is made to chide the Athenians, during the Mytilenean debate, for behaving no better than an audience at a performance of sophists. Everyone, he says, wants to be a orator and have a reputation for quick-wittedness, praising clever remarks before they are out of someone's mouth. But whatever the differences, both contexts were contests where victory went to those who deployed the skills of persuasion to best effect.

The styles of political and legal debate can thus be seen to serve as models and analogues in some philosophical and scientific discussion. On other occasions, to be sure, the product of research into physics, cosmology, or medicine was not cast into the form of a debate. Archimedes' statics and hydrostatics are the outcome of individual, indeed rather isolated, study: the prefaces to some of his treatises implicitly lament the lack of colleagues with whom to correspond. However, in the early stages of Greek speculative thought especially, we may believe that interpersonal exchange, including in the context of formal debate, provided an important framework for some philosophical and scientific research.

As already noted, the influence of rhetoric was greeted by Plato, for one, with some dismay. It is now time to look at the *negative* models that the arts of persuasion afforded to philosophy and science. Both Plato and Aristotle repeatedly contrast the merely persuasive with the incontrovertibly true. As the examples of the lawcourts and political assemblies amply demonstrated, the merely plausible might or might not be true. But what philosophy and science were often held to require was more than just persuasiveness. Of course to claim that your opponents are no more than glib, and that what your yourself deliver is the unvarnished truth, is itself a standard rhetorical move. Long before Plato philosophers such as Parmenides had represented ordinary mortal opinions as the Way of Seeming, while on Parmenides' own story what he offered was the Way of Truth: and similarly Heraclitus too dismissed his rivals, and mankind in general, as fools.

However, the step that introduces a new factor in the possible modes of justification for the philosophers' position is the explicit analysis of the nature of demonstration. Although Plato develops the general contrasts between the plausible and what has been demonstrated, it is Aristotle who offers the first full philosophical analysis of the conditions that have to be fulfilled for a conclusion to be said to have been demonstrated. In the *Posterior Analytics* he points out that demonstrations (which he believed to be syllogistic in form) proceed by valid deduction from premisses that are themselves indemonstrable (on pain of an infinite regress) but true and indeed necessary.

While Aristotle thus provided the first theoretical analysis of demonstration, the work that stood as the example, *par excellence*, of its practice was Euclid's *Elements*, written around 300 BC. Here was the whole of elementary mathematics set out systematically in a network of deductive arguments proceeding from clearly stated axioms (definitions, postulates, and common opinions). The impact of this development is hard to exaggerate. Demonstration *more geometrico* became the ideal not just in mathematics itself but in other fields as well, in the exact sciences such as optics and harmonics, and even in some of the life sciences also. The second-century AD medical writer Galen sought as far as possible to make medicine, too, an exact science. Such basic principles as that nature does nothing in vain were given axiomatic status and, from these and the fundamental definitions, conclusions in anatomy, physiology, and pathology could (he claimed) be rigorously demonstrated, though he recognized, for sure, that much in those enquiries fell short of that ideal.

Here, clearly, we are far removed from the institutions of democracy and the modes of argument favoured by them, and at first sight it seems that this whole prominent strand in Greek philosophy and science can have nothing to do with the political background we described earlier. Yet while most of the applications of demonstration *more geometrico* were indeed independent of *external* influences, we should not lose sight of the point that the *origin* of this whole development owes much to the negative models provided by merely persuasive argument. For, as we said, a recurrent preoccupation of both Plato and Aristotle was to legitimate the contrast between what is merely plausible, on the one hand, and what is incontrovertibly true, on the other, that is, very broadly, between the domain of rhetoric and sophistic, and that of their own styles of high philosophy.

My next two more speculative themes relate to abstraction and to radical revisability. All theory, whether in political philosophy or elsewhere, may be said implicitly or explicitly to involve an element of idealization, the concentration on essential aspects of the data to be explained to the exclusion of other features considered to be accidental. Greek political theorizing, not surprisingly, exhibits a similar fondness for abstract schematic analysis to that manifest in other areas of Greek philosophy and science. However Greek political practice is, at points, exceptional in the extent to which attempts were made to implement schemata arrived at as a result of such analysis. This is not just that the founding of new colonies provided opportunities to set up brand-new constitutions. The constitutional reforms carried out by Kleisthenes at Athens beginning around 508 BC reorganized the entire tribal system on abstract principles. Attica was divided into three regions (city, coast, and inland) and each of the ten new tribes had representative *demes* in each. Even though no direct influences may be involved—in either direction—the geometrization of the political system may be compared to the geometrization of the cosmos. The first attempts at a geometrical model for the heavenly bodies go back to Anaximander around the middle of the sixth century.

In such cases what we see at work is a certain depersonalization of the subject-matter. But the most vivid instance of this, in politics, is in the very principle that lies at the heart of democracy itself, the notion that all citizens are equal and that decisions are to be reached and disagreements resolved by *majority vote*. However familiar such an idea may be to us, the principle of one person one vote represents a radical departure from the Greeks' own earlier social organization, where we may be sure that disputes were resolved if not by the naked exercise of power, certainly with due attention paid to the wealth, prestige, status, and reputation of the disputants. Though less was at stake in scientific theorizing than in political practice, similar tendencies can be seen at work in early natural science, first in the exclusion of personal gods from any account of natural phenomena, and then in the search for the underlying, mathematically expressible, relations as the key to the explanation of such phenomena. The discovery of the numerical ratios corresponding to the main musical harmonies was an early success story, though we must add that the growth of a general realization of the *ideal* of the mathematization of physics was both slow and halting and that many examples of its alleged implementation were no more than numerological fantasies.

My last remarks already take us to my final theme. One striking feature of much early Greek speculative thought is the impression given of the possibility of a radical new understanding of the world, based not on traditional beliefs nor on what was commonly assumed or generally acceptable, but on reason alone. This is partly a matter of the innovativeness displayed or claimed by philosophers, doctors, and mathematicians alike, but partly also of their evident belief in the radical revisability of traditional ideas and assumptions. The new styles of enquiry consciously or otherwise challenged and undermined common religious, moral, and other beliefs. Natural philosophy, the claim was, could give naturalistic explanations of phenomena. Following wherever the argument led, some of the philosophers proposed highly counter-intuitive conclusions (examples from Heraclitus and Parmenides have already been mentioned) but, deploying the potent contrast between *reality* and *appearance*, they insisted that much that was commonly taken as real was no more than a mere appearance.

No doubt the question of the origins of this ambition cannot be given a simple answer. The traditional historiography of philosophy would place the primary emphasis on developments within epistemology itself. However, a further part of the answer may perhaps lie in the political field, since it provided particularly striking instances of the radical revisability of existing constitutional forms. Such revisions certainly punctuate Greek political history, especially in the democracies, even though the dangers of such innovation were also clearly recognized. However, the principle to which the democracies adhered was that anything could be discussed, that any argument would be given a hearing, that every issue would be decided by democratic vote in the sovereign assembly.

Of course the realities of life in the democracies often fell far short of any such ideal, and the freedom of speech that Athens in particular prided itself on had its limits (as Socrates discovered). Yet the ideal expressed in the democratic ideology was not any the less influential for being just that, an ideal. We do not, to be sure, find philosophers and scientists explicitly invoking the democratic ideology themselves. Yet even anti-democrats such as Plato and Aristotle hold to the principle of the very greatest freedom of discussion—at least of *philosophical* issues. As to the influence of political structures on other spheres of experience, Aristotle explicitly recognizes that, if custom and tradition are open to radical challenge in the political domain, that has widespread repercussions elsewhere, indeed on *every* branch of knowledge.

We have suggested a number of ways in which Greek philosophy and science may reflect, directly or indirectly, the institutions of the city-state in general and those of democracy in particular. But we may now attempt briefly in conclusion to test some of those suggestions by means of a comparison and contrast with the ancient Chinese experience. On the one hand, at a period roughly contemporary to classical and early Hellenistic Greece, that is from the Warring States (480 to 221 BC) to the late Han (second century AD), the Chinese produced a variety of philosophical systems, complex medical theories, sophisticated mathematics, and a technology generally far in advance of that in the West. On the other, the political circumstances of ancient China differ markedly from those of ancient Greece. It is true that in the late Spring and Autumn period (sixth century BC) some of the Chinese political units were not much greater than some Greek states. However, the comparison of their political structures with those of Greek city-states reveals more differences than similarities, notably the absence of a sovereign citizen assembly. More strikingly, the *agreed* ideal, throughout Chinese political history down to modern times, was that of the rule of a wise and benevolent emperor. Chinese political theory concentrated on the characterization of such a rule and on how to implement it, and indeed advice on all matters of importance was generally directed to the emperor. Democracy figured as an option neither in theory nor in practice.

Yet, as noted, philosophy and science flourished in classical China as much as they did in Greece. So it is all the more interesting to consider whether or how far the differences in the *styles* of enquiry in those two great ancient civilizations reflect the differences in their political institutions. We may limit these concluding remarks to three of the most striking points.

First, the rivalry expressed between different philosophical systems in ancient China took an altogether less adversarial and exclusive form. While criticism of others' views was often voiced, a common way of doing so was to suggest that one's rivals had found only *part* of the Way, the Dao, not the *whole*. Thus in two early statements of the spectrum of philosophical positions, those in chapter 130 of Si Ma Qian's *Shi Ji* and in chapter 33 of Zhuang Zi, the *partial* successes, even of groups of thinkers for whom no great sympathy is felt, are acknowledged. This highlights, by contrast, the notion of exclusive truth that plays such an important role in Greek intellectual exchanges, following, in that respect (I suggested), the models provided by victory in a court of law.

The second profound difference in styles of enquiry relates to the lack of any preoccupation with the notion of axiomatic demonstration in ancient Chinese mathematics or indeed elsewhere in Chinese thought. Sophisticated mathematical results are set out in extant classical texts of the first century BC (such as the *Nine Chapters on the Mathematical Art*) and in the third century AD commentaries on them (for example those of Liu Hui). Yet thre is no concern to present these in axiomatic–deductive form, indeed no preoccupation with axioms or foundations as such at all. The quest for the incontrovertible, which (I suggested) is in part a reaction, in Greece, to the perceived inadequacies of the merely persuasive modes of rhetorical argument, has no analogue in China; but then neither does the analysis of rhetoric leading to a diagosis of its merely persuasive force.

This relates to my third and final point, to do with the notions of the uses of abstraction, the supremacy of reason and the possibility of radical revisability that are in play both in politics and elsewhere in ancient Greece. Of course the fact that tradition was generally held in considerable honour in China did not mean that new ideas were not introduced, though it was exceptional for these to be trumpeted as the definitive solutions to problems that had defeated everyone else, as sometimes happened in ancient Greece. Rather in China new ideas were often offered as the rediscovery, or the correct interpretation, of earlier lore. But so far as political revisability goes, that was severely circumscribed by the unquestioned ideal of imperial rule. The focus was thus on how to perfect a given system, not how to justify any system by the pure dictates of reason. Equally in other spheres of enquiry, too, the person whose view counted supremely in China was the emperor: he was the preferred target for the sages' efforts at persuasion, and the image of an ideal of free debate among individuals treated, in principle, as equals is to say the least far less influential.

55

Early philosophy and science take different forms, as the contrast between China and Greece exemplifies. But that comparison serves to confirm some of the particular influences, on their Greek forms, that stem from the circumstances of Greek political life, both the actual practice of Greek political institutions and, as much, the ideals or ideology with which they were associated.

CHAPTER 4

The Italian
City-Republics

QUENTIN SKINNER

THE Italian city-republics first began to develop their distinctive political systems as early as the closing decades of the eleventh century. It was then that a number of northern communes took it upon themselves, in defiance of papal as well as imperial suzerainty, to appoint their own 'consuls' and vest them with supreme judicial authority. This happened at Pisa in 1085 (the first recorded instance), at Milan, Genoa, and Arezzo before 1100, and at Bologna, Padua, and Siena by 1140. During the second half of the twelfth century a further important development took place. The consular system was gradually replaced by a form of government centred on ruling councils chaired by officials known as *podestà*, so called because they were granted supreme power or *potestas* in executive as well as judicial affairs. Such a system was in place at Padua by the 1170s, at Milan by the 1180s, and at Florence, Pisa, Siena, and Arezzo by the end of the century.

By the middle of the thirteenth century, many leading communes of Lombardy and Tuscany had thus acquired the status of independent city-states, with written constitutions guaranteeing their elective and self-governing arrangements. Amid the feudal and monarchical structures of western Europe, these developments were of course nothing less than extraordinary. They represented an explicit challenge to the prevailing assumption that government must be regarded as a God-given form of lordship, and thus that hereditary monarchy must be recognized as the only legitimate form of rule. It is not surprising, therefore, to find that the example of the Italian city-republics continued to serve as an inspiration to later enemies of tyranny and absolutism at many subsequent points in modern European history.

We must be careful, however, to avoid the unhistorical assumption that any direct line of descent can be traced from the political arrangements of the city-republics to those of modern democratic states. Two caveats need to be entered. The first is that the city-republics proved to be highly unstable, with the result that their experiments in self-government turned out in almost every case to be sadly short-lived. The main source of their instability lay in the fact that most *podestà* were originally nominees of the nobility, who tended from the outset to dominate whatever ruling councils were set up. This in turn gave rise to a further constitutional development in the first half of the thirteenth century. Citizens who felt excluded started to band together into separate 'societies' and elect their own councils and *capitani* in rivalry with the jurisdictions of the *podestà*. Such *societates* managed to win official recognition at Bologna by the 1220s, at Pisa by the 1230s, and at Florence, Padua, and Arezzo by the middle of the century.

Not surprisingly, the outcome of permitting such divided jurisdictions and loyalties was endemic civic strife. The most famous example (immortalized by Shakespeare in *Romeo and Juliet*) was the twenty-year conflict waged by the Montecchi against the older nobility on behalf of the *popolani* at Verona in the first half of the thirteenth century. But this was only one of many similar struggles. As Giovanni da Viterbo was to put it in his treatise of *c.*1250, *The Government of Cities*, 'practically every city nowadays is divided within itself, with the result that the effects of good government are no longer felt' (Giovanni da Viterbo 1901: 221).

Sometimes, as in the case of Venice, such faction-fighting was effectively contained. But in most cases it prompted a further political development which in turn spelled the end of the city-republics. By the beginning of the fourteenth century, many cities began to forfeit or voluntarily to cede their self-governing constitutions to hereditary *Signori* in the name of securing greater unity and civic peace. By this method the Visconti became *Signori* of Milan as early as 1277 and of Bologna by 1330. The commune of Pisa similarly fell under the control of a series of signorates towards the end of the thirteenth century. The Carraresi were formally accepted as *Signori* of Padua in 1339, while Arezzo finally lost its independence to Florence in 1384. Florence itself remained a republic until the early sixteenth century, but eventually succumbed to the Medici and became absorbed into the Grand Duchy of Tuscany in 1569. Of all the city-states of the Renaissance, only Venice survived as a self-governing republic, a status it managed to retain until its collapse in 1797. By that time, however, it had become a byword for stagnation and faded glory, a mere repository (as Ruskin was to put it in *The Stones of Venice*) 'of gathering vanity and festering guilt'. The gloomy moral drawn by most political theorists of early modern Europe from the history of the Italian city-republics was that self-government is simply a recipe for chaos, and that some form of strong monarchical rule is indispensable if public order is to be maintained.

The second caveat we need to enter is that it would be highly anachronistic to suppose that, even in their heyday, the city-republics ever thought of themselves as upholders of 'democratic' government. During the first century of their development the very term 'democracy' was virtually unknown. Throughout this period the cities drew their main ideological support from the defenders of the ancient Roman republic, especially from Cicero's moral treatises and from Sallust's and later Livy's histories of republican Rome. But none of these writers ever refers at any point to the concept of 'democracy' or 'democratic' rule. The terminology only became central to European political discourse after William of Moerbeke, translating Aristotle's *Politics* into Latin for the first time in the middle of the thirteenth century, chose the word *Democratia* to translate (or rather, to transliterate) Aristotle's term in Book 3 for the rule of the people.

Even after the term became current, the protagonists of the Italian city-republics would have been horrified to hear their constitutional arrangements described as 'democratic'. When Aristotle speaks of democracy, he uses the term to classify what Moerbeke describes as one of the 'transgressions' of good government. According to Book 3 of the *Politics*, there are three lawful forms of rule: monarchy, aristocracy, and 'polity', the rule of either one person or a few or a multitude in the public interest. The three corresponding transgressions are said to be tyranny, oligarchy, and democracy, the rule of one person or a few or a multitude in their own interest. The term 'democracy' thus came to be used—in the words of Moerbeke's translation—as the name of 'a form of government which is conducted for the benefit of the poor rather than in the public interest' (Aristotle 1872: 180).

It was not long before this understanding of the concept came to be formulated in tones of even deeper hostility. One of the earliest and most influential writers to contribute to this development was St Thomas Aquinas in his treatise of *c.*1270 entitled *On Princely Government*. Aquinas shows considerable admiration for the self-governing republics of his native Italy, and even stresses in chapter 4 that 'one sees from experience that a single city administered by elected magistrates who are changed every year is often able to achieve far more than a king who rules over three or four cities' (Aquinas 1959: 20). But this does not in the least make Aquinas disposed to speak in favour of democracies. On the contrary, he insists in his opening chapter that 'a government is called a democracy when it is iniquitous, and when it is carried on by a large number of people.' 'A democracy', he goes on, 'is thus a form of popular power in which the common people, by sheer force of numbers, oppress the rich, with the result that the whole populace becomes a kind of tyrant' (Aquinas 1959: 6).

While it would thus be seriously misleading to think of the Italian city-republics as democracies, there is nevertheless a sense in which we can speak of their contribution to the history of modern democratic theory and practice. They not only engendered a rich political literature in which a number of arguments in favour of government by the people were articulated for the first time in post-classical thought. They also evolved a structure of institutions which bequeathed to sceptics and enthusiasts alike a permanent reminder of the fact that self-government is no mere utopian fantasy, but is capable of being turned into political reality.

Among the principles of popular rule which the city-republics put into practice, the most obvious was the requirement that all political offices should be elective, and should only be held for strictly limited periods of time. This is not of course to say that the city-republics held regular democratic elections in anything approaching the modern sense. The right to vote was restricted to male householders, who also needed to show that they owned taxable property within their city, and that they had been born there or had at least resided continuously for a considerable number of years. Within these limits, however, the principle of election was very widely respected. It was generally used in the first place to establish the membership of ruling Grand Councils. One common method was to divide cities into electoral districts or *contrada*, within which those citizens who were eligible to vote then drew lots to decide who should serve as electors to the council. It was then usual for council members to act in turn as electors of the *podestà*. A common method in this case was for the entire council—generally some 600 strong—to draw lots in order to constitute an electoral committee consisting of around twenty members. This group then put forward three possible names, the final choice being made by a vote of the council as a whole.

These arrangements were celebrated and legitimized in a distinctive political literature to which the city-republics gave rise. The earliest surviving treatises on city government date from the middle of the thirteenth century, the best-known being the work of Dante's teacher, Brunetto Latini. When Latini published his encyclopedic work *The Books of Treasure* in 1266, he included a final chapter entitled 'The Government of Cities', in which he drew on his own experiences both as a Florentine citizen and as an exile in France. Latini opens his discussion by mounting a highly invidious comparison between the virtues of elective government and the tyrannical consequences alleged to follow from systems of hereditary rule. As he observes, 'the people of France and of almost every other country are obliged to submit to the power of kings and other hereditary princes'. But such rulers 'simply sell public offices to the highest bidder, with almost no concern for the good or benefit of their citizens'. This corruption stands in strong contrast with the system 'of governing cities by the year' which prevails in Italy, where 'the citizens, townsfolk and communes are able to elect their own *podestà* or *signore*'. The outcome, Latini insists, is that only in Italy are the people 'able to choose those who will act most profitably for the common good of the city and all their subjects' (Latini 1948: 392).

The same challenge to hereditary government recurs even more powerfully in the other strand of political literature to which the city-republics gave rise. After Aristotle's *Politics* became widely disseminated in the latter part of the thirteenth century, a number of scholastic philosophers began to use his authority to lend additional weight to the defence of communal rule. By far the most important theorist to write in this vein was Marsilius of Padua, who published his celebrated treatise *The Defender of Peace* in 1324, at the very moment when his native city was in the process of losing its traditional system of elective government to the hereditary signorate of the Carraresi. Marsilius opens his treatise by considering the origins and goals of civil communities, and in the course of his discussion mounts a vehement defence of elective as opposed to hereditary rule. All governments, he observes in chapter 9, obtain their authority by either election or succession or conquest. But wherever we find 'temperate' as opposed to 'diseased' forms of rule, this will always be due to the fact that the government in question came to power with 'the consent of the subjects'. It follows, according to Marsilius, that 'non-elected kings rule less voluntary subjects', and thus that 'the elected kind of government is superior to the non-elected'. It is 'by the method of election alone' that one can hope to obtain 'the best ruler' and thereby assure a proper standard of justice (Marsilius 1956: 32–3).

Of even greater interest to students of modern democracy is the fact that this preference for elective government was generally underpinned by a thesis of popular sovereignty. According to the apologists for the city-republics, the fundamental reason for insisting that all public offices must be elective is to ensure that their holders acquire a status no higher than that of salaried representatives of the people who elect them. The best form of government is accordingly held to be that in which the whole body of the people, the *universitas civium*, remains at all times the ultimate possessor of *imperium* or sovereign authority.

Brunetto Latini offers the briskest possible statement of this commitment at the start of his chapter entitled 'Of Signories'. 'There are three types of government', he announces, 'one being rule by kings, the second rule by leading men, the third rule by communes themselves. And of these, the third is far better than the others' (Latini 1948: 211). For the most careful statement of the case, however, we need to turn again to Marsilius of Padua's *Defender of Peace*. 'The best law', Marsilius affirms in chapter 12, 'is made only through the hearing and command of the entire multitude'. One reason is that any law will always be 'better observed by every citizen which each one seems to have imposed upon himself'. But the main reason is that 'the common utility of a law is better noted by the entire multitude', since 'anyone can look to see whether a proposed law leans towards the benefit of one or a few persons more than of the others or of the community, and can protest against it' (Marsilius 1956: 46–7).

With these arguments Marsilius commits himself to the fundamental principle which was later to win him abiding notoriety north of the Alps, but which merely reflected in philosophical language the actual practice of the Italian city-states. 'We may conclude', he declares, 'in accordance with the truth and the counsel of Aristotle', that the ultimate Legislator in any well-ordered community must be 'the people or the whole body of citizens, or the weightier part thereof, through its election or will expressed by words in the general assembly of the citizens, commanding or determining that something be done or omitted with regard to human civil acts, under a temporal pain or punishment' (Marsilius 1956: 45).

Marsilius goes on to draw a crucial inference from this basic argument. When a body of people, acting through a ruling council, agrees to the election of executive and judicial officers, this does not necessarily involve the abandonment of any rights of sovereignty. As Marsilius puts it, the *universitas* or body of citizens remains the Legislator at all times, 'regardless of whether it makes the law directly by itself or entrusts the making of it to some person or persons'. It follows that those whom we elect to govern us 'are not and cannot be the Legislator in the absolute sense, but only in a relative sense and for a particular time and in accordance with the authority of the primary Legislator' (Marsilius 1956: 45). And it follows from this that, as Marsilius underlines in chapter 18, if our rulers subsequently betray their trust and fail to govern in the public interest, it remains the right of the sovereign people to remove them from office and if necessary punish them.

Despite these forthright pronouncements, we must beware of assuming that the ideologists of the city-republics believed in anything resembling a theory of popular sovereignty in the modern democratic sense. As we have seen, they were essentially neo-classical writers, drawing their main inspiration from the philosophers of the Greek *polis* and the historians of early Rome. As a result, their views about the merits of self-government were almost always put forward with small-scale *civitates* or city-states specifically in mind. They rarely commented on the question of whether it would be desirable or even possible to establish similar systems of popular sovereignty in large-scale territorial states. When they did so, moreover, they tended to endorse the sceptical argument originally formulated by Aristotle: that since large nations can hardly be regarded as genuine communities, it hardly makes sense to think of ruling them in a communal style.

There can be no doubt, however, that the city-republics not only developed a genuine theory of popular sovereignty; they also made serious efforts in most cases to put it into operation. This can be seen most clearly if we consider the relationship between the powers of Grand Councils and of *podestà* in the heyday of the city-republics. On the one hand, the figure of the *podestà* was normally assigned a remarkably wide range of jurisdictions. Not only did he rank as the city's chief executive and judicial officer, but he was frequently given authority to act as an ambassador and even to serve as commander-in-chief. On the other hand, his status remained that of a salaried official of the commune. He was generally elected for six months or at most a year, and was thereafter debarred from holding office again for at least a further three years. While in office he was required to work in continuous consultation with the city's ruling councils, and at the expiry of his term he was compelled to undergo a *sindicatus*, a formal scrutiny of his conduct when in power.

There was thus a real sense in which sovereign authority remained vested at all times—as Latini, Marsilius, and others recommended—in the hands of the Great Councils. These bodies remained responsible for drawing up and continually revising the written constitutions by which the executive officials of most communes were bound. And it is clear that, in spite of their unwieldy size, they frequently decided matters of the highest importance on their own initiative. For example, it is recorded of the Genoese *Consiglio Grande* in 1292 that, with some 600 members present, it debated and finally resolved the question of war with Sicily in a session lasting seven days, in the course of which over a hundred citizens spoke.

As well as extolling such methods of participative government, the ideologists of the city-republics put forward an extremely influential explanation of why such arrangements should always be preferred. So important did this part of their argument become that it would probably not be unhistorical in this case to suggest that it may have exercised a direct influence on a number of later theorists of democracy.

The essence of their argument was that some form of popular and participative government is indispensable if one's community is to have any prospect of attaining its highest goals. These goals were in turn said to take the form of civic glory and greatness—greatness of size, greatness of standing, greatness of wealth. The ideal is a distinctively Roman one, and we accordingly find it most fulsomely developed by those writers who owed their intellectual allegiances more to the Roman moralists and historians than to the philosophers of ancient Greece. Among the earliest ideologists of the city-republics, this included both Brunetto Latini and Giovanni da Viterbo, each of whom stresses that, as Giovanni puts it, the aim of a good *podestà* must always be 'to uphold the honour and greatness and welfare' of whatever city is given into his charge (Giovanni da Viterbo 1901: 234).

For the most grandiose statements of the theme, however, we must turn to the political literature that accompanied the rise to civic greatness of the Florentine republic in the course of the Renaissance. We find the ideal of civic glory presented with increasing confidence by such writers as Leonardo Bruni, Matteo Palmieri, and Poggio Bracciolini in the first half of the fifteenth century. But we find it put forward with even greater eloquence in the closing years of the republic's life, and by no one more influentially than Machiavelli in his *Discourses* on Livy's history of early Rome, a work Machiavelli appears to have completed in 1519. As Machiavelli makes clear throughout his commentary, his main reason for focusing on the birth of Rome is in the hope of discovering by what means the city managed, from such small beginnings, to rise to such an extraordinary peak of greatness and thereby to become the glory of the world.

It is of course true that such ideals of glory and greatness have become alien to modern democracies, and have even come to be regarded as intrinsically anti-democratic in character. But it is arguable that modern democratic governments have impoverished the lives of their citizens by their unwillingness to recognize (except in the realm of international sport) that a sense of community as well as achievement can often be gained even by mere spectators of those activities which bring glory to their participants. It is undeniable, moreover, that the modern European democracies have benefited immeasurably from the characteristic preoccupation of their Renaissance forebears with civic glory and greatness. To mention only the most obvious instance, the art and architecture of the city-republics, most of which arose out of an emulative quest for civic glory, have bequeathed to modern Europe a cultural legacy of almost unexampled magnificence.

It was in relation to these goals of civic glory and greatness that the ideologists of the city-republics generally argued in favour of their distinctive way of life. The argument in its classic form may be said to have embodied two basic claims. The first is that no community can ever hope to acquire glory or greatness unless it fosters the liberty and equality of all its citizens, and can thus be said to follow 'a free way of life'. The most influential statement of this principle was undoubtedly owed to the Roman historian Sallust in *The War with Catiline*. Sallust prefaced his account of Catiline's conspiracy with a brief but uniquely influential description of the rise of republican Rome, in which he argued that 'it was only when the city managed to win its liberty that it was able to rise to such greatness in such a short space of time' (7. 3). The suggestion that a free way of life represents a necessary condition of civic glory was subsequently taken up by almost every apologist for the city-republics in the Renaissance. The classic statement can be found at the start of Book 2 of Machiavelli's *Discourses*, the moment at which he spells out in general terms the alleged connections between liberty and civic greatness. 'It is easy to understand', he declares, 'how an affection for living a free way of life springs up in peoples; for one sees by experience that cities have never increased either in power or in wealth unless they have been established in liberty' (Machiavelli 1960: 280).

Sallust was also an important source for the explanation usually given by the ideologists of the city-republics for supposing that civic glory is unattainable in the absence of a free way of life. Cities only become great, Sallust maintains, 'when civic virtue dominates everything', and 'when the greatest struggle between citizens is the struggle to attain glory for themselves' (7. 6). Any city which aspires to bask in the reflected glory of its citizens must therefore ensure that it leaves them as free as possible from unnecessary restrictions or constraints, and thereby leaves them at liberty to develop and exercise their talents and energies to the uttermost. Machiavelli reiterates and develops the same theme at the start of Book 2 of the *Discourses*. He begins by noting that 'all countries and provinces that are able to follow a completely free way of life are able to make immense gains.' This is due to the fact that 'each and every citizen knows not only that he has been born free and not in slavery, but that he can hope to rise by means of his own energies and abilities to become a leader of his community.' This in turn means, Machiavelli goes on, 'that wealth grows and multiplies in such communities as a result of increases both in trade and agriculture. For everyone is willing to increase what he owns and to acquire more goods when he believes that he will be able to enjoy freely what he has acquired. So it comes about that, in emulation with each other, people consider both their own and the public interest, with the result that both the one and the other begin to grow marvellously' (Machiavelli 1960: 284).

Under what form of government can this ideal of living a free way of life, a *vivere libero*, most readily be attained? This brings us to the second major principle enunciated by the ideologists of the city-republics. We already find Sallust expressing it in negative terms when he insists that we can never expect the required civic spirit and competition for glory to flourish under a monarchy. But for the clearest positive statement we need to turn once more to the same crucial passage from Book 2 of Machiavelli's *Discourses*. 'It is truly marvellous to consider', he proclaims, 'what greatness Athens managed to achieve over the space of a century as a result of managing to liberate herself from the tyranny of Pisistratus; but above all it is marvellous to consider what greatness Rome attained once she managed to liberate herself from her kings' (Machiavelli 1960: 280).

The key contention is thus that, in order to preserve a free way of life, it is indispensable to avoid hereditary monarchy and to uphold a republican form of government. So central to the self-image of the Italian city-states did this claim become that their apologists eventually sought to argue that liberty is actually the defining characteristic of republics. When the citizens of Lucca wished to celebrate their self-governing regime, they carved the word *Libertas* over the gates of their city. When the defenders of Florence's traditional government sought to oppose the rise of the Medici in the course of the fifteenth century, they took as their battle-cry the phrase *Popolo e Libertà*. And when the people of Siena wished to remind their councillors of their duty to uphold the city's republican constitution, they inscribed the word *Libertas* over the portals of the council chamber in the Palazzo Pubblico.

So firmly did this equation between republicanism and liberty become entrenched that, within the English republican tradition in particular, it became customary to describe republics simply as 'free states'. When Marchamont Nedham wrote in 1656 to commend the abolition of the English monarchy and the establishment of a republican constitution, he entitled his proposal *The Excellency of a Free State*. Likewise, when John Milton sought in 1660 to explain how the impending restoration of King Charles II could be forestalled by organizing England into a federation of self-governing *civitates*, he called his treatise *The Ready and Easy Way to Establish a Free Commonwealth*.

If we ask how the protagonists of the city-republics defended this central contention to the effect that republics alone promote liberty and hence greatness, we again find that Sallust's argument in *The War with Catiline* exercised an overwhelming influence. As we have seen, Sallust insists that monarchical regimes can never be expected to leave their subjects with sufficient freedom to develop their talents and abilities. This failing he attributes to the fact that 'kings always treat good men as objects of even greater suspicion than the wicked, since their talents and abilities invariably appear as a threat' (7.2). But Sallust also regards the encouragement of such free and emulative behaviour as the key to glory for both individuals and the cities that nurture them. His thesis is thus that it is because cities ruled by princes find such freedom threatening that they can never hope to rise to greatness.

This argument was again taken up and given its classic shape by Machiavelli in Book 2 of the *Discourses*. Machiavelli begins by remarking, in characteristically ironic tones, that 'whenever a tyranny supervenes upon a free way of life, the smallest of the evils that befalls the city is that it can no longer go forward, and is unable to grow greater either in power or in wealth; usually or almost always it falls into decline'. The basic reason, he goes on to explain, is that 'even if by chance there should arise a tyrannical ruler of real talent and ability, someone who manages by courage and force of arms to increase his dominions, this never results in any benefit to the community, but only to the ruler himself.' And this, he adds, 'is simply because, not wishing to have any cause to feel jealous of those over whom he is tyrannizing, he will find it impossible to give honourable employment to the best and most valiant citizens.' Lacking the necessary freedom to exercise their abilities, the citizens will be unable to increase the glory of their city by winning glory for themselves (Machiavelli 1960: 280).

As the protagonists of the city-republics recognize, the claim that civic liberty can only be securely enjoyed under a self-governing republic carries with it an important corollary. It follows that a willingness to participate in the political process, to seek one's own highest goals within the public sphere, must in turn be a necessary condition of securing one's own liberty. When Machiavelli speaks of those too lazy or self-interested to perform their civic duties, he invariably describes them as corrupt; and corruption he takes to be fatal to liberty, just as participation is indispensable to maintaining it. This explains why Jean-Jacques Rousseau, the greatest of Machiavelli's disciples among later theorists of popular rule, was to insist in *The Social Contract* that the people of England can only be described as slaves. Apart from exercising their freedom to vote, they are granted no place in the political process at all. However, as Rousseau cannot resist adding, the use they make of their freedom shows that they deserve their servitude.

From the perspective of the modern democratic citizen, this final argument is apt to appear a paradoxical one. Recent liberal theorists of freedom and citizenship have generally been content to assume that the act of voting constitutes a sufficient degree of democratic involvement, and that our civic liberties are best secured not by involving ourselves in politics but rather by erecting around ourselves a cordon of rights beyond which our rulers must not trespass. None of this is thought to vitiate the democratic character of our politics, partly because our rulers are still obliged to seek election, and partly because it is also said (though generally with less assurance) that they remain accountable at all times to those who have elected them.

It may well be, however, that the unfamiliar connection drawn by the ideologists of the city-republics between freedom and participation represents the most significant lesson we can hope to learn from them. Ordinary citizens in modern mass societies often find it impossible to make their political will felt, and even to act in defence of their individual liberties. This makes it correspondingly easy for modern governments, even of purportedly democratic allegiances, to act without proper regard for the will or even the rights of their own citizens. But if this is so, then it ceases to be at all paradoxical to suggest that, if we could somehow improve the level and extend the methods of political participation, this might offer us a safer if more roundabout route to the preservation of our own liberties. Increasingly the suggestion wears the air of a straightforward if disquieting truth.

Far from merely bequeathing us a paradox, the ideologists of the city-republics may thus be said to remind us of one of the most powerful if pessimistic arguments in favour of democracy. Put at its simplest, the argument states that, if we remain content to leave the business of government to ruling individuals or groups, we must expect them to rule in their own interests rather than in the interest of the community as a whole. The moral, according to the writers we have been considering, is that we must never put our trust in princes. If we wish to ensure that governments act in the interests of the people, we must somehow ensure that we the people act as our own government.

REFERENCES

Aquinas, St Thomas (1959), *De Regimine Principum* in *Aquinas: Selected Political Writings*, ed. A. P. D'Entrèves (Oxford), 2-82.

Aristotle (1872), *Politicorum Libri Octo*, trans. William of Moerbeke, ed. F. Susemihl (Leipzig).

Giovanni da Viterbo (1901), *Liber de Regimine Civitatum*, ed. C. Salvemini in *Bibliotheca Juridica Medii Aevi* (Bologna), iii. 215-80.

Latini, Brunetto (1948), *Li Livres dou Trésor*, ed. F. Carmody (Berkeley, Calif.).

Machiavelli, Niccolò (1960), *Il Principe e Discorsi*, ed. S. Bertelli (Milan).

Marsilius of Padua (1956), *The Defender of Peace*, trans. and ed. A. Gewirth (New York).

Sallust (1921), *The War with Catiline*, in Sallust, *Works*, trans. J. C. Rolfe (London), 1-130.

CHAPTER 5

The Levellers

DAVID WOOTTON

HE Levellers are the first modern political movement organized around the idea of popular sovereignty. They are the first democrats who think in terms, not of participatory self-government within a city-state, but of representative government within a nation-state. They are the first who want a written constitution in order to protect the rights of citizens against the state. The first with a modern conception of which rights should be inalienable: the right to silence (torture to extract a confession was a normal judicial procedure over most of Europe) and to legal representation; the right to freedom of conscience and freedom of debate; the right to equality before the law and freedom of trade; the right to vote and, when faced with tyranny, to revolution. The Levellers are thus not merely the first modern democrats, but the first to seek to construct a liberal state. Not only do their objectives have a contemporary ring, but the very language they use is often indistinguishable from our own.

We cannot have any sense of how extraordinary their proposals are unless we remind ourselves that not a single one of their key demands had previously been recognized by any actually existing government in the Old World; even the right to freedom of conscience had achieved only the most tenuous institutional entrenchment in the New. In England the government had been largely successful in imposing religious uniformity, and highly successful in carrying out pre-publication censorship of the press, until 1642. In most constituencies only some 10 per cent of adult males had the vote, and no one had an automatic right to legal representation when charged with a criminal offence: lawyers were only entitled to intervene if what was in question was an issue not of fact, but of law, and Sir John Davies was happy to argue that English law was superior to Roman because it did not 'allow counsel unto such as are indicted of treason, murder, rape, or other capital crimes' (Wootton 1986: 141). The Levellers were trying to construct a political and social world quite unlike anything that had ever existed before; quite unlike anything that had ever been envisaged before. The ideas that they invented are those which still guide our actions three and a half centuries later. Now all but one of their demands seems practical, all but one is generally recognized as a precondition for political legitimacy; the exception is their determined opposition to conscription.

The Leveller movement was short-lived: it lasted, at the most generous count, no more than four short years, from the autumn of 1645 to the autumn of 1649. But at its height it could muster the support of thousands of signatories to petitions, could call out large demonstrations in London, and could claim to speak on behalf of many of the soldiers in the Parliamentary army. The movement began as it became clear that the royalist army was going to go down in defeat in the first civil war; it ended as Cromwell and the Rump consolidated power after the execution of the king. It existed, in other words, only when there was a power vacuum, with no clearly established legitimate authority, no institution able to lay claim to a monopoly of force. By November of 1649, when Lilburne was released from one of his many spells in prison, it was clear that England's new rulers no longer felt they had anything to fear from the Leveller movement. Of the Levellers' four leaders, Lilburne, the younger son of a gentleman, was to die in 1657 where he had spent much of his life, in prison, a convert to Quakerism. We last hear of Richard Overton, once a Cambridge student and at one time an actor, when a warrant for his arrest is issued in 1663 for printing an attack on the government. William Walwyn, once a successful merchant, was to die in 1680, by then a quack doctor and long retired from political life. John Wildman, son of an Anabaptist, was to make a fortune from speculating in the confiscated estates of royalists, to become a knight, but to return again and again to anti-government plotting up until his death in 1693.

If there was no doubt at the time that the autumn of 1649 marked the Leveller movement's collapse, it is only with hindsight that we can talk about a movement dating back to 1645, for at first the Levellers had no name. The first time the name appears in print it is in a declaration written by the King (11 November 1647): it is immediately seized on by the royalist propagandist Marchamont Nedham as a most apt title for such a despicable and desperate knot to be known by, that endeavour to cast down and level the enclosures of nobility, gentry and property, to make us all even, so that every Jack shall vie with a gentleman and every gentleman be made a Jack. (*Mercurius Pragmaticus*, 9–16 Nov. 1647)

A Leveller was thus someone who set out not only to destroy rank but also to subvert private property, particularly private property in land: the term had traditionally been applied to anti-enclosure rioters defending popular access to the commons. 'By levelling,' said Harrington in 1658, 'they who use the word seem to understand: when a people rising invades the lands and estates of the richer sort, and divides them equally among themselves' (Harrington 1977: 460). By December of 1648 there were, indeed, Levellers to be found who wanted to level men's estates: they were soon calling themselves True Levellers or Diggers. But what we now term the Leveller movement always insisted it had no intention to level estates or introduce communism. The Levellers were in favour of levelling ranks, but not property (see e.g. Wolfe 1944: 288).

What they favoured was political equality. They did not say they wanted 'democracy'. Everybody knew that democracy was the worst form of government. Aristotle, it is true, had recognized some good forms of democracy, but what impressed medieval and early modern readers was the vivid picture he had painted of the tyranny of the lawless multitude, and it was to this that they were usually referring when they used the term 'democracy'. Harrington, in 1656, was to take a major step towards rehabilitating the idea of democracy by employing it as the term for good popular government and introducing the term 'anarchy' for corrupt democracy (Harrington 1977: 162). A few years later we find William Petty defending democracy as the best form of government in his private papers (Wootton 1986: 39–40). But when Harrington and Petty talked about democracy it was the political proposals of the Levellers they had in mind: they, like us, were searching for a convenient label for the new ideal of popular representative government. To talk about a Leveller movement before the autumn of 1647, to call the Levellers democrats: these are anachronisms, but harmless ones.

Behind these anachronisms there lurks, however, a larger one. Our interest in the Levellers derives from the fact that they seem to foreshadow the world we live in. They were of much less interest to historians in the eighteenth and nineteenth centuries who never expected to see democracy become the norm. Hume made only one reference to them as a group in his *History of England*; eighteenth- and early nineteenth-century radicals such as Catherine Macaulay and William Godwin gave them more space, but the Putney Debates were not published until the 1890s, and the first book on the Levellers did not appear until 1916. Brailsford, born in 1873, rightly said, 'To our generation fell the good fortune of rediscovering the Levellers' (1961: p. xi). Historians of the generations after Brailsford's were bound to suspect that what they needed was a picture of the Levellers, not as our precursors, but as eccentric members of an alien world. But the truth is that we are still waiting for a satisfactory account of the Levellers which will succeed in making their apparent modernity seem no more than an illusion of perspective.

There are four obvious ways in which one might try to restore the Levellers to their age. One might argue that they were far from being democrats; one might argue that they were far from being modern because their mode of thought was religious, not secular; one might argue that they were not forward-looking, but backward-looking, not out to create a new political order, but seeking to restore a mythical past; and finally one might argue that the Levellers were far from having a modern conception of the political process: they may have been a movement, but they did not think in terms of party politics.

C. B. Macpherson was the first to try to smash the link between the Levellers and democracy (1962). They were not, he claimed, interested in winning the vote for all adult males. They intended to exclude from the franchise all servants and beggars, and by servants they meant all wage-workers, by beggars all those on poor relief. The result would have been to give the vote to only a small minority of economically independent adult men. Now there is no doubt that on at least one occasion the Levellers were willing to accept a franchise of this sort. But there is also no doubt that it is not what they originally wanted or usually advocated.

At Putney, in November of 1647, representatives of the rank and file in the army together with leaders of the Leveller movement met with the army officers to debate what the army's political objectives should be, now the king had been defeated and now the majority in Parliament had made clear that they wanted to disband the army without making good the arrears of pay owing it, and that they wanted to preserve political oligarchy and reimpose religious uniformity. The assumption on both sides was that the Levellers and their supporters were arguing for one man one vote, or something very close to it. One of their supporters, Colonel Rainborough, himself an officer, a gentleman, and a Member of Parliament, was quite unambiguous:

I think that the poorest he that is in England has a life to live as the greatest he; and therefore truly, sir, I think it's clear, that every man that is to live under a

government ought first by his own consent to put himself under that government; and I do think that the poorest man in England is not at all bound in a
strict sense to that government that he has not had a voice to put himself under.
(Wootton 1986: 286)

And again a few minutes later: 'I do hear nothing at all that can convince me why any man that is born in England ought not to have his
voice in election of burgesses' (ibid. 288–9). If the Levellers were in the
end prepared to retreat from this position, it was because their prime
objective was to secure a vote for every household—living-in servants
(nearly all young and unmarried) were in their eyes comparable to
women and children, whose political interests were represented by the
head of the household. Only under acute pressure, and only momentarily, were they prepared to retreat from a householder franchise, which
would have given the vote to the poor, to a franchise which would
exclude those who were not self-employed.

The Levellers were, then, nearly democrats. Was their mode of
thought so deeply religious as to be unlike our own? John Lilburne was
always the most prominent of the Levellers, and his first appearance on
history's stage is positively reassuring. In April 1638, aged 22 or 23, he
had been arrested by the prerogative court of Star Chamber for import-
ing books which argued that, because the Church of England had bishops, it was a scion of Antichrist. Laying claim, as Puritans before him had
done, to a right to silence, he was condemned for his contempt to be
whipped at the cart's tail the length of the Strand, and pilloried in Palace
Yard, Westminster. But Lilburne was difficult to silence when he wished
to speak. As he was whipped, he cried out against the bishops. As he was
pilloried, he sought to scatter abroad pamphlets attacking them as
antichristian which he had hidden in his pockets. Eventually bound and
gagged, he continued 'to stamp with his foot and gesticulate in order to
show the people, that, if he had it in his power, he would still harangue
them' (Hume 1983: 244).

Yet what a world of difference there is between the Lilburne of 1638
and the Leveller leader. In the innumerable pamphlets Lilburne published
between 1645 and 1649 Antichrist has no role to play. Nor is Christian
theology at the heart of his concerns. It is true we find his close associate,
Richard Overton, insisting in July of 1646 that in the eyes of God all
men were equal, and that true Christians should treat each other as
equals. Amongst the first Christians there would have been no scope for
titles such as 'gracious lords' or 'favourable lords', for they recognized 'no
ruler, nor government, but by common election and consent' (Wootton

1991: 427). It is true too that many of the Levellers had probably belonged to 'gathered' or separatist Churches, in which they had played a role in determining their own constitution and selecting their own authorities, had witnessed democracy, or something close to it, in action. But the Christian model, whether exemplified by the early Church or embodied in contemporary practice, was not the crux of the Leveller case. For this was a model that could apply only to the saints, the saved, the elect. From the early Church and from the sects backsliders were excluded by excommunication. What the Levellers were proposing, however, was a democratic constitution for society as a whole, sinners as well as saints. What they were opposed to was any measure which would reserve power in the hands of the self-selected godly. What they wanted was not a Christian, but a secular democracy, and for this they had no theological models. William Walwyn, the most radical and subversive mind amongst them, questioned the very idea that some would be saved and others damned; but the Levellers certainly did not think that their political programme could only be accepted if one rejected the central principles of orthodox religion.

Where the Levellers entered most directly into religious debate was over the question of toleration. Unlike almost all their contemporaries they were prepared to tolerate Catholics as well as Protestants, pagans and even atheists too. In order to defend this view, they had to insist that it was not the magistrate's duty to enforce the Ten Commandments and ensure that his subjects had no other God but the true God. They had to insist on a fundamental difference between the ancient kingdom of Israel, where Church and State were united, and any Christian state, where religion must be voluntary and dissent tolerated. The sects maintained that there were theological reasons for separating Church and State. But it was not those reasons which the Levellers stressed. At the Whitehall Debate of December 1648, when all those opposed to the King and the Presbyterians gathered to plan a new constitution, Wildman argued that the reason why the magistrate should not be allowed to choose the religion of his subjects was simple: there was no reason to be confident he would choose aright. Such choices were best left in the hands of each and every individual (Woodhouse 1938: 161). He couched his arguments in terms of probabilities, quite unhandicapped by the fact that probability theory had yet to be invented (Hacking 1975).

Thus the arguments of the Levellers are not only democratic, they are strikingly secular. Overton dismissed the claims made by the Independents to divine inspiration as hocus-pocus. 'They are not flesh and blood,' he mocked, 'as are the wicked, they are all spiritual, all heavenly, the pure chameleons of the time' (Morton 1975: 204). Overton was reporting how he had been arrested at between 5 and 6 in the morning of 28 March 1649 by a party of soldiers under an Independent officer. This officer had claimed he had found Overton in bed with another man's wife. Overton vehemently denied the charge. But he also thought it was no business of the army's to enquire into his sleeping arrangements. In a world in which there was virtually no such thing as privacy—where bedrooms were reception rooms, beds shared, dressing and undressing done in public—Overton was trying to articulate a distinction which we would call a distinction between private and public, but for him was a distinction between sin and crime:

> As I am in myself in respect to my own personal sins and transgressions, so I am to myself and to God, and so I must give an account; the just must stand by his own faith. But as I am in relation to the Commonwealth, that all men have cognizance of, because it concerns their own particular lives, livelihoods and beings, as well as my own; and my failings and evils in that respect I yield up to the cognizance of all men, to be righteously used against me. So that the business is, not how great a sinner I am, but how faithful and real to the Commonwealth; that's the matter concerneth my neighbour, and whereof my neighbour is only in this public controversy to take notice; and for my personal sins that are not of civil cognizance or wrong unto him, to leave them to God, whose judgement is righteous and just. And till persons professing religion be brought to this sound temper, they fall far short of Christianity; the spirit of love, brotherly charity, doing to all men as they would be done by, is not in them. (Morton 1975: 223)

The argument is a Christian one, but it is an argument for the radical secularization of the state and of the criminal code. All men are to be regarded as sinful; but this is perfectly compatible with their being good citizens. If Overton is not a secular thinker, his argument can be translated without distortion into secular terms. Once one has separated private and public as he does, it is only a short step to Mandeville's claim that private vices, properly regulated, are the securest foundation for public benefits.

Perhaps we will have better luck with the Leveller attitude to time. Men and women in the seventeenth century were taught deference; the Levellers laid claim to equality. They were taught respect for tradition and the status quo. Their legal system was grounded in the common law, which recognized past practice as the only unchallengeable authority. Did not the Levellers too argue constantly from precedent and past practice? The only language within which one could conceive of radical change, in the pre-revolutionary age, was eschatological, and that, we have seen, the Levellers avoided. Overton was as quick to make fun of the language of eschatology as of that of divine inspiration, mocking the 'counterfeit dialect' by which the Independents had 'dressed out to the people in the sacred shape of God's time' their political opportunism, their resolve 'to rest themselves in the large and full enjoyment of the creature for a time, two times and half a time' (Morton 1975: 205).

Here too we seem at first to be on a promising line of enquiry. Again and again the Levellers associated contemporary oppression with a particular historical event: the conquest of England in 1066. Under the Anglo-Saxons government had been in the interests of the people. The law, in particular, had been designed to protect the innocent, not reward the powerful. There were no lawyers; the laws were known and understood by all; juries had the ultimate authority in the courts; justice was prompt and local, not dilatory and centralized. William had brought into existence an extensive apparatus of repression, symbolized by a law in the conqueror's tongue, the tongue still spoken in the common lawcourts, 'law French' (Hill 1958).

But the Leveller arguments in no way depended upon the claim, often reiterated, that they were simply seeking to reinstate the historical rights of free-born Englishmen. One version of this claim was to appeal to Magna Carta as the embodiment of the people's rights, a restatement of Anglo-Saxon liberties; but when Lilburne did this in 1645, Walwyn corrected him. The oppressed are in error when they 'with one consent, cry out for Magna Carta (like great is Diana of the Ephesians), calling that mess of pottage their birthright, the great inheritance of the people'. This is 'to call bondage liberty, and the grants of conquerors their birthrights'. But Walwyn's response was not to go back to the rights of the people before the Conquest. It was to appeal to 'the universal rules of common equity and justice' by which 'all men and all authority in the world are bound'. 'That liberty and privilege which you claim is as due unto you as the air you breathe in' (Walwyn 1989: 148–9). Walwyn's arguments were later taken up by Overton:

Whatever our forefathers were, or whatever they did or suffered, or were enforced to yield unto, we are the men of the present age, and ought to be absolutely free from all kinds of exorbitances, molestations, or arbitrary power. . . . You know the laws of this nation are unworthy a free people and deserve from first to last to be considered and seriously debated and reduced to an agreement with common equity and right reason, which ought to be the form and life of every government. (Wolfe 1944: 114, 124)

'We are the men of the present age' was not an appeal to history, or to rights and liberties shaped over time; it was an appeal against history to universal standards and abstract principles. We are, in the Leveller proposal for an Agreement of the People, only a short step from a Declaration of Rights.

On the fourth question, that of the Leveller view of the political process, we seem, at last, to be within sight of an easy victory. The Levellers may have been a movement, they may have had a manifesto, but they were not a political party. They never stood for election; they never presented themselves as the prospective rulers of the country. They always saw themselves, not as participants in a political process, but as advocates of a certain set of rules which ought to govern the participation of others. Far from seeing their own activities in political terms, they insisted that they were opposed to politicians and to the setting up of parties. They represented not a partial interest, but a common interest, 'an unanimous and universal resolution in all well-minded people' (Haller and Davies 1944: 182).

The failure of the Levellers to think in terms of party politics certainly decisively sets their view of democracy at odds with our own. The first modern political party was to be forged by Shaftesbury in the 1670s; the first defence of party was Burke's *Thoughts on the Causes of the Present Discontents* (1770). The Levellers were advocating representative government without having the least idea of how, in practice, representative government would have to be conducted. But if their failure to think in party-political terms represents one respect in which we can decisively locate them in an alien historical past, it also serves to remind us of the fundamental paradox of modern democratic government. In representative democracies, it is not the people who govern, but political parties. And political parties themselves do not simply represent their members; they also reflect the priorities of interest groups while simultaneously seeking to articulate the concerns of the wider public. Had the Levellers been able to foresee the modern political party it is doubtful they could have approved the queasy mixture of principle, interest, and expediency from which it takes its being. But a sense of distaste at the workings of our political process would not mark them out as visitors from another culture: it is one of the fundamental characteristics of our own view of our politics. The Levellers may not have had a modern conception of politics; but then few of us have reconciled ourselves to the institutions which shape our lives. Once again, the gap between the Levellers and ourselves is less than at first sight appears.

I have surveyed four strategies for trying to establish that the Levellers belong to a different and alien political culture. Each of these strategies is, in practice, partially successful. The Levellers were happy to think in terms of the representation of households, not individuals; keen to appeal to Christian principles; eager to lay claim to ancient rights; incapable of thinking in party terms. Yet, at the same time, none of these strategies really pays off: for the Levellers are concerned with the rights of each and every individual; their fundamental arguments are secular not religious; they are determined to throw off the dead hand of precedent; and, if they failed to think in party terms, so, time and again, do we.

We are thus faced with a persistent difficulty. Since Burckhardt, historians have been primarily concerned with portraying alien worlds. They have ventured across time, as anthropologists have across space, to find ways of thought and modes of behaviour at odds with our own. How to discuss, how to explain, individuals who insist on inhabiting, not their world, but ours: who are, in Marvell's phrase, 'rational amphibii' (Marvell 1972: 99)? Dragged from their world into ours, the Leveller texts remain stubbornly alive.

In the first half of this chapter we have explored a number of strategies for pushing the Levellers back into the past, working on the assumption that the seventeenth century was an alien world, theocentric, hierarchical, conservative. We have seen that these strategies are not unfruitful, but they are inadequate to their primary task: they fail to render the superficial modernity of Leveller texts illusory.

Is the problem that we are working with a mistaken set of assumptions about the seventeenth century? Are the Levellers in fact spokesmen of a new social order, emerging within the interstices of the old? David Underdown has argued (1985) that seventeenth-century England was not really one society but two. On the one hand there were arable areas with nucleated villages, functioning manor courts, and great landlords: here deference and hierarchy were the norm, and support for monarchy and the Church of England was strong. But on the other there were woods, uplands, marshes, areas of mixed agriculture, rural industry, and scattered settlement, where individuals had much greater freedom and social differences were much more fluid. Here support for Parliament, for Puritanism, and for the Levellers was to be found.

The bulk of support for the Levellers, however, came not from rural England, but from London and from the army. Seventeenth-century London was to a remarkable degee a society of immigrants, each trying to make his or her way in an alien world (Wrigley 1967). The New

Model army was to a considerable degree a volunteer army, in which there was extensive opportunity for advancement through ability. In these societies egalitarian principles made sense; self-government seemed a practical objective; tradition seemed an irrelevant hindrance. The Levellers were thus addressing these new communities of 'masterless men', and if what they have to say seems strangely familiar to us it is because we all now live in such mobile, contractual, egalitarian societies (Herzog 1989).

There is, almost certainly, a good deal of truth in this argument. It is particularly striking that the last political act of William Walwyn, the most socially egalitarian of the Levellers, the one most hostile to wealth, power, and privilege, was to pen a forceful plea for freedom of trade. Walwyn looked forward to the day when there would be merchants 'in every haven and town', trading not 'in a stately manner upon set days', but engaged in a continuous 'strife and emulation'. Trade would no longer be confined to wealthy men restricting their activities to 'a beaten road', but would soon involve each and every individual and flood through 'all creeks and haven towns': 'every ten shillings, as in some countries, would be improvable; even servants would adventure their wages' (Walwyn 1989: 449–51). The Levellers did not envisage a commercial society of the sort that was actually dominant in early Stuart England, a society of chartered companies and great capitalists; they hoped rather to establish a nation of shopkeepers.

But it is worth remarking that the Levellers and their fellow radicals were not speaking only for masterless men, but also for those with masters. Walwyn wants to create opportunities for servants. Jeremiah Burroughs was proud that 'There is no country in the world where country men, such as we call the yeomanry, yea, and their farmers and workmen under them, do live in that fashion and freedom as they do in England; in all other places they are slaves by comparison': he was thinking of the arable heartlands, with their hierarchy of landlord, tenant, and labourer, and of the rights of workmen to equal consideration alongside their employers (Wootton 1990: 667). Rainborough's famous words:

truly, sir, I think it's clear, that every man that is to live under a government ought first by his own consent to put himself under that government; and I do think that the poorest man in England is not at all bound in a strict sense to that government that he has not had a voice to put himself under (Wootton 1986: 286)

are usually read simply as a statement of egalitarian principles. But it is worth pausing to ask what he is thinking of when he speaks of putting oneself under government. He certainly is not thinking of a political act, for we normally find ourselves under government. He has some other model to which he wants to make politics conform. The obvious occasion when a man put himself under government, particularly when a poor man chose who was to govern him, was when he was indentured as a servant. Rainborough's paradigm of freedom is the freedom of the employee to choose an employer and to agree the terms of employment with him. Walwyn, Burroughs, and Rainborough are not thinking in terms of masterless men, but of men free to choose their masters, and free, in principle, to become employers themselves. And this, as we have seen, was characteristic of the Leveller movement as a whole: it demanded a right to choose its rulers, rather than to rule.

We can make some progress, then, by recognizing that the Levellers inhabit a surprisingly fluid, commercial society, and that the social policies they advocated were intended to expand economic opportunities and increase social mobility. We can also make progress by recognizing that they did not live in a world where everything conspired to encourage deference to authority. There were powerful intellectual traditions which could be appealed to against the claims of absolute authority. Brian Tierney (1982) has convincingly shown that the principles of constitutional government put forward by Parliamentary spokesmen such as Samuel Parker had medieval roots. Johann Sommerville (1986) has demonstrated that the arguments of the early 1640s were foreshadowed in the 1620s and 1630s, even if no one explicitly defended a right of rebellion before the meeting of the Long Parliament. There was nothing novel in the notion of limited government, a mixed constitution, or an ultimate right of rebellion. What was novel is the claim, which we first find being made by two clergymen, Burroughs and Bowles, in the winter of 1642/3, when it seemed possible that Parliament would concede victory to the King, that, faced with tyranny, men find themselves as if in a pre-social state, armed with the rights of nature, and entitled to construct a new political order on abstract principles of natural right (Wootton 1990). Neither medieval political thinkers nor early Stuart Parliamentarians had thought of the state of nature as something other than a useful device for explaining how limited governments had first been established, had thought of declaring that tyranny restored the state of nature and all the freedoms that went with it. By appealing to the rights of nature, Burroughs and Bowles asserted the equality of all men, pushed to one side the biblical arguments for obedience, and broke the chains of precedent. It is this decisive move, which makes possible a radical egalitarianism where even those denied the franchise under the existing constitution could lay claim to a right to be heard, which separates the Levellers, and their immediate precursors, the diehards of 1642/3, from all those who had gone before.

How is one to explain this extraordinary paradigm shift, which marks the birth of modern political theory? A good deal depends upon what sort of obstacles one thinks had to be overcome in order to make it. It seems unlikely that the obstacles were intellectual: Sir Robert Filmer complained in 1631 that all the teaching of the universities for the last hundreds of years amounted to nothing other than a defence of equality and men's right to choose their own government (Filmer 1991: 2–4). This was a grotesque exaggeration, though it shows that at least one conservative feared there were considerable intellectual resources to which radicals could lay claim. But Filmer's attack on subversion is also an example of phenomenon discussed by Stephen Greenblatt, who has been one of the most fertile writers on the theme of power and authority in early modern England in recent years. Greenblatt's landmark essay 'Invisible Bullets' argues that when we encounter what seem to be subversive voices in the texts of Shakespeare's day we need to be aware that subversion and disorder is usually only voiced in these texts so that it can be contained. Disturbing vistas are glimpsed only so that they can be closed off. Greenblatt seems to claim that there is no such thing as a subversive text in Renaissance England; only texts that seem subversive to us (1988: 21–65; but see his disavowal, 1990: 165–6). Filmer's debate with radicalism is typical in that it is one-sided. If this is the case, if the Elizabethan and early Stuart 'world picture' left no space for subversive speculation, if subversive arguments were conjured up only so that they could be exorcized, then a deep and unbridgeable chasm would lie between the genuinely subversive texts of the Civil War and all that went before them.

That subversive texts are few and far between before 1642 is unquestionable. But is this because subversive ideas were in the end incredible— that one could imagine, to use Greenblatt's example, that other people could be atheists, but never become one oneself? Or is it rather because the price for giving voice to subversive ideas was too high? A classic example, which deserves to be more widely studied, is that of Étienne de la Boétie's *Discours de la servitude volontaire* (Greenblatt 1989). La Boétie's text has come to be regarded as one of the founding texts of anarchism because of its bitter attack on all authority which denies equality and concentrates power in the hands of a few. Why, La Boétie wants to know, do people tolerate the tyranny embodied in all forms of government when the tyrants are so few, the victims so numerous? La Boétie does not seek to close off the subversive vista he has opened up; there is no process of containment here.

After La Boétie's death in 1563 his friend Montaigne wanted to publish a fitting tribute to his memory. It was with this in mind that he set out to write the *Essays*. At the heart of the *Essays* he planned to publish an essay on friendship; and within the frame provided by that essay (the image is Montaigne's) he intended to contain the text of the *Discours*. This plan was doomed to failure. Huguenot rebels published La Boétie's text before Montaigne could do so, and it was condemned to be burnt. It became unpublishable, even within the complex container which Montaigne had devised for it.

Thus the line between an argument which can be safely contained and one which is too dangerous to handle is a thin one: it is a line which La Boétie's text crossed as Montaigne worked on packaging it for public consumption. By the same token, readers may often have unpacked texts, and found within them subversive meanings which their authors believed they had rendered innocuous. Walwyn found in Montaigne, his favourite reading, ideas which Montaigne had derived from La Boétie, and restored to them their subversive implications (Walwyn 1989: 399–401).

A censored text can look as if it has been safely 'contained', but others may be able to unpack the subversive meaning hidden within it. The complex play of containment and censorship on the one hand, and creative reading on the other, means that it is impossible to say, without reference to a particular context, which texts are subversive, which supportive of authority (Ginzburg 1980: 28–51). Sir Henry Marten, father of the regicide, for example, entertained Parliament in 1628 with a story from Aesop's *Fables*, about a lion, a donkey, and a fox, the moral of which was far too dangerous to be put in words, for it was that one should never trust the King (Patterson 1987: 279–80).

Our detour through Renaissance literature brings us, at last, back to the Levellers. I have several times referred to Overton's contribution to *The Picture of the Council of State*, a work written in prison by the Leveller leaders when they were rounded up in March of 1649. It is easy to read that brilliant essay with an eye only to the political theory to be found embedded in it; but to do so is to miss its point. Overton's objective is to write an essay which is the mirror image of the texts discussed by Greenblatt: here the voices of authority appear, often verbatim, sometimes, as we have seen, mocked and satirized; but they do so precisely so that they can be contained, subordinated, made to serve the purpose of a subversive argument. Overton, who had spent years on the stage, re-enacts the drama of his arrest and interrogation in order to subvert the values of his captors and ensure that his own voice be heard over theirs. The techniques of inversion pioneered by Overton were to be put to brilliant use by a former Leveller, Edward Sexby, in *Killing No Murder* (1657), which begins with a mock panegyric of Cromwell, but is in fact a bitter cry for his assassination: 'All this we hope from your Highness's happy expiration, who are the true father of your country: for while you live we can call nothing ours, and it is from your death that we hope for our inheritances' (Wootton 1986: 361).

Sexby ended: 'Courteous reader, expect another sheet or two of paper of this subject if I escape the tyrant's hands . . .', giving rise to the myth that Cromwell's troops had burst in on him while he was in the act of writing. Sexby, indeed, died in prison. Overton was soon released in 1649; but he had played the role of martyr before Sexby, concluding his essay with the motto *Dulce est pro patria mori*. Overton wrote 'from my aristocratical captivity in the Tower of London.' He knew that he was now held where More and Raleigh had been imprisoned, and that they too had turned to writing in captivity. But what struck him, as it must strike us, was how the world had changed: now the most important enemies of the state were not Catholics or aristocrats, but representatives of the common people. Imprisonment in the Tower was for Overton a triumph, proof that the Levellers had to be taken seriously.

What we standardly read to learn about the Levellers is the Putney Debates; but they mislead us because, for a brief moment, Levellers and oligarchs spoke to each other as equals. In 1649 Overton urged on his captors such a 'fair and moderate discourse' between equals (Morton 1975: 209). But he knew perfectly well the army was engaged in 'inconsiderately devolving all law, right and freedom betwixt man and man into their sword', and he sought to parry this sword, proving himself, rather than his captors, 'as quick and as nimble as an Hocas Spocas, or a fiend in a juggler's box', with nothing more than the story, the petty drama, of his captivity (ibid. 202, 204).

If we read the Levellers as if they were contemporaries, we miss the extraordinary faith they placed in the power of words, a faith that seems ludicrous to us, but not perhaps to men who had been raised on Foxe's *Book of Martyrs* and found there models, not only of how to defy authority fearlessly (compare, for example, Hill 1975: 29, with Foxe 1861–89: vii. 519–20), but also how to win ultimate victory by reporting that defiance (Haller 1963). When the troops came to arrest Overton he hid some incriminating books in 'the beds betwixt the sheets (and the books were all the persons he [the arresting officer] found there in the beds, except he took us for printed papers, and then there were many)' (Morton 1975: 200). The joke is a sour one: no one could mistake a book for a person, or think Overton was in bed with a woman because a book was in his bed. But at that same time Overton *is* a printed paper and printed papers *are* persons; thanks to printing there are innumerable Overtons to be scattered abroad, numerous spokesmen for subversion. Overton's bedroom was more crowded than it seemed.

In July of 1609 an English ship, after many storm-tossed days at sea, was wrecked on the island of Bermuda (Greenblatt 1988: 129–63). On it was a party of colonists bound for Virginia, under the command of the new Governor, Lord La Warre. The men, however, soon realized that life in Bermuda, land of eternal spring, was easier than ever it would be in Virginia, and threatened to rebel. On 24 January 1610, Stephen Hopkins, 'a fellow who had much knowledge in the Scriptures, and could reason well therein', sought to win over recruits to the conspiracy,

and alleged substantial arguments, both civil and divine (the Scripture falsely quoted) that it was no breach of honesty, conscience, nor religion, to decline from the obedience of the Governor, or refuse to go any further, led by his authority (except it so pleased themselves) since the authority ceased when the wreck was committed, and with it they were all then freed from the government of any man; and for a matter of conscience, it was not unknown to the meanest, how much we were therein bound each one to provide for himself, and his own family (Purchas 1906: xix. 30–1).

Hopkins was seized, court-martialled, and sentenced to be shot; but he played the part of a penitent well, and was eventually pardoned. What little we know of him comes from one of those who pleaded for his life, and the account is remarkably ambiguous: Hopkins's arguments are both substantial and false, addressed to others and to ourselves; he was both rightly condemned and rightly pardoned. Our narrator, Sir Thomas Gates, both silences Hopkins and invites us to reconstruct his line of reasoning. We cannot tell if, in his 'substantial arguments, both civil and divine', he referred to the rights of nature, but it seems likely he did. What is clear is that when the English ship of state went on the rocks in 1642, there were, as in Bermuda in 1609–10, men quick to argue that the original contract had been dissolved, that all were now equal, and should be governed only by authorities of their own choosing. It would be easy to conclude that every ship contained a silent Hopkins, every village a mute Lilburne, each waiting his opportunity to speak. Yet in seventeenth-century Europe there were numerous civil wars and only one Leveller movement. In the Caribbean there were numerous wrecks, and (as far as we know) only one Hopkins.

Did Hopkins construct his arguments as the months passed, as Bermuda came to feel like home? Or were they already contained concealed in the learning he carried with him? The choice is certainly a false one. Jesuit monarchomachs and Calvinist tyrannicides had provided a conceptual tool-box with which it was as easy to construct an argument for freedom as it was for Lord La Warre, with the material tools he had rescued from the wreck, to construct a pinnace to take his stranded subjects on to Virginia. But such arguments were more fragile even than ships, as fragile as the people who gave voice to them. Until, that is, the printing press came to their assistance, and gave to Lilburne and Walwyn, Overton and Sexby the chance to be in more than one place at a time, to be many persons not one. And here again the record of the Putney Debates, important as it is, distracts attention from the main thing, which is not that the Levellers believed in equality, or spoke for it, but that they were able to get their beliefs into print. It is only because they were able to put the printing-press to work that they became so powerful that it was necessary to make a verbatim transcript of a debate between them and their superiors. We know what they thought because they had already made their views known to thousands of their contemporaries; we never will know what Stephen Hopkins thought, for even Sir Thomas Gates would not tell us, and many of his fellow castaways can have known nothing of his arguments until he was brought forth in manacles before the assembled company to plead for his life. Under such circumstances there could be no *patria* to die for, no prospect of the immortality earned by those who die in a good and public cause.

If the Levellers appear to be the founding fathers of modern democratic theory, it is because they are the first to address themselves, not to the republic of letters, but to the republic of the lettered. Indirect democracy is inconceivable without the printing-press. The Levellers did not pause to meditate upon this fact: Overton's joke about the books in his bed is one of the few indications that (for all the time and labour they must have spent carrying presses from one hiding-place to another, all the days and nights spent setting type and printing) they had given it any thought at all. Behind Overton's joke, though, there lies a passage in Milton's *Areopagitica* (1644), a passage which shows how Civil War radicals had grasped the power of the press:

For books are not absolutely dead things, but do contain a potency of life in them to be as active as that soul was whose progeny they are; nay, they do preserve as in a vial the purest efficacy and extraction of that living intellect that bred them. I know they are as lively, and as vigorously productive, as those fabulous dragon's teeth; and being sown up and down, may chance to spring up armed men . . . as good almost kill a man as kill a good book. Who kills a man kills a reasonable creature, God's image; but he who destroys a good book kills reason itself, kills the image of God, as it were in the eye. (Milton 1958: 149–50)

Overton, writing from his imprisonment in the Tower, knew that he could be killed, but that it was too late to destroy his books. 'I know I am mortal and finite,' he told his captors. 'But, Gentlemen, I humbly desire yet a word or two' (Morton 1975: 214). He was bound, but he could not be gagged.

For a moment, indeed, as we read Overton we seem to achieve the impossible: we seem to hear the dead speak. But, of course, the dead are silent, as Greenblatt reminds us (1988: 1). The peculiar form of survival after death that printed texts make possible was best defined by Sexby. He presented *Killing No Murder* as a statue erected in memory of his friend Sindercombe, who had died silently in prison after trying to assassinate Cromwell. Not a statue erected in a public place, but one constructed by every reader in his or her mind's eye. Men are silenced; their papers are burnt; their bodies perish. The printed book survives; new Sindercombe statues are constantly constructed; once again we lend our voices to the dead. To our surprise, the language that they speak is sometimes indistinguishable from our own.

REFERENCES

Brailsford, H. N. (1961), *The Levellers and the English Revolution* (London).
Filmer, R. (1991), *Patriarcha and Other Writings*, ed. J. P. Sommerville (Cambridge).
Foxe, J. (1861–89), *Acts and Monuments*, 8 vols. (London).
Ginzburg, C. (1980), *The Cheese and the Worms: The Cosmos of a Sixteenth-Century Miller* (Baltimore).
Greenblatt, S. (1988), *Shakespearean Negotiations* (Berkeley, Calif.).
—— (1989), 'Anti-Dictator', in D. Hollier (ed.), *A New History of French Literature* (Cambridge, Mass.), 223–8.
—— (1990), 'Resonance and Wonder', in S. Greenblatt, *Learning to Curse* (New York), 161–83.
Hacking, I. (1975), *The Emergence of Probability* (Cambridge).
Haller, W. (1963), *Foxe's Book of Martyrs and the Elect Nation* (London).
—— and Davies, G. (eds.) (1944), *The Leveller Tracts: 1647–1653* (New York).

Harrington, J. (1977), *The Political Works of James Harrington*, ed. J. G. A. Pocock (Cambridge).

Herzog, D. (1989), *Happy Slaves: A Critique of Consent Theory* (Chicago).

Hill, C. (1958), 'The Norman Yoke', in C. Hill, *Puritanism and Revolution* (London), 50–122.

—— (1975), *The World Turned Upside Down* (1st edn., 1972; Harmondsworth, Middx.).

Hume, D. (1983), *The History of England*, 6 vols., Liberty Classics (Indianapolis).

Macpherson, C. B. (1962), *The Political Theory of Possessive Individualism* (Oxford).

Marvell, A. (1972), *The Complete Poems*, ed. E. S. Donno (Harmondsworth, Middx.).

Milton, J. (1958), *Areopagitica*, in J. Milton, *Prose Writings*, ed. K. M. Burton (London), 145–85.

Morton, A. L. (ed.) (1975), *Freedom in Arms* (London).

Patterson, A. (1987), 'Fables of Power', in K. Sharpe and S. N. Zwicker (eds.), *Politics of Discourse* (Berkely, Calif.), 271–96.

Purchas, S. (ed.) (1905–7), *Hakluytus Posthumus*, 20 vols. (Glasgow).

Sommerville, J. P. (1986), *Politics and Ideology in England, 1603–1640* (London).

Tierney, B. (1982), *Religion, Law and the Growth of Constitutional Thought, 1150–1650* (Cambridge).

Underdown, D. (1985), *Revel, Riot, and Rebellion: Popular Politics and Culture in England, 1603–1660* (Oxford).

Walwyn, W. (1989), *The Writings of William Walwyn*, ed. J. R. McMichael and B. Taft (Athens, Ga.).

Wolfe, D. M. (ed.) (1944), *Leveller Manifestoes of the Puritan Revolution* (New York).

Woodhouse, A. S. P. (ed.) (1938), *Puritanism and Liberty* (London).

Wootton, D. (ed.) (1986), *Divine Right and Democracy* (Harmondsworth, Middx.).

—— (1990), 'From Rebellion to Revolution: The Crisis of the Winter of 1642/3 and the Origins of Civil War Radicalism', *English Historical Review*, 105.

—— (1991), 'Leveller Democracy and the Puritan Revolution', in J. H. Burns (ed.), *The Cambridge History of Political Thought, 1450–1700* (Cambridge), 412–42.

Wrigley, E. A. (1967), 'A Simple Model of London's Importance in Changing English Society and Economy, 1650–1750', *Past and Present*, 37.

CHAPTER 6

Democracy
and the
American
Revolution

GORDON S. WOOD

THE American Revolution is the single most important event in American history. Not only did it legally create the United States, but it defined most of the persistent values and noblest ideals of the American people, including their commitments to equality, and constitutionalism. Most important, the Revolution created American democracy, indeed, made Americans (despite the contradictory persistence of slavery until the middle decades of the nineteenth century) the first people in the modern world to possess a truly democratic government and society. With the Declaration of Independence in 1776 Americans threw off hereditary monarchy and all that monarchy implied of aristocratic hierarchies of blood and family and quickly established new republican governments in which all citizens were presumed to be equal. The American revolutionaries not only erected governments in which all parts, including in some cases even judges, were made elective by the people, but they soon expanded the right to vote to a degree that most Europeans scarcely conceived of. But even more important to democracy than this expansion of the suffrage was the way Americans in the revolutionary era brought common people into the affairs of government—not just as voters but as actual rulers. In fact, as a consequence of the Revolution Americans gave to ordinary workaday people a cultural and social significance that they had never before had in history. In the end this celebration of common people in government and society became the essence of American democracy. By the early nineteenth century the huge sprawling and bustling money-making democracy that had emerged out of the American Revolution was new and improbable enough to startle the world. And it was not long before curious European intellectuals—Tocqueville being only the most famous—began journeying across the Atlantic to investigate just what the New World had wrought.

In the eighteenth-century Anglo-American world democracy, as it always had, referred to government by the people—not simply government electively derived from the people, which was a republic, but government actually administered by the people. It was, as James Otis of Massachusetts said, 'a government of all over all', in which the ruled became the rulers and the rulers the ruled. Enlightened Britons on both sides of the Atlantic might agree that ideally the people ought to govern themselves directly, but they realized that democracy in this literal sense had been approximated only in the Greek city-states and in the New England towns; actual self-government or simple democracy was not feasible for any large community. As one American polemicist stated in 1776, even the great radical Whig Algernon Sidney had written that he had known of 'no such thing' as 'in the strict sense . . . a pure democracy, where the people in themselves and by themselves, perform all that belongs to government', and if any had ever existed in the world, he had 'nothing to say for it'. In fact, most eighteenth-century Britons in Europe and America were so uneasy over the impracticality and instability of pure democracy that democracy was commonly used vituperatively to discredit any untoward tendency towards popular government.

Still, all Britons were convinced that the people had a necessary role to play in government; indeed, without the people's presence government would inevitably become tyrannical. But in a large modern state how was their presence to be felt? Out of the impossibility of convening the whole people of the society, it was thought, arose the great British discovery of representation—'substituting the few in the room of the many', as some Americans put it. Through their representation in the House of Commons, and for the colonists their representation in their provincial assemblies, Britons in the Old World and the New believed they had achieved institutional bulwarks for protecting their liberties that other peoples could only dream of. Narrow though the suffrage was by modern standards and unrepresentative of the society as the eighteenth-century

House of Commons and the colonial assemblies may have been, they were for their day the most popular governmental bodies in the world. They constituted, and people understood them to constitute, what they called 'the democratical parts' of their mixed or balanced constitutions.

Englishmen in the mother country thus participated in government through their House of Commons just as the colonists participated in their provincial governments—their 'little models of the English constitution'—through their lower houses of representatives. This was what the eighteenth-century English-speaking world essentially meant by democracy. Democracy was not yet a faith, not an ideology, not an ethic; it was still a technical term of political science describing popular participation in government in a manner that was not all that different from the way the ancient Greeks had used it. For Britons as for Aristotle or Plutarch this popular participation ideally constituted only a part of their government. Much though the British people valued their participation in their House of Commons and their colonial assemblies, few of them thought that such popular participation by itself was sufficient for the working of a proper constitution and the protection of liberty. Some sort of mixture of democracy with monarchy and aristocracy was necessary.

Indeed, eighteenth-century Britons used the term 'democracy' almost always in conjunction with 'monarchy' and 'aristocracy'—as an essential part of the mixed or balanced constitution of Great Britain. The theory of mixed or balanced government was as old as the Greeks and had dominated Western political thinking for centuries. It was based on the ancient categorization of forms of government into three ideal types, monarchy, aristocracy, and democracy—a classical scheme derived from the number and character of the ruling power: the one, the few, or the many. Each of these simple forms possessed a certain quality of excellence: for monarchy, it was order or energy; for aristocracy, it was wisdom; and for democracy, it was honesty or goodness. The maintenance of these peculiar qualities, however, depended on the forms of government standing fast on an imagined spectrum of power. Yet experience had tragically taught that none of these simple forms by itself could remain stable. Left alone each ran headlong into perversion in the eager search by the rulers, whether one, few, or many, for more power. Monarchy lunged toward its extremity and ended in despotism. Aristocracy, located midway on the band of power, pulled in both directions and created faction and division. And democracy, seeking more power in the hands of the people, degenerated into anarchy and tumult. The mixed or balanced polity was designed to prevent these perversions by including each of the classic simple forms of government in the same constitution; the forces pulling in one direction would be counterbalanced by other forces and stability would result. Only through this reciprocal sharing of political power by the one, the few, and the many could the desirable qualities of each be preserved.

Through its expression in the eighteenth-century British constitution this theory of balanced government attained a vitality and prominence it had not had since antiquity. The division of British society into the three estates of king, nobles, and people and their constitutional embodiment in Crown, House of Lords, and House of Commons seemed almost miraculously to fulfil the ancient dream of balancing the simple forms of monarchy, aristocracy, and democracy within a single constitution. State and society were made one. No wonder theorists everywhere, including Montesquieu, viewed the eighteenth-century British constitution with admiration and awe.

Most American revolutionaries in 1776 had no intention of abandoning this celebrated theory of mixed or balanced government—even though they were throwing off monarchy and establishing republics. They still believed that their new republican state governments, although now elective, ought to embody the classic principles of monarchy, aristocracy, and democracy. Consequently, in nearly all of their new state constitutions drafted in 1776-7 the revolutionaries created republican versions of a balanced constitution—with single though considerably weakened governors to express the one; with upper houses or senates to express the few; and with powerful and enlarged houses of representatives to express the many. In fact, it was the granting of so much power to the popular houses of representatives that led some Americans, like Richard Henry Lee of Virginia in 1776, to conclude that their new governments were 'very much of the democratic kind', even though 'a Governor and second branch of legislation are admitted'.

In several states, particularly in Pennsylvania, some revolutionaries deliberately rejected incorporating the theory of balanced government in their new state constitutions. Radical forces in Pennsylvania in 1776 argued that a mixed government that included a governor and senate implied the existence of monarchical and aristocratic elements in their society that the republican revolution supposedly had abolished. 'There is but one rank of men in America,' the Pennsylvania radicals argued, 'and therefore . . . there should be only one representation of them in government.' The creation of a senate, they warned, would lead to the rise of a house of lords. Consequently, the constitution-makers in Pennsylvania, in emulation of what they believed was 'the Ancient Saxon constitution', erected a simple government composed of a single legislative body with no governor and no senate or upper house. It was as close to an eighteenth-century version of democracy as seemed feasible for a large community.

This 1776 democratic constitution of Pennsylvania aroused a storm of controversy that did not subside until the constitution was changed a decade and half later. Debate over this radical state constitution provoked some of the most illuminating ideas of the entire revolutionary era and helped to transform American thinking about mixed government and democracy. Opponents of the Pennsylvania constitution thought that the state had created a political monster that ought mercifully to be put to death. They could not imagine a government without a single chief executive and an upper house of the legislature. But at the same time, in the egalitarian atmosphere of the republican revolution, opponents of the Pennsylvania constitution quickly came to realize that they could not easily justify establishing a governor and a senate for the state in the traditional terms of mixed or balanced government—as embodiments of monarchy and aristocracy. They were repeatedly forced to deny that their proposal for a senate meant they wanted to establish a hereditary aristocracy in Pennsylvania; they did not desire a house of lords, they said, but only a body that would incorporate into government the wisdom of the natural élite of the society and help to maintain a balance in the mixed republic. But the distinction was hard to sustain, and in the end the opponents of the Pennsylvania constitution had to abandon the theory of balanced government outright and to justify the existence of an upper house on the grounds that it was in no way an aristocracy but merely 'a double representation of the people'. Bicameralism was now explained, not as the embodiment of different social estates or of Aristotle's simple forms of government, but as the division into two branches of a mistrusted legislative power.

The implications of such an argument were immense. If the senates were thought simply to be another kind of representation of the people, then it was possible for other parts of the government—governors and judges, for example—to be likewise considered as representatives of the people. If this were the case, then the once clear distinction between a republic—where all authority flowed from the people—and a democracy—where the people were the rulers—would collapse.

At the outset of the constitution-making in 1776 Americans had not thought that their governors and senates, though elected by the people (sometimes in the same manner and by the same electorate as the lower houses of the legislatures) were thereby considered to be representative of the people. Election was incidental to representation; it was not supposed to be its source. The mutuality of interests between the representative and those for whom he spoke was the proper measure of representation. Although the elected chief magistrates and the elected senates *derived* their authority from the people, they presumably did not share a mutuality of interests with the people and thus they did not *represent* them; that privilege belonged exclusively to the correctly named houses of representatives, whose members supposedly did share common interests with the people. But developments in their ideas of representation, initially revealed in the imperial debate with Great Britain in the 1760s, had already prepared Americans for a momentous shift in their thinking.

In justification of Parliament's right to tax the colonists spokesmen for the British government in 1765 argued that all Englishmen, whether or not they actually voted for Members of Parliament, were virtually represented in the House of Commons and thus in effect consented to the taxation. The colonists immediately rejected this claim that they were represented in Parliament in the same way non-voters in England were. What purpose is served, asked James Otis of Massachusetts in 1765, by the continual attempts of Englishmen to justify the lack of American representation in Parliament by citing the examples of the burgeoning new cities of Manchester and Birmingham, which returned no members to the House of Commons? 'If those now so considerable places are not represented, they ought to be.' Out of their experience in the New World Americans had come to believe in a very different kind of representation from that of the British—a kind of actual representation that made election and voting not incidental but central to the process. In America the rights and interests of a person seemed so particular and so personal and the mistrust of superiors so pervasive that only the strongest possible ties between him and the representative who spoke for him in government could suffice. Although actually voting for that representative was the least of those ties—local residential requirements for the representative and the instructing of the representative were others—the right to vote inevitably became more and more important to Americans.

By the 1780s many Americans had become convinced that only by actually voting for an official could a person guarantee his sense of being represented. This had the effect of making election the sole criterion of representation; as James Wilson put it, 'the right of representing is conferred by the act of electing.' Consequently, Americans had become increasingly used to thinking of all elective parts of their republics as somehow or other representative of the people. Federal and state officials, the president, national senators, governors, state senators, even judges—any body that even derived its authority from the people—were now considered to be different kinds of representations of the people. To be sure, the members of the houses of representatives were thought to be the more 'immediate representatives', but they were no longer the full and exclusive representatives of the people. The people were represented everywhere and by all officials in America's governments.

By extending representation through all parts of their governments Americans were able to justify their new federal system with its multiplicity of officials at both the state and national level: all were now agents, limited agents, of the people who remained outside of the entire system of government. Because the so-called houses of representatives had lost their exclusive role of embodying the people in government, democracy as Americans had understood it in 1776 disappeared from their constitutions. The people ruled everywhere, or, from a different perspective, they ruled nowhere. The people, it seemed, did not actually participate any longer in the American governments as they continued to do, for example, in the House of Commons. Americans had taken the people as a social estate out of the government altogether and had thereby destroyed the identity between state and society that theorists since Aristotle had cherished. The 'true distinction' of America's governments—the element that separated them from the ancient republics—wrote James Madison in *The Federalist*, No. 63, 'lies *in the total exclusion of the people, in their collective capacity,* from any share' in the government. America, he said, possessed no democracy at all; it was a republic through and through—a republic for Madison being a government 'in which the scheme of representation takes place'.

Americans now told themselves that no people before them, not even the British, had ever understood the principle of representation as they had. The world, said James Wilson in 1788, had 'left to America the glory and happiness of forming a government where representation shall at once supply the basis and the cement of the superstructure . . . diffusing this vital principle throughout all the different divisions and departments of the government'. Representation, said Madison in *The Federalist*, was 'the pivot' on which the whole American system of government moved.

Because their governments were so new and distinctive, Americans groped for terms adequate to describe them. Many turned Madison's perspective around and, because the people were represented every-where, described the new system as thoroughly democratic. Indeed, said John Stevens of New Jersey, election by the people, and not the strength of the lower chambers in the legislatures, made 'our govern-ments the most democratic that ever existed anywhere'. Yet others real-ized that democracy, as eighteenth-century political science had understood the term, was not an entirely accurate word to describe their new governments. They were better depicted as 'democratic republics', by which was meant, said Alexander Hamilton in 1788, 'a *representative democracy*'.

Although frightened conservatives in subsequent years continued to use the word 'democracy' pejoratively, increasingly they found more and more Americans not only willing to accept but to celebrate democracy as the most precise way of characterizing their political system. 'The government adopted here is a DEMOCRACY,' the renegade Baptist leader Elias Smith told his fellow Americans in 1809. 'It is well for us to under-stand this word, so much ridiculed by the international enemies of our beloved country. The word DEMOCRACY is formed of two Greek words, one signifies *the people*, and the other the *government* which is in the people . . . My Friends, let us never be ashamed of DEMOCRACY!' For many Americans in the early nineteenth century democracy had become identified with the nation. It was the faith they had come to believe in.

Yet this cursory analysis of the way democracy changed its meaning for Americans in the revolutionary era does not do justice to the full significance of what happened. It is perhaps too formal and theoretical, too concerned with the meanings of words and institutions, and too pre-occupied with elections and voting to capture the substantial changes in society and politics that made post-revolutionary America the most com-pletely democratic nation in the world. Although Americans themselves are often the last to realize the fact, democracy has come to mean much more than the counting of votes and electing representatives. Beneath the transformation of constitutions, the increase in elections, and the broad-ening of the suffrage in the revolutionary era lay more fundamental changes in the way Americans organized their politics and their society. These changes created the real and sustaining sources of America's democracy.

At the outset in 1776 the revolutionary leaders had a republican, not a democratic, conception of political leadership. They sought to destroy the monarchical reliance on family and kinship and to open up govern-ment to those who were not only talented but virtuous. To be virtuous meant to possess the willingness to sacrifice private interests for the sake of the public good—a willingness not everyone in the society could muster. To be virtuous in this way, men had to be independent and free of the occupations and petty interests of the market-place. The ideal political leader since antiquity was always someone who was capable of rising above selfish commercial interests and was not burdened by the necessity of actively having to make a living. Hence, as Aristotle had said, those who had to 'live a mechanical or commercial life' could not be political leaders, since such leaders had to have 'leisure to develop their virtue'. In the eighteenth-century Anglo-American world many concluded that the best leaders and most virtuous citizens for a commonwealth were landed gentry who, as Adam Smith said, did not have to exert themselves for profit, and independent farmers who, as Jefferson said, were free of 'the casualties and caprice of customers'.

Some concluded that in an ideal republican world the public leaders ought to be virtuous enough to serve without salary. Office-holding, as Jefferson said, ought to be in accord with the 'Roman principle'. 'In a virtuous government . . . public offices are, what they should be, burthens to those appointed to them, which it would be wrong to decline, though foreseen to bring with them intense labor, and great private loss.' Receiving profits from a public smacked of interestedness and tainted the office-holder's virtue. Which is why the radical Pennsylvania constitution of 1776 abolished all 'offices of profit' in the government. For the same classical reasons George Washington was anxious that he not be paid a salary as commander-in-chief or as president.

This age-old emphasis on the leadership of a leisured landed gentry who did not have to work for a living lay at the heart of America's classical republicanism: only those who were capable of standing above the swirl of private market-place interests could make disinterested judgements on behalf of the public good. Therefore the idealistic goal of American republicanism in 1776 was to remove these private interests from politics or at least create a political system that would allow its gentry leaders to transcend these interests.

This republicanism, however, contained the seeds of its own transformation into democracy. The equality that was so crucial to republican citizenship had a permissive significance in America that could not be restrained, and ordinary people, whose meanness and need to labour had made them contemptible in the eyes of their superiors from the beginning of history, found in republican equality a powerful justification for their self-esteem and self-assertion. As a consequence, the important age-old distinction between leisured gentlemen and common working people, which the revolutionary leaders continued to try to honour, was repeatedly blurred and eventually dissolved. At the same time the American people, as the republican source of all authority, proved unwilling to be represented exclusively by gentlemanly leaders, no matter how educated, leisured, or enlightened. They showed that they wanted their consent to be continual and explicit, and had said so at the very beginning of the imperial debate. In fact, the Americans' initial emphasis on actual rather than virtual representation in 1765 was a striking harbinger of future democratic developments.

The conceptions of actual and virtual representation that emerged in the 1760s presumed two very different sorts of society. Virtual representation made sense only in a society organized hierarchically where those on the top could meaningfully speak for those below them. It assumed that the people were a homogeneous body whose interests were capable of being discerned by an enlightened élite as one—as a unitary public good. But despite the hopes of many of the revolutionary leaders that America might be represented by disinterested gentlemen who could transcend the different interests and parties and promote a common good, American society proved in fact to be much too diverse and pluralistic, the lines of authority much too vague and tenuous, and the gentry leadership itself much too vulnerable to challenge from below for any sort of virtual representation to be sustained. Virtual representation may have still been meaningful in aristocratic and hierarchical Britain, but it made less and less sense in egalitarian America.

As the debate over the Constitution in 1787–8 eventually made clear, American society even within a single state was increasingly seen not as a unitary entity with a single common interest but, as a Marylander put it in 1788, a heterogeneous mixture of 'many different classes or orders of people, Merchants, Farmers, Planters, Mechanics, and Gentry or wealthy Men', all equal to one another. Although the new federal Constitution was designed to create a political system that would allow enlightened and virtuous leaders to transcend these clashing interests, the opponents of the Constitution acutely realized that the pluralism and egalitarianism of American society would prevent any élite, no matter how talented and enlightened, from speaking for the whole. Men from one class or interest, they said, could never be acquainted with the 'situation and wants' of those from another. The interests of the society were in fact so diverse and discrete that only individuals sharing a particular or partial interest could speak for that interest. The conception of actual representation that was implicit in American life from the beginning was now drawn out to the fullest.

The opponents of the Constitution may have lost the battle over the new national government created in 1787–8, but in their understanding of the need for the most explicit form of consent possible they were more in tune with the future direction of American politics than were the supporters of the Constitution. It was foolish, they said, to tell people, as the proponents of the Constitution did, that they ought to overlook their personal and local interests when personal and local interests were all there really were. 'No man when he enters into society', said James Winthrop of Massachusetts in 1788, 'does it from a view to promote the good of others, but he does it for his own good.' Since all individuals and groups in the society were equally self-interested, the only 'fair representation' in government, declared the 'Federal Farmer', the most distinguished of the writers opposed to the Constitution, ought to be one where 'every order of men in the community . . . can have a share in it'. Consequently any American government ought 'to allow professional men, merchants, traders, farmers, mechanics, etc. to bring a just proportion of their best informed men respectively into the legislature'. The only way for a person to be fairly and accurately represented in government was to have someone like himself with his same interests speak for him; no one else could be trusted to do so. Indeed, such mistrust was a major impulse behind the development of American democracy. Americans thus concluded that only an explicit form of representation that allowed Germans, Baptists, artisans, farmers, and so on each to send delegates of its own kind into the political arena could embody the democratic particularism of their society.

Ultimately, the logic of this extreme form of actual representation determined that no one could be represented in government unless he had at least the right to vote. Thus expanding the suffrage became a major reform in the early Republic. At the time that Europeans were still struggling with the problems of embodying estates and other social groups in government, Americans rapidly opened up voting to almost the entire white adult male population. By 1825 nearly all the states had achieved universal white manhood suffrage.

But this extreme form of actual representation had other consequences besides expanding the suffrage. It eventually justified the participation of very ordinary people in government not merely as voters but as rulers. The early Republic of America saw the emergence into political leadership, especially in the state legislatures, of the very merchants, artisans, and businessmen who theorists from Aristotle on had said were ill-equipped for such responsibilities because of their involvement in the market-place and lack of leisure to develop their virtue. Such mean men who worked for a living were presumably barred from government because they were partial and narrow-minded and had private interests to promote. Bringing such private interests directly into the operations of government, however, became central to the meaning of American democracy.

One of the crucial moments in the history of American politics—maybe the crucial moment—occurred in 1786 during several days of debate in the Pennsylvania assembly over the rechartering of the Bank of North America. The debate centred on the role of private interest in public affairs.

The principals in this debate were William Findley, a Scotch-Irish ex-weaver from western Pennsylvania and a promoter of the debtor and paper-money interests in the state, and Robert Morris, the wealthiest merchant in the state, who had aristocratic aspirations and was a major supporter of the rechartering of the bank. In attempting to acquire another charter for the bank Morris and his genteel Philadelphia ilk continually tried to pose as disinterested gentlemen in the classical mould, who were above cross market-place interests and concerned only with the public good. But Findley and his plebeian western colleagues, who certainly had to work for a living, refused to let Morris and the aristocratic supporters of the bank get away with this pose. These supporters of the bank's rechartering, Findley charged, were themselves interested men; they were directors or stockholders of the bank and thus had no right to claim that they were neutral, disinterested umpires only deciding what was good for the state. The advocates of the bank 'feel interested in it personally, and therefore by promoting it they were acting as judges in their own cause'.

There was nothing new in these charges. To accuse one's opponent of being self-interested was conventional rhetorical strategy in eighteenth-century debates. But Findley went on to pursue another line of argument that was new—astonishingly new. He accepted Morris's and the other bank supporters' interestedness in the bank. There was nothing unusual or improper in their supporting rechartering of the bank, he said. They were, after all, directors and stockholders in the bank, and their promotion of the bank was only to be expected. 'Any others in their situation', said Findley, ' . . . would do as they did.' Morris and the other investors in the bank had every 'right to advocate their own cause, on the floor of this house'. But, said Findley, they had no right to protest when others realize 'that it is their own cause they are advocating; and to give credit to their opinions, and to think of their votes accordingly'. They had no right, in other words, to try to pass off their support of their personal cause as an act of disinterested patrician virtue. The promotion of private interests in politics, said Findley, was quite legitimate, as long as it was open and above board and not disguised by specious claims of genteel disinterestedness. Precisely because no one in the society was capable of promoting an exclusive public interest that was distinguishable from the private interests of people, Findley suggested that the promotion of private interests necessarily was what American electoral politics was all about.

Findley was not content merely to expose and justify the reality of interest-group politics in representative legislatures. He glimpsed some of the important implications of such interest-group politics, and in just a few remarks he challenged the entire classical tradition of disinterested public leadership and set forth a rationale for competitive democratic politics that has never been bettered. If representatives were elected to promote the particular interests and private causes of their constituents, then the idea that such representatives were simply disinterested gentlemen, squire worthies called by duty to shoulder the burdens of public service, became archaic. It may have been meaningful in the past, when such virtuous men did exist, for such a disinterested representative to make no effort on his own behalf and simply stand for election. But now, said Findley, in the democratic America of many interests where the candidate for the legislature 'has a cause of his own to advocate, interest will dictate the propriety of canvassing for a seat'. Such interest-group politics meant that politically ambitious men, even those with interests and causes to advocate, now could legitimately run and compete for electoral office and thus become what Madison (in *The Federalist*, No. 10) most feared—parties who were at the same time judges in their own causes.

In this one radical suggestion in 1786 Findley was anticipating all of the modern democratic political developments of the succeeding generation in America: the increased electioneering and competitive politics, the open promotion of private interests in legislation, the acceptance of the legitimacy of political parties, the extension of the actual and direct representation of particular groups in government, and the eventual weakening if not the repudiation, of the classical republican ideal that legislators were supposed to be disinterested promoters of a public good that was separate from the private market-place interests of the society.

Under the pressure of these democratic developments the character of America's public officials had to change. Although many revolutionary leaders ideally wished to see their offices, as Jefferson and Washington did, as burdens from which they should receive no monetary reward, they did not have the large plantations and hundreds of slaves to support them that Jefferson and Washington did. Consequently, from 1776 on many of them found themselves in the awkward position of having to urge their republican governments not only to pay salaries but to keep raising them. Although Members of Parliament were not paid salaries until 1911, members of American governments received salaries from the beginning of the Republic. This had an immense effect on the character of American political leadership.

In order to justify their salaries American officials began arguing that serving in government was no different from being a lawyer or doctor or even a businessman; it was another means of making a living. But seeing public office as just another occupation from which one earned a living was a long way from classical republican thinking. It effectively destroyed the two thousand-year-old inhibition against mechanics, businessmen, and other ignoble and commercially interested men serving in government.

As early as the 1780s ambitious men who worked for money, like the scrambling but wealthy businessman Matthew Lyon of Vermont, began attacking the leisure that gave educated gentlemen both the time and responsibility for public service. Leisure, meaning not having to work for a living, had been for ages a principal source of gentry distinctiveness and of the gentry's obligation to serve in government without pay. In the decades following the Revolution this leisure was labelled idleness and was subjected to scathing criticism—criticism that went beyond anything experienced in Britain or Europe in these years. Before this criticism ran its course in the early decades of the nineteenth century, there was nobody left, in the northern part of the United States at least, who dared publicly and proudly to claim that he did not work for a living. And, as foreign visitors discovered to their astonishment, this included even public officials.

In America, said Tocqueville, not only did everyone work for a living but everyone thought that work itself was honourable, even 'work specifically to gain money'. In Europe the classical republican tradition of political leadership by a disinterested leisured aristocracy was still very much alive. In Europe, said Tocqueville, there were 'hardly any public officials who do not claim to serve the state without interested motives. Their salary is a detail to which they sometimes give a little thought and to which they always pretend to give none.' But in America public service and profit were 'visibly united'. In fact, observed Tocqueville's

French compatriot Michael Chevalier, 'the idea of service and salary are so inseparably connected' in Americans' thinking that in their 'almanacs it is common to see the rate of pay annexed to the lists of public offices'.

All this stress on the fact that, in Tocqueville's words, 'every man works for his living' had immense consequences in making people feel equal. It was this equality in working in order to consume goods that had hitherto been the preserve of the tiny minority of leisured gentry that gave Americans whatever satisfaction they had in their busy lives: 'every day confers a number of small enjoyments on every man.' With everyone alike in working for profit, no one, including servants, said Tocqueville, had to 'feel degraded because they work'. Who could be humiliated by working for pay when even the president of the country 'works for a salary'?

Perhaps nothing separated early nineteenth-century Americans more from Europeans than their attitude toward labour and their egalitarian and democratic sense that everyone must participate in it. With everyone claiming to work and no exclusive working class, it is not surprising that the development of a socialist movement in the United States was inhibited. In America it seemed that everyone had to have an occupation, and beginning with the 1820 census every adult male was asked his occupation. All people became labourers and all activities, including public office-holding, were reduced to the making of a living—a severe and unprecedented levelling that no other society in the modern world quite duplicated. It gave American democracy a basic social power that the simple extension of the ballot and the mere counting of heads could never have achieved. Ultimately, this common preoccupation of Americans with making a living and consuming goods—pursuing their private happiness, many might say—has made their society even today, despite great disparities of wealth, one of the most democratic the world has ever seen.

CHAPTER 7

Democracy and the French Revolution

BIANCAMARIA FONTANA

I

FROM its very beginning the French Revolution of 1789 was perceived by contemporary observers as an epochal event which completely transformed the social and political identity of the civilized world. It marked the sudden collapse, within less than three years, of the grandest and proudest of the monarchies of the Old Regime, the destruction of one of its most ancient and splendid aristocracies and of the secular power of the Catholic Church. It created the first republican government to rule over a large, densely populated European country, and together with it laws and institutions which today are still a model for democratic governments throughout the world.

Conservatives all over Europe witnessed with astonishment the apocalyptic ending of a civilization, of those values of honour, nobility, respect, paternal authority, and religious faith which had ruled the West since the advent of Christianity. Sympathizers of the revolution, in France as outside it, saw in it the overdue destruction of a regime which rested upon prejudice and abuse, and the advent of a new age of law, right, and justice, of a modern society founded upon liberty and equality of its citizens. Both sides identified the central feature of this catastrophic or triumphant turning-point with what Edmund Burke described as the 'upturning of the edifice of society': what we might see, more soberly, as a process of rapid democratization, the sudden extension of political power and political rights to large sections of the population previously excluded from these.

As is generally the case with historical landmarks, there is an element of arbitrariness in focusing upon a particular date or set of events as crucial moments of change: many ideas, aspirations, and sentiments currently associated with the revolution had been slowly maturing within European society for several centuries; and many features of the Old Regime survived long after the storming of the Bastille by the Parisian mob. Even if we allow for the inevitable over-simplification of historical reconstruction, to say that the French revolutionary events of the summer of 1789 mark the beginning of modern democracy in Europe raises a set of intricate and difficult questions.

If we retrace for example the unfolding of the revolutionary process—from the convocation of the Provincial Assemblies and the Estates General to discuss the financial deficit to the decision of the deputies of the Third Estate to challenge royal authority; from the mobilization of the people of Paris in defence of its representatives to the bloody struggle amongst political factions in the National Assembly—we are confronted with entirely different dimensions of political experience. It is debatable whether democratic practices really took shape in the restricted space of the Assembly and of the political clubs, in the streets of Paris, or in hundreds of town halls, churches, village squares, and workshops all over France.

For Goethe the history of the new world dawned on the battlefield of Valmy in 1792, when the French republican armies defeated the forces of reaction unleashed against their country; but it is at least as plausible to see greater long-term significance in the Declaration of the Rights of Man, the abolition of feudal rights, or the extension of the electoral suffrage to millions of French citizens. Another obvious area of disagreement is the relation between the achievements of the revolution and the means through which its new laws and institutions were enforced. It is possible to regard the politics of terror which marked the height of the revolutionary movement—the long, bloody list of arrests, massacres, private and public violence—as inevitable, if regrettable, side-effects of an otherwise beneficial process, or, alternatively, as aberrations which perverted and undermined those very democratic values of liberty, equality, and justice which they claimed to serve.

Most of what historians have written in the last two hundred years to describe the revolution, explore its causes, and assess its results implies some judgement on the agents and instruments, on the value and extent of this process of democratic transformation as well as its impact upon future political experience. The workers' movement of the nineteenth century, the socialist revolutionary parties of the twentieth, the defence of the rights of ethnic and religious minorities and of women have as legitimate a claim to the heritage of 1789 as the prosperous bourgeois liberal republic of President Mitterrand, with its fast trains and Plexiglass pyramids.

II

There are two fundamental ways in which it is possible to consider the role of democracy in the French Revolution. The first stresses the participation 'from below' of large sections of the population in revolutionary events: it explores the political and social identity of these collective agents—crowds, classes, parties, occupational groups—analyses their beliefs, interests, and expectations, and attempts to define the part which they played in the revolution. The second approach focuses instead on the procedures and instruments upon which modern democracy has come to rest: it looks at the way in which the new political system was defined in constitutional terms, considers its legislation, its institutions, and their functioning.

Both these aspects have been studied extensively by historians and both of course contribute to our understanding of the dynamics of the revolution. Yet the choice between the two is not just a matter of random preference or professional expertise. In adopting one or other perspective interpreters have made an implicit judgement on what they regarded as most vital in the making of modern democracy: the experience of political participation and the exercise of power on the part of large social groups—the nation in its multiform living reality—or the definition of a set of rules through which this power could be safely and efficiently delegated by the nation to 'abstract' political agents and institutions.

In its most traditional form the study of the historical agents of democracy assumed the existence of well-identified social groups and classes whose interests and ideological attitudes could be expected to conform to given patterns. The interpretation of the revolution then pivoted on the leading role played by one or other of these social entities—bourgeoisie, proletariat, artisans, or peasantry. This viewpoint goes back to the early Whig reading of 1789 as the advent of a new 'stage' of historical development, in which commerce and the middling ranks had come to replace the political and social dominance of a feudal aristocracy. But in its more recent and influential socialist and Marxist version the revolution became the magic moment in which the dispossessed—peasants without land, exploited urban workers, militant artisans, starving lumpenproletarians—gained brief access to political power only to have it taken away from them, once their support was no longer needed, by the manipulative intervention of the propertied classes.

For the Whig historians the 'excesses' of popular insurrection were the inevitable (and temporary) side-effects of necessary change, while the succumbing of mob-rule to bourgeois control after the fall of Robespierre was the re-establishment of the new natural order of society. Marxist history did not in fact substantially alter this view, although it reversed the implicit preference which underlay it: 1789 was the prefiguration of a socialist revolution which had failed to reach its ultimate ends because the 'times' (the socio-economic position and political awareness of the agents) were not yet 'ripe' for it. As Sylvain Maréchal wrote in 1796, 'The French revolution is only the forerunner of another, even greater, that shall finally put an end to the era of revolutions.'

The massive research of the last few decades on the social and economic conditions of France during the revolution (to which Marxist scholars have made such a decisive contribution) has given us a far more accurate and complete picture of the past, but it has also seriously undermined these familiar sociological assumptions. In the light of this new work the supposed conflict and even the separation between 'aristocracy' and 'bourgeoisie' appears far less sharp than was previously believed, and the involvement of large sections of the nobility in the revolutionary movement of crucial importance. The urban bread riots and peasant revolts of the years of the revolution are hard to distinguish in character from their predecessors under the Old Regime. The role of artisans within Parisian uprisings has lost its previous prominence. Popular attitudes towards religious belief, women's rights, or conscription have proved hard to identify. A whole series of historical stereotypes of the direct economic interests, political allegiances, and beliefs of the French population in the late eighteenth century have proved unreliable or confused. The more complete our knowledge becomes, the more blurred and tangled the picture of the revolution which it gives us.

In the last two decades historians have shifted their attention increasingly from the social and economic background of the actors of the popular movement to their behaviour in the collective political activities in which they shared. Instead of focusing upon their supposedly stable identity as members of a social class, historians have looked at the temporary identity these actors acquired as crowds of protesters and rioters, participants in municipal assemblies in the districts of the city of Paris or in the meetings of the political clubs. This is often harder to study convincingly. Even relatively organized political activities like the electoral or municipal assemblies or the discussions in the Jacobin Club have left fewer records than the debates of the National Assembly, and even these are more likely to concern important speakers and decisions than to capture the feelings and contributions of the mass of the participants. It is easier to discover roughly how many people practised a given trade in Paris in the 1790s, and assess their probable living standard, than to judge their level of literacy, political indoctrination, or religious commitment.

At the beginning of the revolution contemporary witnesses were struck by the sudden cascade of print—pamphlets, journals, and newspapers discussing the political and social issues of the day. Behind this lay a vigorous tradition of clandestine subversive writings under the Old Regime which flooded into the open as soon as the censorship was lifted. Many people felt at the time—and for good reasons—that the 'force of public opinion' had played a crucial role in bringing on the revolution, undermining the credibility of established authority and spreading new ideas of religious scepticism, social criticism, and reform. Yet even this seemingly decisive factor in shaping the experience of the participants in the revolutionary movement is hard to pin down—despite extensive debate in the National Assembly over the liberty of the press—since we know very little about who had access to any particular texts and still less about who actually read them and was affected by their arguments.

It is clear nevertheless that it is a real advance to see the advent of democracy in France during the revolution not as the predetermined outcome of socio-economic forces, but as a set of genuinely creative collective practices, in which the energies of different groups of people coagulated around immediate political issues. In this respect the novelty and inventiveness of the Parisian sansculottes can scarcely be exaggerated: the extraordinary sight of artisans and shopkeepers, soldiers and flower-sellers, respectable petty bourgeois in cockades, ragged men and women crowding on the benches of ancient convents to deliberate on the fate of the republic.

In some respects, however, this new perspective undermines, rather than enhances, the role of 'immediate' and 'spontaneous' popular participation. Seeing politics as a set of organized collective activities inevitably shifts attention from the masses to the militant élites who through the network of the assemblies of the forty-eight Parisian districts and the clubs formed the backbone of the revolutionary organization. Centuries of despotic monarchical rule had prevented the formation in France of stable political parties like those that controlled English political life in the same period. The sudden collapse of the regime gave unrestrained scope to the aggressive initiative of revolutionary militancy.

The ideal of 'direct democracy'—*démocratie pure* in the language of the time—was very prominent in the context of 1789 and continued to exercise a powerful influence upon the revolutionary movements of the nineteenth and twentieth centuries. In the absence of more accessible historical examples of democratic governments, the French revolutionaries found their inspiration in the models of the Greek city-state (the *polis*) and of the Roman republic—perpetuated within Western political tradition by historians of classical antiquity and republican writers. In the idealized reconstructions of its admirers this model embodied the active and constant participation of the citizens in political decisions, their complete dedication to the service and defence of the republic, and their profound identification with collective values of honour, patriotism, and virtue. Although this ideal of ancient republicanism exercised a great influence upon the collective imagination, rhetoric, and imagery of the actors of the revolution, the events of 1789–94 also underlined its impracticability in the real social and economic circumstances of late eighteenth-century France.

It is of course true that large sections of the population took part in the revolution who had little if any previous contact with political ideas and activities—a phenomenon made more striking by the distance between the central government in Paris and the provinces which marked French political life both before and during the revolution. The impossibility of sustaining a permanent mobilization, the forced imposition, through police measures, of values of republican virtue and austerity, the disruption of economic activity by the demands of state security and defence, and the persecution of traditional religious beliefs in the name of a new republican faith were decisive factors in the collapse of the Jacobin dictatorship in the summer of 1794.

Marxist writers have always emphasized the continuing opposition between the popular movement and 'dictatorship' of the masses on the one hand and the organization of a revolutionary party with its factions and leaders on the other—between the 'sansculottes' and the 'Jacobins'. If the spontaneous popular uprising of the early stages of the revolution was soon taken over by the most efficient and well-organized militant group, centred on the Jacobin Club, political leaders continued to turn to the Parisian sections for support against their political opponents competing for control of the Assembly and the executive Committee of Public Safety.

Whenever a political crisis or confrontation arose, its outcome was decided by the spontaneous intervention of the Parisian mob (the historian Michelet described their anonymous leaders as 'ghosts without name, without character, without antecedents, without followers') who took to the streets to impose their views on the government. It was the people of Paris who decided the victory of the Assembly against the King, occupying the Hôtel de Ville and the Bastille in July 1789, forcing the royal family to return to Paris from Versailles in October of the same year, and virtually reducing them to an undignified imprisonment after their attempted escape to Varennes in July 1791. It was the Parisian crowd who decided the desperate defence against the Prussian occupation on 10 August 1792 and swept off the last supporters of the monarchy. It was again, the people of Paris who in the *journées* (the day-long riots) of May and September 1793 decided the struggle between the factions of the Jacobins and the Girondins in favour of the former. The end of the revolution, in the summer of 1794, coincided precisely with the moment in which, for the first time, the people failed to intervene, abandoning its leaders Robespierre and Saint-Just to the revenge of the 'moderate' majority of the Assembly.

The Jacobins can be seen as a 'bourgeois' élite who exploited and betrayed the genuinely 'proletarian' soul of the revolutionary movement, but may also be seen as a necessary intermediary who alone could give political coherence and efficacy to inherently shapeless popular protest. The dispute which began in the early 1790s was fated to last as long as social movements and revolutionary parties in the modern world. Even for those who did not share the socialist faith in the prospect of the proletarian revolution, the myth of direct democracy lived on, surfacing whenever groups of people dared to challenge a hated social order and dreamed of replacing it with a new community of justice and equality. But whatever value we attach to such feelings, it is essential to recognize that the French Revolution also struck the first of a series of deadly blows to their historical credibility in modern society. The outcome of 1789 gave a dramatic proof that democracy in a modern state could no longer spring from the worn myths of the ancient republic and the selfless dedication of its free citizens to the service of their community, but must be pursued instead through a new theory and practice of political representation.

III

As early as 17 June 1789, when the rebellious deputies of the Third Estate, assembled in an empty tennis court in Versailles, along with some representatives of the Nobility and the Clergy, founded the National Assembly, the revolution proclaimed its first and central principle: popular sovereignty vested in the whole of the French nation. In itself the idea of the sovereignty of the people was not a new one in late eighteenth-century Europe, though until then even its most liberal advocates had been inclined to see it as largely symbolic, and its exercise as permanently delegated by the people to the monarch and a combination of hereditary and elective bodies. Only in the exceptional case in which the sovereign was guilty of some major abuse of his authority would the people be justified in resisting his commands.

In France, however, the monarchy had remained firm in its claim that the King received his authority from God alone: a claim which the Bourbon dynasty continued to defend, through all the constitutional concessions forced upon them, until the revolution of 1830 which brought Louis Philippe of Orleans to the throne. Naturally the absolute power of the French monarch was restrained by tradition, by the principles of Christian morality, and by the *ius gentium* (what today we would call international law); but the King did not derive his authority from popular consent, nor did he share it with any other magistrate or institution. When the Estates General were called in spring 1789—for the first time since 1614—their deputies had originally been summoned from all over France only to inform and advise the monarch on the financial crisis and other matters of public concern, not to exercise any kind of deliberative authority.

The principle of popular sovereignty influenced the legislative work of the Assembly in two different ways. In the first place the deputies examined the consequences of this new conception of political legitimacy for society at large, offering a definition of the rights of the citizens and undertaking an extensive reform of the legal apparatus of the Old Regime, since in this new perspective the great majority of laws, customs, and practices of absolute monarchy appeared obsolete and impossible to justify. But they also faced the difficult question of how the sovereign nation could express its will and exercise its power through a novel set of institutions, procedures, and rules. They had, in other words, to confront the issue of political representation.

The Declaration of the Rights of the Man and Citizen, proclaimed by the Assembly on 26 August 1789 and subsequently prefaced to all revolutionary constitutions, reproduced in innumerable illustrations, monuments, and allegories, is one of the most familiar symbols of the revolution and has continued to influence the political history of the modern world. Unlike the words 'Bill' and 'Charter'—which suggest the idea of a legal statement or of a contract—the term 'Declaration' deliberately echoed the solemn formula of royal pronouncements. Its first purpose was to confer on popular sovereignty the sacredness which had always accompanied the acts of the monarchy by appealing to universal principles and the authority of God.

As a piece of legislation the Declaration is in fact difficult to place. Drawing on a long tradition of writings produced over centuries by the philosophers of natural jurisprudence, the document proclaimed the individual rights of personal liberty, political equality, security of property, legal guarantees, and liberty of thought, not as the specific entitlements of French citizens but as the 'natural' and 'imprescriptible' rights of mankind at large. According to it all individuals in all countries at all times must be free to do anything they chose to, provided it did not cause direct injury to anyone else. All citizens had the right to profess any opinion or religion of their choice and to feel that their property was secure. Nobody could be accused, arrested, imprisoned, or killed by the political authority without evidence and without a regular trial.

The extensive discussion and redrafting of the articles of the Declaration in the Assembly became an ambitious philosophical debate which seems now surprisingly academic in the circumstances of a pressing political crisis. For week after week, under the puzzled eyes of the rest of the world, the French deputies argued at length about such questions as the existence of God, the origins of property, the respective importance of happiness and interest in human society. In the end, because of its universal claims, the Declaration was not a set of legal prescriptions which the French state could in any way hope to enforce. The French government could take responsibility only for its own laws and its own citizens, not for mankind at large. Unlike the American Bill of Rights, which had some influence on French legislators, it was introduced not to spell out and specify the content of an existing constitution, but to serve as the ideological premiss to any future legislative activity.

Many thought at the time that the Declaration was the single most important achievement of the revolution, the basis upon which the entire political and legal structure of the Old Regime was effectively reconstructed, and the foundation of the new modern conception of citizenship.

They believed that it was the Declaration which effectively ended the long-established abuses of feudal society—from legal torture and arbitrary imprisonment on royal command to religious discrimination and aristocratic privileges—and caused them to be replaced by a modern system of civil and penal legislation.

In contrast with this opinion other contemporary observers thought that the Declaration was little more than a rhetorical exercise, a philosophical profession of faith which had an ostentatiously ideological appeal, but which in itself had very little impact upon the real position of French subjects in relation to the state. They believed that the rights thus acknowledged by the Assembly would remain purely nominal unless they were effectively embodied in the constitution and in the positive laws of the country. The notion of natural individual rights indicated the abstract limits of state authority, but without institutional mechanisms to guarantee the division and control of political powers this limit would be overstepped whenever it was convenient for the political authority to do so. It was useless to proclaim solemnly that people *must* be free if the citizens themselves could not effectively check what their governors were doing. In point of fact, moreover, in the course of the revolution the Declaration did little, if anything, to prevent the adoption of arbitrary and abusive measures on the part of the regime.

The role of the Declaration as one of the founding myths of modern democracy cannot be seriously disputed. By translating the results of several centuries of philosophical reflection into a kind of civic catechism, the legislators of the Assembly provided future generations with a vivid and accessible model, which the subsequent military conquests of the French republic helped to spread all over Europe and in the colonies. But in the light of the Terror, the views of the Declaration's critics retain a dramatic urgency. In spite of its formal commitment to human rights, between 1792 and 1794 the Jacobin government arbitrarily arrested and murdered thousands of citizens, persecuted their religious beliefs, and confiscated their property, justifying its actions on the grounds of public safety and collective interest—the old arguments of the despotic 'reason of state'. (Notably, however, legal or police torture as well as rape seem to have been completely absent from this first French experience of terrorism.) To those who had survived the revolutionary tribunals and the guillotine it was all too clear that, in order to be enforced, the universal rights of man needed the support of effective representative institutions.

IV

The absolute authority which the French monarchy had enjoyed for centuries had left no solid heritage of public offices and laws to form the basis for the exercise of popular sovereignty. Under the Old Regime France had no written constitution, only rather hazy traditions concerning the mythical origins of the kingdom. Its assemblies—the ancient Estates— illustrated the symbolic presence of the medieval orders of society—the Nobility, the Clergy, and the Commoners or Third Estate—in the deliberations of the Crown. The opening ceremony of the meeting of the Estates General on 5 May 1789 had shown an odd contrast between the ostentatious display of traditional pomp and pageantry and the new eagerness of the majority of the deputies to take active part in political decisions. The rejection of their traditionally subordinate role by the deputies of the Third Estate gave them ample scope for initiative but exposed them also to all the risks inherent in establishing entirely new political practices and institutions.

Unlike some of the Jacobin leaders in the later stages of the revolution, the legislators of 1789 did not delude themselves that a population of 27 million people (the largest in Europe after that of Russia) could exercise its sovereignty directly through some formula of universal participation in political activities. The delegation of power to some minority— hereditary or elected—was necessary to make popular sovereignty at all viable. One of the most influential theorists of the Assembly—the Abbé Sieyès—explained this necessity through a comparison with economic labour: in large, commercially developed modern societies ordinary people could not be involved in politics full-time any more than they could grow their own food or make their own tools. The mass of the population must rely on the services of 'professional' political representatives just as they did on those of cobblers, peasants, or schoolteachers. Once designated, this minority of representatives would not merely act as spokesmen of the people, voicing their complaints and requests to the Crown according to the formula of the 'imperative mandate', as had been the practice of the Estates General. As members of the new national legislative body the deputies would be invested with real authority and enjoy autonomy of initiative and decision.

If the founders of the Assembly agreed from the start that their role as deputies must give them the effective power to make independent decisions, they did not agree at all when it came to deciding the overall shape of future institutions, and in particular the question whether deputies should be chosen by election or heredity. The abolition of the monarchy on 22 September 1792, followed by the trial and execution of the King and Queen on the guillotine, is probably the best-known single event of the revolution, the one which made the most dramatic impact upon the imagination of contemporaries and future generations. Yet in 1789 the republican tradition in France was very feeble: all existing national sentiment was connected with the traditions and grandeur of the monarchy, and militant republicans were a negligible minority.

Conservatives and reformers alike believed that France was a large modern nation, too different in any respect from the small city-states of antiquity to flourish under republican institutions. The large majority of the deputies of the National Assembly of 1789 were committed not to the destruction of royalty, but to the transformation of France into a 'limited' or 'constitutional' monarchy. It was largely the impact of external factors—in particular the war declared against France by Prussia, Austria, and the émigré nobility, growing popular unrest and domestic violence, combined with the ambiguous position of the King and his family—which resulted in the collapse of the monarchical authority. Even then France retained the constitutional form of a kingdom with a deposed monarch rather than that of a true republic.

With the disappearance of the King the absolute power previously exercised by the monarchy was not shared out amongst a number of different institutions—one or more legislative assemblies, an executive, and a body of judicial officials (as in the English government), but was instead transferred undivided to the National Assembly itself, becoming easy prey to the factions and individual leaders who successively gained control over it. The totalitarian democracy of the Jacobins was the result not just of external popular pressure, but also of the lack of any effective division of powers in the constitutional system, a feature which turned the Assembly into a mirror image of monarchical absolutism. After the failure of the constitutional compromise of 1789, French legislators found they could only choose between restoring the monarchy in its absolute form (as did Napoleon when he became Emperor) or accepting a republican government.

If in 1789 the hereditary power of the monarchy had still enjoyed a high degree of popularity, the same cannot be said of the monopoly exercised by the aristocracy upon French society and government. Under the Old Regime France was dominated by the experience of aristocratic privilege, which manifested itself not only in the relatively inoffensive form of social pomp and prestige enjoyed by the aristocracy, or by granting to the nobility a high degree of immunity in relation to penal offences, but more poignantly through the exclusion of commoners from a wide range of careers and positions in the civil, military, and religious administration of the country.

Although there were in fact many members of the nobility sitting on the benches of the Assembly, the majority of the deputies agreed that aristocratic privilege was in conflict with the very principle of popular sovereignty. They argued that the nation was a community in which people were supposed to have the same political (if not social or economic) interests. A closed oligarchy enjoying privileges determined by birth (unlike wealth and other distinctions which could be acquired through individual exertion) would have interests which conflicted in principle with those of the community at large. Having agreed to the abolition of feudal rights in August 1789, and to that of hereditary nobility in June 1790, the deputies refused to allot a share of legislative power to a hereditary assembly of nobles. The members of the so-called English party—those who wished for the introduction of a second hereditary chamber like the English House of Lords—were defeated by the majority of the Assembly who wanted just one elective chamber.

Having established that representation must be based upon election rather than heredity, the legislators of the Assembly insisted also on the necessity of frequent elections (the Assembly should be renewed every two years) and of a wide electoral suffrage. The revolutionary constitution of 1791 established an electoral franchise which was very close to universal male suffrage. The property requirements to be a voter were very low: it was sufficient to pay a tax contribution equivalent to three days' wages. Only domestic servants (who were thought to be too dependent on their masters to have autonomous political opinions) and vagrants and beggars (whose place of residence could not be established) were effectively excluded. Some members of the Assembly, like the philosopher Condorcet, were in principle in favour of extending voting rights to women, but in the end it was agreed that public opinion would be too prejudiced against it.

In practice the electoral mechanism embodied in the constitution of 1791 (which gave voting rights to about 4 million male citizens) proved quite difficult to operate. France had no tradition of direct election, in which people all over the country would simply vote for the members of parliament: voters elected the members of local assemblies which then returned the deputies to the Estates General. This complicated system was maintained to elect the representatives to the National Assembly.

The Assembly was formed by 745 members, of whom one-third were in proportion to the population, one-third were in proportion to tax returns, and one-third corresponded to geographical districts. In principle this system (which seems very cumbersome to us) was not more awkward than the one employed in the same period to elect the members of the British parliament. But because in France before the revolution there were no political parties with stable local interests in the constituencies, the elections proved chaotic.

Without electoral lists to choose from and without party discipline there were frequent disputes as to which candidates had in fact been elected. The practice of renewing the Assembly every two years was also unsettling, since it meant almost continuous general elections, and in the post-revolutionary period it was replaced by the even more objectionable solution of renewing at each election only one- or two-thirds of the deputies. The radical constitution of 1793, voted at the height of the revolutionary period and never enforced, made even greater concessions to democratic participation and further accentuated the instability of the system. The suffrage was extended to all citizens, the deputies nominated on a proportional basis alone (one deputy for 40,000 inhabitants), and elections were expected to be annual. After the coup of Thermidor, which liquidated Robespierre and the surviving Jacobin leadership, the new constitution of 1795 marked a hasty retreat towards a restricted, property-based franchise. The number of electors was lowered to about 100,000 and continued to be confined to a minority of relatively prosperous proprietors and taxpayers until universal male suffrage was finally reintroduced after the revolution of 1848.

To a large extent the defects of the revolutionary system of representation were due to external rather than internal factors: the war and the economic crisis, the growing fear of the propertied classes, the famine which threatened the poor, the growing pressure of political terrorism. The absence of any previous experience of general elections and political deliberation did not help. In a poisonous attack on the National Assembly the British politician Edmund Burke described it as a gathering of litigious provincial lawyers, unused to the exercise of power, inebriated by their own rhetoric, all eager to make a name for themselves by proposing measures of legislation which were as demagogic as they were impractical. It is probably true that the most serious structural defect of the new French constitutional design was the excessive importance it attached to legislative activity, to the detriment of the executive function: in other words, deputies were more anxious to make far-reaching new laws than they were to work out how they could be applied.

To make its decisions effective, the revolutionary government was often forced to resort to extraordinary measures and decrees (which were strictly speaking illegal), following a pattern familiar from the despotic monarchy of the Old Regime. Discussion and deliberation in the Assembly were supplanted by the swift and efficient intervention of the Committee of Public Safety, which had no legal status and was in effect merely the executive summit of the revolutionary party. After the collapse of the Jacobin regime, those members of the political class who had survived the Terror hastened to reverse this commitment, pursuing the ideal of a strong executive power as the only chance to re-establish law and order. Within a few years the republican institutions lost all credibility and were ready to fall into the hands of a victorious general, Napoleon Bonaparte.

For all the faults of their constitutional design, the achievement of the French legislators was a most remarkable one, effecting an almost instant transition from monarchical power and pomp and the aristocratic society of orders to a political space markedly closer to our own. Our contemporary constitutions, electoral practices, courts, and laws, in Europe as in the new democracies of Africa, Latin America, and Asia, are still largely based upon ideas set forth by the rebellious deputies of 1789, ideas which many of their contemporaries had dismissed as wildly utopian, the product of some kind of passing collective madness.

V

In their efforts to transform France into a modern republic the legislators of 1789 were inspired by the example of the recent American Revolution of 1776. The French monarchy had been the natural ally of the American colonies in their struggle against British imperialism. To French reformers, America offered the exciting image of a new society and a free and egalitarian political world. Although the two young republics made a great display of mutual admiration and enthusiasm, in practice American institutions proved difficult to imitate. At the outbreak of the revolution France had been for two hundred years a strongly centralized state. Regional differences and aspirations had remained alive since the unification of the kingdom by Henry IV, but the possibility of a federal constitution had never gained political credibility. If anything, the revolutionary government had reinforced and perfected the centralized administration of the Old Regime. America was seen by French observers as a land of plenty, in which every citizen could become the owner of a small farm. In France such generalized distribution of property was unthinkable: when the revolutionary government confiscated the lands of the Church and of the *émigré* nobility these were not redistributed to the peasants but sold off to rich commoners. If the radical fringes of the Jacobin movement were inspired by dreams of social justice, the revolutionary government itself remained stalwartly committed to the defence of private property. There was, moreover, a further important difference between the two republics, which contemporaries were quick to point out: once they had chased their former colonial rulers from the national territory, Americans were well protected from the threat of foreign invasion by their geographical position, while France was exposed to the attacks of her powerful European neighbours.

The military intervention of Prussia, Austria, and later Britain and Russia in support of the King of France against the rebellious government of the Assembly had decisive consequences for the fortunes of the revolution. When the Prussian army entered French territory in 1792 the threat of a foreign occupation elicited a passionate national response and led to mass recruitment in the army and to a large-scale mobilization of the civil population to support the war effort. In spite of the examples of classical antiquity, both the practice of conscription and the involvement of civilians in the war were a quite new phenomenon in late eighteenth-century Europe. Their impact upon French society and world opinion was enormous and it would be impossible fully to understand the democratic implications of the revolution without taking them into account.

Like all other European powers before the revolution (with the sole exception of the Swiss republics) France had employed a professional army, supplemented by a number of regiments of foreign mercenaries. Under the Old Regime aristocratic patronage and the limited chances of advancement open to commoners had weighed heavily on the officer class. After 1789, when the nobility began to emigrate, only a minority amongst the officers and the higher ranks of the army defected to the royalists. Even so the number of soldiers under arms was too low and the economic resources of the state were insufficient to sustain a war with the rest of Europe. In 1789 the National Guard, the bourgeois militia, commanded by a veteran of the American war, General Lafayette, played a key role in the Parisian uprisings. When in summer 1792 the general in chief of the foreign coalition, the Duke of Brunswick, issued a manifesto threatening the rebellious subjects of the King of France with a bloody repression, the Assembly replied with a dramatic appeal to national resistance, '*La Patrie en danger*'. Regiments of volunteers from different parts of the country converged on Paris and took part in the assault on the Tuileries which led to the deposition of the King, now viewed as an enemy agent. A few months later, in February 1793, the volunteers were integrated—not without some friction—into the regular army.

The general conscription called in 1793 soon brought the number under arms from about 200,000 to 900,000, while civilians of both sexes and all age groups were employed to service the war economy. There was naturally some resistance to this mobilization, especially in the countryside and in some regions like the Vendée, peasants and deserters engaged in a widespread guerrilla struggle against the revolutionary army. However the presence of troops of enthusiastic patriots and militants (whose level of education was generally above that of the average soldier), the opportunity for rapid promotion from the ranks, and the technological superiority of French artillery rapidly turned the motley battalions of 1792 into a formidable war machine. Soon France succeeded not only in liberating her national territory, but in occupying large portions of the enemy empires, creating—in Italy, Germany, Switzerland, Holland, Spain—satellite states on the model of the Jacobin republic. The conquest was led by brilliant young officers of revolutionary sympathies, risen from the ranks, and it was one of them, General Bonaparte, who gained control over the tottering political institutions with the coup of Brumaire in December 1800.

The military adventure of the French republic—which lasted almost without interruption from 1792 to the final defeat of Napoleon at Waterloo in 1815—is probably the most ambiguous aspect of the revolution's democratic heritage. Conscription revived the classical ideal of the citizen-soldier, naturally inclined to peace but always ready to fight for the defence of his hearth and country, dependably at one with the political sentiments of the nation, where the soldier of the Old Regime had been an alien mercenary, often a foreigner. At the same time it showed the aggressive potential of mass mobilization and of an army founded on careers open to talent, especially when the war economy became a ready solution for unemployment and commercial competition.

The new French republic showed that modern democracies would not be, as many had hoped, exclusively committed to commerce, quiet living, and peaceful relations with their neighbours. On the contrary, they could prove more aggressive and imperialistic than any of the monarchies of the Old Regime. The partisans of Greek, Italian, and Hungarian independence in the nineteenth century, the Red Army at St Petersburg, the thousands of names on the mass graves on the Somme, aggressors and resistance fighters of 1939–45 all found themselves following in the steps of the ragged battalions who marched through Paris in the summer of 1792 singing for the first time the 'Marseillaise'.

CHAPTER 8

Democracy since the French Revolution

CHARLES S. MAIER

AFTER THE REVOLUTION: POLITICAL DANGERS AND SOCIAL TRENDS

Two and a half millennia after the canonic date established for the introduction of democracy into Athens, at a moment indeed of democratic triumph, when almost every authoritarian regime has ceded to a government based on popular will, it requires formidable historical effort to recall the fear of democracy that pervaded polite society after the collapse of the Napoleonic Empire. Even on the eve of the French Revolution the term had ambivalent connotations; afterwards it was associated with Jacobin dictatorship, Terror, and continuous French military aggression. 'I am of that odious class of men called democrats,' Wordsworth wrote in 1794. With the collapse of the few dozen Democratic Societies in the mid 1790s, discredited by their support for France and tarred by President Washington as accomplices of the Whisky Rebellion, the term disappeared in American usage until the founding of the Jacksonian Democratic Party in the late 1820s.[1] In most places attitudes toward democracy depended upon one's stance towards the evolving French events, which the revolutionaries themselves alternatively termed republican or democratic. The term retained some positive resonance in the Netherlands. In the Italian Jacobin republics, so ephemerally established between 1796 and 1800, *governo democratico* might briefly evoke enthusiasm. Not for long, however. 'In the last years,' noted the German Campe in 1813, 'the friends of absolutism and the nobility have made the word Democrat into an insult.' None the less, in the diverse lexicons of the era up to 1830, authorities strove for a neutral meaning: 'believing in freedom', or 'citizen of a state in which the people rule themselves through representatives . . . believing in free citizens, friend of freedom, friend of the people' (Hans Maier in Koselleck and Maier 1972: 854–61; Palmer 1953: 203 ff; for the Democratic Societies, Hofstadter 1969: 92–5).

Naturally enough the aristocratic and military élites who reimposed their control over European politics after 1815 distrusted appeals to broad currents of public opinion—whether a Metternich who glorified a 'stability' that would preserve his complex monarchy, or a Wellington who disdained what he perceived as the mob. On the morrow of Waterloo, democracy seemed at best the luxury of a rustic republic at the edge of the world or a few city-states—more likely a sort of regime that must degenerate into mob rule, mass violence, despoliation of property, and legal terror. For the men of the centre, it reflected legitimate grievances, but threatened to degenerate. 'Democracy', Guizot wrote in 1837, 'is a war cry; it is the banner of the many situated below against the few placed on high. A banner raised sometimes in the name of the healthiest rights, sometimes in the name of the crudest and outraged passions, sometimes against the most iniquitous usurpations, sometimes against the most legitimate superiority' (Rosanvallon 1985: 83–4). How have these attitudes and perceptions come to change so radically during the intervening century and three-quarters?

The history of democracy in the nineteenth and twentieth centuries involves the story not so much of making the world safe for democracy, as Woodrow Wilson wanted it, but of making democracy safe for the world. Why could not democracy simply be resisted? Such was the intention of many of the political leaders and thinkers of the Restoration. But more perspicacious observers understood that democratic trends could not be suppressed indefinitely. The reason was that society itself was evolving democratically. Political forms followed changes in social structure. If, as Tocqueville (following the Marquis d'Argenson) claimed, all history tended towards the destruction of aristocracies, there could be no long-term societal barrier to a government of and by the people. 'A great democratic revolution is at work among us . . . it is universal, it is durable, it escapes human intervention every day; every event, like every man, furthers its development' (D'Argenson, 1764, in Brunner *et al.* 1972: 844; Tocqueville 1951: i. 1. 1 and 1955: p. xii). In 1859 Mill argued similarly, 'There is confessedly a strong tendency in the modern world towards a democratic constitution of society, accompanied or not by popular political institutions' (Mill 1910a: 143). The point, however, was that they would be so accompanied. Political forms would tend in the long run to recapitulate social trends. The rulers of 1815 might not have agreed on the egalitarian thrust of social evolution. Still, after repeated revolutions, the growth of an urban working class, the abandonment of serfdom in the East European countryside and of slavery in the colonies, and finally in the cotton, sugar, and mining territories of the Americas, this trend was hard to deny. Simple counter-revolution thus seemed more and more impossible. The power of democratic passions, so it was understood, depended less upon political reason and the argument of inherent equal rights than upon social evolution. Democracy presupposed equal participatory rights; the trends in industrial society apparently were working towards the diffusion of property and education that would underlie such a political development. To be sure, the actual historical tendency was far more complex. The progress of industrial society and bureaucratic administration would partially widen the bases for emerging social hierarchies; it certainly would not eliminate them outright. Revised rankings and new élites could provide strongholds for resisting democratic politics. None the less, it was the apparent levelling that so struck mid-nineteenth-century observers. They drew their political conclusions from a simplified sociology.

But two different conclusions might be drawn. If one believed that social levelling would lead only to a diffusion of yeoman status or middling property (the promise of American life, but after all America had free land!), then the political democratization that ensued might be stable and acceptable. All the more so, since nineteenth-century theorists increasingly suggested that a modern government could include a democratic ingredient (incorporated in the lower parliamentary house) alongside an aristocratic or monarchical component. Politics need not be all democratic or reactionary. On the other hand, if the observer feared that social levelling would continue toward proletarianization, then the advance of democracy must appear an alarming trend. For this would suggest, as will be seen, that all democracy must in effect tend towards social democracy. That is, the advent of popular government and expanded electorates would ineluctably lead to programmes for further social equalization and redistribution of wealth. Democracy as a stable, continuing (but contained) element of the modern state, or democracy as a voracious mass confiscatory force? The perceived outcome often hung upon sociological prediction. As another political lexicographer wrote at mid-century:

not only the political but also the social foundation of the hitherto condition of society is undergoing a transformation, that the possessing classes, the bourgeoisie, are losing not merely the political privileges they have enjoyed, but also the material bases of these privileges, i.e. their property, in favour of the propertyless classes, and that therefore not only a complete political but also a material and social equality of all social classes must be produced. In this sense people have spoken of a social democratic state, of a democratic and social republic as the necessary tendency of the development of the democratic principle. (*Brockhaus*, 8th edn., iii. 312 (1840), cited by Hans Maier, in Brunner *et al.* 1972: 868–9).

The first half of the revolutionary year 1848 would bring these movements into prominence *seriatim*. Tocqueville asked the Chamber of Deputies, in early 1848, if they did not really understand that mass passions had passed from political to social? Could they not perceive that the people were 'gradually forming opinions and ideas which are destined not only to upset this or that law, ministry, or even form of government, but society itself, until it totters upon the foundations on which it rests today?' (Tocqueville 1959: 11–12). The June Days (as supposedly the Paris Commune almost a generation later) were 'not strictly speaking a political struggle, in the sense which until then we have given to the word, but a struggle of class against class' (ibid. 150).

Was socialism and class conflict really inevitable? The year 1848 was an exceptional moment, soon to be overcome. Even before 1848 liberal spokesmen, who insisted on the power of legislatures to restrain the prerogatives of 'throne and altar', began to make distinctions. Some of them separated a menacing direct democracy from a limited or representative democracy. Direct democracy meant the illiberal restraint of opinion, the curbing of individuality and of culture, the mobilization of mass sentiment to dominate policies and personnel. It remained continually vulnerable to despotism, whether exerted by the mob or a tyrant, as it had been since Aristotle and Montesquieu. On the other hand, liberals also recognized, representative democracy might be constructed with restraints and guarantees. This required establishing by constitutional prohibitions that certain human rights were not subject to majority will: the practice of constitutional or liberal democracy. The demonstration that such a restrained popular government might be established—and in a large territory, not merely the city-states of ancient Hellas or modern Switzerland—was the achievement of the American constitutional founders, pre-eminently James Madison and his colleagues. By 1815 the American republic had navigated through the Napoleonic wars without civil war, fragmentation, or disastrous international setbacks. It had overcome a brief temptation to depart from its constitutionally enshrined freedoms of the press and speech. Perhaps most crucial for its future, it had peacefully transferred power from one embryonic party to an organized opposition.

But were American conditions replicable in Europe? Some of the lessons, such as the so-called separation of powers, the founding fathers of the United States had learned from European theorists such as Montesquieu. They could be reimported. Other institutional models might include geographical federalism, the vigour of local government, the *esprit de corps* of the legal profession, separation of Church and State. As a youth, Tocqueville believed some of these models could be applied at home. By the 1850s, disillusioned with the advent of an authoritarian regime once again, he was less sanguine. The French loved equality more than liberty; they connived in centralization (Tocqueville 1955). Moreover, some salient American advantages could not be instituted in Europe. America, in Goethe's famous line, 'had it better' because of accessible land, middling fortunes, buffers to social polarization. Without a yeoman social basis, democracy might careen toward despotic socialism. For those who kept a liberal-democratic faith, however, institutional cleverness might contain the levelling impulse. Mixed government, instituted through bicameral representation, promised the best chance to contain democratic passions.

American developments, however, also suggested another negative aspect to the encroachment of democracy. For conservatives, or even those liberals poised in the political centre, democracy could undermine individual culture and values. Tocqueville and John Stuart Mill alike expressed the concern about the tyranny of the majority. To be sure the potential was mixed. Individual brilliance might gleam most brightly under an aristocratic monarchy. None the less, both thinkers recognized just as forcefully that the average intelligence of a community, its civic culture, depended upon its members' active participation in public affairs. Without a role in government, men would turn inward, become selfish, grasping, and anomic. Tocqueville, Constant, and the French liberals emphasized liberty as the prerequisite of intellectual and cultural development; Mill stressed active participation: 'the ideally best form of government is that in which . . . every citizen [is], at least occasionally, called on to take an actual part in the government, by the personal discharge of some public function, local or general' (Mill 1910b: 207). The opposite of representative government, he repeatedly warned, was bureaucratic administration. It might assure some good results but led to routine and the suffocation of public intelligence, and was itself internally despotic.

The first element of good government, therefore, being the virtue and intelligence of the human beings composing the community, the most important point of excellence which any form of government can possess is to promote the virtue and intelligence of the people themselves . . . A representative constitution is a means of bringing the general standard of intelligence and honesty existing in the community, and the individual intellect and virtue of its wisest members, more directly to bear upon the government, and investing them with greater influence in it than they would in general have under any other mode of organization. (Mill 1910b: 193, 195. On the evils of bureaucracy, pp. 246–8; also Mill 1910a: 165–70)

Conservatives, however, did not concede that democratic government might raise the average cultural level of a community, stressing instead only its debasing and levelling effects. Indeed this complaint has remained the most persistent criticism of democratic trends. Long after it was unfashionable to complain about democratic institutions *per se*, it remained (indeed remains) perfectly acceptable to lament the degradation of public or aesthetic discourse: from Matthew Arnold to T. S. Eliot and Ernst Jünger, the masses remained debasing. Many democrats reject the élitism that remains encoded in this aesthetic appeal. But others who might distance themselves from the cultural critique of democracy still hope to keep certain privileged spheres of values off limits to democratic politics. The desire to limit the intrusiveness of the majority remains strong in discussions of education today, just as during the 1970s it persisted in terms of economic institutions. Whether it is school curricula, or control of the money supply, or the preservation of ecological resources, there are always some areas of collective life that many of us wish to shield from majority rule.

CONSTITUTIONAL DEMOCRACY AND POLITICAL PRACTICE

Democracy after the French Revolution meant, if nothing else, that numbers were the major resource of politics. Quantity counted, whether in counting votes or filling the streets. 'Quality'—whether inherited nobility or education—might be appealed to, but in theory could enjoy no special privileges. No single citizen's preferences or wisdom could be ranked higher than another's; hence decisions required aggregating preferences and deciding majorities. Democracy—so the revolutionaries and their successors read Rousseau—also meant more than mere majoritarian decision rules. In the revolutionaries' reading, democracy implied an effort to make citizens think not just more alertly, as Mill would stress, but 'correctly', to share right beliefs. Prior to Kleisthenes, after all, lurked the patriarchal figure of Solon: founder, legislator, and educator all at once. Even for would-be democrats the Spartan Lycurgus retained an aura of moral authority. Washington offered a modern counterpart. The appeal of such founders could justify a search for moral consensus. Between education and indoctrination, however, lay a subtle and easily transgressed boundary. Democracy might be—to use the locution of the 1940s—potentially totalitarian. (Talmon (1955) argued that an ineluctable line led from Rousseau and other Enlightenment democrats to Communist dictatorship.) And if it was not totalitarian, it was certainly repressive.

'Two very different ideas are usually confounded under the name democracy. The pure idea of democracy, according to its definition, is the government of the whole people by the whole people, equally represented. Democracy as commonly conceived and hitherto practised is the government of the whole people by a mere majority of the people, exclusively represented' (Mill 1910b: 256). So Mill tried to distinguish between true and false democracy: false democracy was just majority imposition; true democracy was institutionalized through representative government. In turn representative government gave voice to minority currents. We should pause over Mill's distinction, which ultimately proved difficult to sustain. Mill understood that class legislation (whether by majority or institutionally entrenched minority) was one of the major defects of government. In envisaging it as a majority abuse he echoed James Madison's diagnosis of 'the violence' or 'the mischiefs of faction', faction meaning 'a majority or minority of the whole, who are united and actuated by some common impulse . . . adverse to the right of other citizens, or to the permanent and aggregate interests of the community' (Madison 1788). Madison's answer was to reject 'pure democracy'—by which he meant the local assembly of the whole—and to resort to federally organized representative government. Mill took up schemes of proportional representation that allowed minority currents to find a place in the legislature. Implicitly for Mill the right to have some representation within the legislative body was all the citizen might legitimately claim.

But suppose such representatives were constantly outvoted? Mill did not fret about the grievances that arose from perpetual minority status. Nevertheless, his position meant that the problem of a tyrannical majority was merely shifted from the polity as a whole inside the parliament. The most acute critic of democracy in the early nineteenth century did not let this problem pass. John C. Calhoun envisaged with deep gloom the continued outvoting of the Southern slave states in the United States Congress. In response he proposed to provide the South with a continuing veto over policy by requiring approval for measures by a concurrent majority (that is, the Southern delegates)—a procedure that would have given the U.S. all the cohesiveness of contemporary Lebanon (Calhoun 1854: 25–30). But Calhoun was ruthless in his rejection of majority rule. The possibility of being overruled or outvoted, that is, of losing, was what constituted democracy and Calhoun did not wish to accept it. In the last analysis—and in this respect the critics were more ruthlessly to the point than the defenders—democracy required counting votes.

Given the power of number, the most effective way to avert social upheaval was not by attempting outright reaction, but by patiently weaving restraints on the possible abuses of pure democracy. Middle-of-the-road critics (liberals) envisaged two sorts of restraint. One might limit the electorate, or one might restrain their power. In the first case, if modern politics required an appeal to numerical preponderance, the universe of those to be counted might still be bounded. The National Assembly of 1789 distinguished passive from active citizens: all were to enjoy constitutionally enshrined liberty, negative liberty; only some might vote. Property qualifications remained enforced, though progressively broadened, throughout the nineteenth century. The restored *monarchie censitaire* rested upon approximately 100,000 electors; the revolutionaries of 1848 and the Third Republic would finally open the rolls to all adult males. The British progressively widened the parliamentary suffrage across a century; the Italians followed a similar pattern, but relied on literacy not property to limit access (until 1912). From 1867 on, Bismarck allowed a national suffrage for all males, but restricted the power of the body elected. The US pattern was most intriguing. In early removal of property qualifications from the founding through the Jacksonian era, the Americans forged ahead in opening the suffrage. But by enforcing residence restrictions and, in the case of blacks, arduous civic and literacy tests, diverse American regions reconstructed informal patterns of exclusion. Throughout the West, however, national restrictions on male suffrage seemed less and less justifiable as the century went on. The inherent rights enjoyed by individual males outweighed their different capacities. And if they were to be conscripted into mass armies it became harder to deny them the franchise.[2] The argument for enfranchising women could be resisted longer by appealing to their domestic vocation, their alleged dependence on men, and indeed to all the supposed inferiorities that exclusion from the polls was designed to perpetuate. But New Zealand (1893), Australia (1902), and Norway led the sporadic process of granting them the vote in the twentieth century.

Besides restricting the electorate, liberal states set out to restrict governmental power. The most fundamental restraints involved guaranteeing individual rights over and against their government, what Benjamin Constant called 'the liberty of the moderns' and Isaiah Berlin would later term 'negative liberty' (Constant (1819) in Holmes 1984; Berlin 1958). More systematically than the venerable British precedents, the early amendments to the United States Constitution of 1787 enumerated these basic rights. Originally conceived as protection against monarchical abuses, they were henceforth envisaged as guarantees against abusive majorities: constitutional liberties for discussion, the press, and religion, as well as guarantees of due process. Once stipulated in the Constitution, such rights were not easily removed. Written constitutions required a two-thirds vote of the legislature (or in the United States an even more complex series of hurdles) for amendment. The lesson of the American convention of 1787 was that a constituent assembly could restrain the passions of future legislatures; it expressed a particularly solemn moment of national covenanting. Defenders of this procedure argued that the enhanced status given to constitutional provisions was not anti-democratic. Rather, to protect basic constitutional rights involved the recognition that democracy presupposed every individual had an inherent worth.[3]

The Americans went so far as to declare some efforts to criminalize political behaviour simply illegal. In theory discussion and diffusion of ideas was immune from prosecution (in practice there had to be a continuing testing and retesting of limits). In contrast, French and other Continental guarantees usually stipulated that governments might infringe rights only in line with general and universally binding law. This was a more conditional grant of liberty, although these appeals to law were intended to invoke normative connotations of due process and restraint.

In addition to liberal civil rights, a good representative government had to include structural restraints. The power of democratic majorities might be contained by insisting on what since Aristotle had comprised the best restraint on tyranny: mixed government. But what was the mixing designed to achieve? Liberal theorists on the Continent had demanded mixed government to offset monarchical prerogative. 'Dualists' (to use a German term for constitutional liberals) had spoken for estates and legislatures *vis-à-vis* the executive. But increasingly, the preoccupation was the opposite. After the revolution it seemed less urgent to defend legislative power against executive or judicial authority than the other way around. An upper house would likewise brake the tendencies of the most directly elected representative chamber. These upper houses might represent federal divisions, appointed notables, hereditary peers, or just involve cross-cutting constituencies. Their right of absolute veto was slowly whittled away, but they were still designed to force reflection and sobriety, to cool hasty democratic passions.

Constitutional arrangements were hardly the only critical influence on democratic politics. Social trends spilled over into politics; hence the organization of civil society became important for assuring political outcomes. French liberals, especially, became preoccupied with organizing society to provide a ballast against the revolutionary political upheavals that had characterized their recent history. Political life must incorporate the middle class, repository of talent and common sense; the government must reconstruct the associations that the disciples of Rousseau found so subversive. From the 'doctrinaires' of the Restoration to the 'Progressistes' of the Third Republic the narrow strand of liberal thinkers insisted on making associations less invertebrate, entrusting society with overcoming the anarchic impulses that were so politically inflammable. (Cf. Rosanvallon 1985; Donzelot 1984; and for the biography of a paradigmatic Progressiste, Sorlin 1966.) Sociology from Comte to Durkheim represented, in effect, an intellectual project for encouraging an organization of civil society that might stabilize an increasingly democratic politics. And not only in France: the collection of social statistics, the enquiries into agrarian and industrial conditions carried out throughout Europe and in the American states, presupposed a heightened awareness of social change and social complexity. State agencies and church organizations, new settlement houses and progressive employers, worked to map the terrain of sweatshops and slums, alcoholism and illness. In an era of democratization, the state in effect had to work at constructing its own ideal society to assure stability.

As for governmental mechanisms in their own right, democratic regimes—or the democratic component of mixed regimes—worked by virtue of an institution unprovided for by constitutions, but increasingly central to their operation: the political party. Party development testified to the advance of democracy. Party division had originated in England: it emerged as the form by which political friends secured policies they believed in and offices they coveted. Party made politics into a predictable living and an instrument of governance. Party also performed another function: it transformed opposition from conspiracy into acceptable dissent. In effect it channelled a virulent and potentially lethal rivalry into a workaday and tolerable antagonism of ins and outs. Within a few years of inaugurating a federal republic the Americans had defined two party nuclei around the major foreign-policy alternatives facing the new nation. Within a generation thereafter they had made national parties the key network for organizing elections. Party became the mechanism by which numbers and majorities were organized, brought to the polls, mobilized for policy contests. 'The Democracy' became the title for Andrew Jackson's supporters and America's oldest continuing political organization. The name identified the instrument of governance with the type of regime. 'Any party can rule in fact, but only a democratic party can rule by right,' wrote the contributor to the major German liberal handbook of the 1840s (Schieder 1962: 88). To admit the legitimacy and constitutional role of parties was to sanction the principle of political division. Parties in short reconciled parts and wholes: they could never speak for all the interests in a state (although totalitarian parties would claim to speak for the only legitimate interests). But their partiality was sanctioned by numbers. Democratic legitimacy did not require unanimity or consensus (except to establish constitutional principles); a simple majority was enough.

By the close of the century, parties had become permanent organizations with professional staffs and offices that remained active between elections. They had evolved from gentlemen's parliamentary coalitions into disciplined organizations that kept in touch with constituencies and supervised a network of loyal newspapers. European political observers found the frank dominance of party in American life the key to understanding modern democratic politics. 'The spirit and force of party', wrote Lord Bryce in the 1890s, 'has in America been as essential to the action of the machinery of government as steam is to a locomotive engine' (*The American Commonwealth*, cited in Hofstadter 1969; 71). Max Weber, Moisei Ostrogorski, and others examined American parties, then discovered that the political machines so prominent in the New World also characterized the old. In the generation after the Second Reform Bill (1867), British parliamentary life fell into a routine rivalry organized by Conservatives and Liberals, occasionally racked by internal conflict, and increasingly perturbed by the Irish representatives who sought to swing the balance. By the end of the century French Radical Socialists, middle-of-the-road secular liberals, and working-class socialists all organized parties to contest the Chamber elections and cope with the polarized issues of Church and State. Even in Germany, where the federal Reichstag exerted less influence, strong party organizations grew up around religious and class cleavages. They included a massive working-class Social Democracy, a Catholic Party (the Centre), Prussian agrarian conservatives—and the Protestant town-fathers, national bureaucrats, businessmen, and professionals of the pro-government National Liberals or the dissenting Progressives. By the end of the nineteenth century, democracy meant party government. Those at odds with its triumph worried less about any revolutionary danger than its alleged debasing of public life.

THE RECURRING CRITIQUES: POPULIST AND TECHNOCRATIC

There was ample evidence for those who feared corruption. Liberal regimes seemed increasingly tainted by unholy bargains from the 1870s and 1880s on. Abuses ranged from outright scandal, such as afflicted President Grant's White House and marked the French Panama scheme, to a more pervasive abandonment of principles—the *turno politico*, *trasformismo*, and *toutes les places, toute de suite*, to cite just the cosy or cynical slogans of late nineteenth-century 'Latin' democratic praxis. Even more dangerous from the perspective of rightist critics, democracy was opening the way for the triumph of Marxist parties. Although the revolution of 1848 and the Commune of 1871 had failed to destroy private property, the mass suffrage might achieve the objective more insidiously. Since the disadvantaged were numerically preponderant, democracy involved a craven appeasement that must lead to social democracy and thence to outright socialism. 'In the course of the nineteenth century,' wrote Georges Sorel with his prophetic fusion of left-wing and right-wing radicalism, 'the bourgeoisie was so worried by the fear of revolution that it resigned itself to accepting the claims of a democracy, whose inevitable triumph had been predicted by so many ideologies' (Sorel 1917: 17).

Of course, the opposition to democratic tendencies did not simply fold its tents. Russia might rely on autocracy and censorship; but the advent elsewhere of press freedom and a broad suffrage meant that opposition to democratic tendencies could not simply advance a reactionary electoral programme to reinvest power in traditional élites. Forcible resistance seemed an even less promising strategy. Only regimes where the military still played a major domestic role could actually stage interventions against elected governments. This was the case frequently in Iberia, where generals had intervened both on the Left and Right and would continue to do so through the Spanish Civil War and the Portuguese New State. It was also a recourse in Argentina and other Latin American republics. But most of Europe would have found such conduct simply unacceptable. Allegedly one Junker declared that his emperor must always be in a position to take a few soldiers and dissolve the Reichstag. But this was hardly feasible politics, not even in Germany.

Intellectuals could seek to discredit democracy in theoretical terms. Outright reactionaries, such as the French authoritarian monarchist Charles Maurras, just claimed that democracy was feeble, ineffective, self-divided, anti-national. In so far as democratic theorists claimed that democracy rested not just on the inherent equality of all men (how could one legitimately discriminate among their policy preferences?) but on their essential goodness or rationality, political writers could protest. The late nineteenth-century opponents of democracy responded that men behaved collectively as irrational and easily swayed creatures. Gustave Le Bon in *The Crowd* proposed that such supposed forums for reasoned discussion as legislatures and juries, as well as street mobs, obeyed their murkiest emotions. The Italian theorist Gaetano Mosca and the economist Vilfredo Pareto argued that all democratic parties were based on pretence: only small élites exerted rule. Even those who spoke for allegedly democratic or progressive tendencies were just seeking to organize new élites to hold power. Inside the parties, Roberto Michels agreed, oligarchic tendencies prevailed. Ostensibly neutral sociology thus supposedly demonstrated that democracy was an ideological myth, an illusion, or in Pareto's term a derivation.

All very well, but what political remedies did these disillusioned and sometimes proto-fascist critics propose? Some revelled in visions of apocalyptic violence that might invigorate an otherwise Milquetoast middle class. War and imperialism, so the Futurists suggested, were hygienic. The mass strikes of the first decade of the new country were promising: whereas a Rosa Luxemburg on the Left felt they would stimulate working-class militance, George Sorel on the radical Right believed they might dissipate mushy democratic sloth. All the more so, Pareto agreed, if they involved labour violence. Political health apparently depended more on the adrenal than the cerebral cortex. Longings for domination, whether channelled into imperialism abroad or acted out in confrontations at home, gradually replaced the Victorians' celebration of discussion. Sensing these urges, William James called for a moral equivalent of war. He was in a race with those who envisaged war as the moral equivalent of politics.

Demagogic electoral campaigners were learning to exploit democratic competitions to undermine liberal and parliamentary regimes. By the end of the 1870s and the 1880s, they were playing on new Darwinian currents of militarist nationalism, ethnocentrism, and often a rising political anti-Semitism to rally mass support. Karl Lueger mobilized Viennese shopkeepers, artisans, and white-collar voters against the city's liberal élite in the mayoralty elections of 1879 and entrenched his Christian Social Party by means of populistic, anti-Semitic campaigns. Francesco Crispi sought to rule Italy in the 1880s and 1890s with a mixture of enthusiasm for imperial adventure and authoritarian suppression of dissent. At the end of the 1880s traditional French conservatives recognized that the mass appeal of General Boulanger's nationalism might serve to undermine the Third Republic. By the first decade of the new century a series of racist demagogues rallied the white electorate of the American South with mixtures of populism and white supremacy.

Such tactics revealed the darker side of broad-based electoral politics. The campaigners played on widespread grievances, promised an assault on wealth and privilege, and tapped currents of nationalism and xenophobia. But they exploited their appeals precisely to undermine the liberal ground-rules of parliamentary government. It was fitting that the young Hitler watched Lueger's electoral campaigns in Vienna. When the attack on liberal-democratic government culminated between the world wars, it was justified in terms of a genuine popular will that had supposedly been distorted and frustrated by parliaments, trade unions, and liberal and social-democratic parties.

In the last analysis, so the new rightist critics maintained, democracy failed because it was a regime of useless discussion and insufficient action. The criticism was old. 'Representative assemblies are often taunted by their enemies with being places of mere talk and *bavardage*,' noted Mill, and he added, 'There has seldom been more misplaced derision' (Mill 1910b: 240). Parliaments were designed to talk. But the confidence of the Victorians in discussion or public opinion had ebbed by 1900, certainly on the Continent, and in Britain, too, when it came to the Irish and other intractable issues. Discussion implied that interests might be bridged. The claims of organized religion, however, or of political secularism, the welter of nationality conflicts (in Ireland, Austria-Hungary, Spain), or the menacing stance of the organized working classes did not appear susceptible to compromise. If no compromise were possible, discussion was misplaced; action by audacious minorities was crucial. The turn of the century brought a longing for such decisive minority currents to offset the languor and indolence of democracy. Male action—whether conquering African wastes, competing at the Olympic Games revived in 1896, making cavalry charges in Third World wars, planning revolution—returned to fashion after a generation of pacifism. The quest for *élan vital* pervaded philosophy and glimmered as a personal orientation.

Fascism and Nazism would be the culmination of this post-democratic authoritarian reaction. To the authoritarian critiques that had become so rife by 1914, these new movements added the experience of combat in the First World War. Without the immense toll of the war, anti-democratic thinking and appeals might well have remained just a troubling dissent from workaday liberal accommodation. After the war, so even demoralized liberals might concede, the soldier whose resoluteness had been tempered in the trenches, not the intellectual or politician, deserved to run the harsher world that emerged. And if not the soldier, at least the new experts from the domains of technology and production. The Italian Nationalist (and then Fascist) theorist, Alfredo Rocco, argued that the principles of 1789 had posited an abstract equality among men, which in fact provided no real basis for political cohesion. Like-minded champions of authoritarianism insisted on new communal foundations for politics: brotherhoods of combat, technical expertise, or even more mystically, the soil and race. These collective loyalties would be aggregated by a single national movement entrusted with total power. As political competitors, these movements might take the label of party, but they envisaged putting a quick end to pluralism. 'The party' (and the same transformation had taken place on the Communist Left) had evolved from an association construed as one association among many to a monolithic bloc designed to transform politics and society. The party was also to prepare its national society for the unceasing struggle among states that the war had revealed anew.

This powerful inter-war assault on liberal democracy burned itself out with the horrors of the Second World War. For at least four decades afterwards, civilians in the West could not really challenge the commitment to democracy as a political form. Neo-fascist movements enjoyed occasional double-digit electoral breakthroughs, but failed to make their gains permanent. (And through the 1980s, to be sure, would-be military saviours felt entitled to speak for the higher values of the nation from Iberia to Africa, Latin America, and in Asia.) Still, disturbing echoes of anti-liberal, electorally based xenophobia did resurface periodically in the post-war period. By the beginning of the 1990s, European and American voters' preoccupation with issues of migration and ethnic origins, urban crime and economic security were once again reviving electoral appeals that had first made their mark a century earlier. Periodically it seemed democracy could be its own worst enemy.

Over the course of the last century, finally, there has been another counter-current to the progress of mass democracy—less violent, more persuasive, and well suited for an age of technological advance. To many of its modern critics, by 1900 democracy appeared irrelevant and harmful. Democracy sought to build policy around majority will; what was important was to build it around knowledge. This 'technocratic' approach to government envisaged government by expert or institutional engineer. Much of this thinking permeated British Fabian socialism, giving it the flavour of a more élitist crypto-socialism. It also characterized the urban élites of the United States who distrusted the new immigrant electorate, feared urban patronage and corruption, and longed for government by a professional managerial class. These innovations were not seen as hostile to mass aspirations; they embodied the higher wisdom (an engineering general will, so to speak) that properly enlightened citizens must also want, assuming that they wished to maximize social peace and economic well-being. This technocratic managerialism, curiously enough, could be combined with a belief in such new democratic institutions as the referendum and direct election: both strategies together aimed at undercutting machine politics and legislative corruption. Real democracy in short had to be rescued from masses not yet mature or informed enough to govern themselves. Disinterested expertise was required in large, modern societies, but it was always threatened by demagogic tendencies. As Walter Lippman wrote in Public Opinion (1922), it was no longer possible to believe in the 'original dogma of democracy: that the knowledge needed for the management of human affairs comes up spontaneously enough from the human heart' (Steel 1980: 181).

Did Lippman set the terms of the debate fairly? He envisaged (at least at this time) a huge, mass society that could be co-ordinated only from above. John Dewey focused on the perspective from below and the assets of the head, not the deficiencies of the heart. In the local community, he remained confident, democracy could thrive on continuing experimentation, freedom from dogma, and a progressive education. (For the ideas behind progressive democracy see Kloppenberg 1986.) Dewey's was the more 'American' faith. None the less, the technocratic belief that wise government must be shielded from the mass electorate remains a potent critique of democratic commitments. To be sure, it was and still is contested. As noted above, such a view is shared more broadly than is usually acknowledged. Aside from the basic constitutional rights that most citizens believe enjoy an a priori sanctity, many commentators would place other areas of modern decision-making off limits to majorities. Control of the money supply, school curricula, hospital investments, state funding of art and science are among the areas that are often alleged to be too sensitive for democratic rule-making. By the 1970s such theories were intellectually refurbished and popularized under the concept of 'overloaded democracy'. Popular demands on the public purse could not, so it was argued, be successfully resisted in a modern welfare-state democracy (Barry 1985). Political economists and so-called public-choice theorists likewise claimed that in a democracy special interests would extract concentrated benefits whose costs would be charged almost imperceptibly to taxpayers as a whole. Democracy would thus continually tend to generate more claims than it could finance. By the end of the 1970s this democratic pessimism enjoyed widespread resonance among European and American élites. But the fact that opponents of welfare-state tendencies managed to win crucial elections in the early 1980s at least temporarily eclipsed the appeal of such generalized democratic disillusion. Democratic majorities, it seemed, were not so wedded to the short-sighted welfare-state dismantling of capitalism as had been feared.

DEMOCRACY AFTER 1945:
PEOPLES', CHRISTIAN, SOCIAL, PARTICIPATORY

Cruelty, repression, the persecution of dissenters, the glorification of force and racial hierarchy, war, and finally crushing military defeat had all discredited the authoritarian attacks on liberal democracy by 1945. But the process by which democratic governments had succumbed to dictatorship between the world wars also had taught some hard lessons. For the Communists, so ambiguously poised between authoritarian longings 'in the name of the people' and efforts at wooing mass support, a new strategy beckoned. The Communist leaders who returned to France, Italy, and Germany from Soviet exile at the end of the Second World War called for 'people's democracy' or 'democracy of a new type' or 'progressive democracy'.

Democracy of a new type derived from the legacy of the Popular Front and the Soviet concern about rising Nazi power in the mid- and late 1930s. Rather than stress revolution, post-war Communist spokesmen defined their goals as the cementing of broad anti-Fascist coalitions that would reinstitute democratic government. The coalitions would allegedly rely on electoral politics to confirm their historical role. This concept seemed to govern Communist strategies in Western and Eastern Europe until 1947. Communists initially accepted electoral results in Hungary and Czechoslovakia that limited their parliamentary delegations. None the less, they kept pressing Social Democratic elements to merge with their own party organizations. Some socialists accepted the bid, others fiercely resisted, fearing a simple takeover. Local tensions added to the global Cold War disagreements that drove apart the Soviet Union and the United States. After 1947 Communists were removed from Western political coalitions, but began to impose harsh Party domination on the Eastern European countries where Soviet power could enforce decisive control. Those who would not comply were driven into exile or put on trial. Despite the repression, the rhetoric of anti-Fascist popular democracy still provided the dominant rationale. Democracy, however, meant enforcing Party rule. Only reactionaries, it was claimed, could wish to dissent at the polls. The role of elections was to integrate the forces of officially recognized civil society. Labour unions, now safely led by compliant leaders, youth groups, tamed intellectuals, and other Party-dominated groups, met to nominate members for the electoral slates and to encourage a massive ratification of the single slate at the polls.

Outside the Soviet bloc, Communist adherents could still claim some working-class support in France, Belgium, and above all Italy. Leftist intellectuals found it hard to renounce the old appeals to anti-Fascist unity. Most other voters and leaders in Western Europe gravitated toward the new, encompassing Christian Democracy that claimed the centre and centre-right of politics or supported a national variant of social democracy on the centre-left. These alternative commitments both had anti-Fascist credentials. A broad-based Christian Democracy was the real innovation of post-war politics. Influenced by the Catholic humanism of Jacques Maritain, Alcide de Gasperi, the Italian Christian Democratic leader and prime minister, combined concepts of Stoic and Christian humanism, an appeal to a collective 'people' and to 'democracy', and a continuing belief in Italian civilization. Konrad Adenauer insisted that parliamentary democracy meant the strong leadership of the majority party and robust debate even as he struggled to restore Germany's international standing.

For both these senior statesmen, the era of dictatorship had provided long years for reflection. The pre-war history of Catholic democrats had been episodic and troubled. The concept of Catholic democracy went back to the mid-nineteenth-century churchman Félicité de Lammenais, whose rapturous efforts to reconcile the Church with liberalism were condemned by Rome in the 1830s. After the long, unyielding papacy of Pius IX, the more liberal Leo XIII finally encouraged French Catholics to 'rally' to the Third Republic in the early 1890s and urged a progressive stance on labour issues. But it proved difficult to stabilize a Catholic political stance in Latin countries torn by Church–State conflict. Sizeable Catholic parties gathered around 30 to 36 per cent of the vote in the Netherlands and Belgium. In Germany the Catholic Centre Party originated as an instrument designed to thwart Protestant domination; its cautious reformism was balanced by conservatism and it stirred up no heretical waters. In France and Italy political Catholicism emerged as far more problematic for Rome. (Indeed it has remained a prickly issue up to today's Latin American clergy and its Liberation Theology.) Leo's successors wanted Catholic workers kept immune from Marxist appeals; they endorsed social reformism but feared any revolutionary or collectivist claims. Such efforts at Catholic Democracy as the pre-1914 French 'Sillon', and the Italian Partito Popolare from 1919 to 1925 ended up rejected by the Vatican and conservative bishops.

After Fascism, however, Catholic political initiatives emerged in a new climate. The post-war leaders had shared common dangers and aspirations with Communists and Socialists in the Resistance. Their hostility to socialism mattered less since they accepted, at least initially, an interventionist welfare state. Electorally the Christian Democrats benefited from the discrediting of right-wing alternatives: until the 1950s conservatives had few other promising political choices. The new parties consciously sought to minimize overt links with the hierarchy, above all in Germany where the Christian Democratic Party (CDU) was designed after 1945 to attract Protestant as well as Catholic voters. Nevertheless, German bishops issued pastoral letters during electoral campaigns for a 'Christian politics'. And throughout the continuing pontificate of Pius XII (until 1958), the Italian Church was frankly drawn upon to mobilize voters against Communism and for the Christian Democrats (DC).

The most venerable mass political alternative in post-war Europe remained socialism and its variants. The Socialist Party had governed Sweden since 1932; the British Labour Party nationalized key industrial sectors and instituted major welfare-state provisions, including a National Health Service, after its 1945 electoral triumph. Elsewhere socialists played a less commanding role until the 1960s. In Eastern Europe, if they resisted the Communists' pressure to join an umbrella 'progressive' coalition, they were hounded as reactionaries. If either naïve or worn-down, they sought to work within the new party fronts—as did important East German Social Democratic (SPD) leaders in 1946—they were soon forced into subservience. Socialists in Italy split along similar lines. Pietro Nenni's Socialist Party left the cabinet with the Communists in 1947 and became a Communist electoral ally until the end of the 1950s. The smaller Social Democratic Party, supported in part by American funds, became a coalition partner of the DC. Despite brief co-operation during the Popular Front and the Resistance, French Socialists soon became staunchly anti-Communist after 1945.

As many political commentators pointed out, by the 1950s no great differences of principle divided social democrats from Christian Democrats. (Only in Britain were domestic political alternatives clear-cut.) What, then, did social democrats stand for? Their programmes generally had two major thrusts: one involved control, the other welfare. Socialist programmes envisaged placing leading economic sectors (banks, transportation, key industries) under democratic political control, whether through outright nationalization or extensive regulation. The West German SPD could never push through early 'planning' concepts, though the labour union federation did win the right of labour delegates to sit on corporate boards. But electoral defeats throughout the 1950s tempered the collectivist impulse in Britain and Germany. By the 1960s the 'welfare' agenda largely superseded the objectives of democratic 'control'. It seemed more crucial to guarantee continuing high employment and the progressive expansion of public services—health and education—for all citizens. Advocates for the welfare state expressed the modern agenda of social democracy most eloquently when Richard Titmuss pleaded for a responsible society or T. H. Marshall explained the historical emergence of the three dimensions of citizenship: first liberal rights, later political participation, and most recently economic entitlement (Marshall 1950). The later 1960s, in fact, witnessed the zenith of the social democratic achievement. The conservative political coalition of the 1950s gradually gave way to more reformist politics. In Italy, the Church opened towards social democracy with the accession of John XXIII (1958–63) and the reforms of the Second Vatican Council. That transformation encouraged the 'opening to the Left', with inclusion of the former pro-Communist Socialists in the governing coalition. In the United States, the Kennedy and Johnson administrations departed from Eisenhower's fiscal conservatism to attempt more expansionist and redistributive economic policies. British Labour returned to power in 1964 after a thirteen-year opposition; and by the end of the decade Willy Brandt's SPD had finally displaced the Christian Democrats.

The mid-1960s seemed briefly to resolve the age-old tension between instituting a fully democratic political order and guaranteeing the conditions for property—or in this case modern capitalism. Social democrats governed with the mission of making capitalism efficient and humane. Between Christian Democracy and Social Democracy (or Conservatives and Labour, or Republicans and Democrats), only differences of degree seemed at stake. Both sides of the acceptable political spectrum accepted democratic ground rules; they lived easily with the appeal to majorities, because fundamental upheaval seemed undesirable. Challenges to democratic consensus arose only on national and colonial issues—as in France's conflict over Algeria. For some who remembered the ideological politics of the 1930s there was almost a wistful regret at this 'waning of opposition' (Kirchheimer 1957: 128–56; and 1966: 237–59). It did not wane for long, however.

If European socialism now seemed thoroughly domesticated, the emergence of social movements outside parliamentary parties—first students and the American civil rights movements, then increasingly women and peace organizers—strained this democratic equipoise of the 1960s. Social democratic achievements seemed to the new dissenters too manipulative and bureaucratic. Nor did Lyndon Johnson's war on poverty preclude growing involvement in the Vietnam War and the continuing arms race. University expansion facilitated the mobilization of a younger generation in politics that idealized liberation movements in the 'Third World' and the American ghettos. The 1962 Port Huron statement of the fledgling Students for a Democratic Society adumbrated the new themes of the Left:

We seek the establishment of a democracy of individual participation . . . In a participatory democracy, the political life would be based in several root principles: that decision-making of basic social consequence be carried on by public groups; that politics be seen positively, as the art of collectively creating an acceptable pattern of social relations, that politics has the function of bringing people out of isolation and into community; that the political order should . . . provide outlets for the expression of personal grievance and aspiration . . . so that private problems . . . are formulated as general issues. (Sale 1973: 52–3)

Tocqueville would have agreed on the need to overcome isolation, but the fusion of the personal and the political more closely echoed Rousseau. And it was precisely the erosion of the distinction between private and public concerns that characterized the style and objectives of the new movements, the most significant legacy of what became 1968.

The conflicts associated with 1968 ushered in two major developments. One involved the realm of values, the other economic dogma. The clashes of 1968 did not bring victory to the Left; but they did establish that political contention might revolve around such issues as cultural lifestyles, family structure, minority entitlements, and the Cold War stasis. The concept of democracy grew more encompassing in its cultural and social implications. The right to vote was not enough. Democratic politics involved contesting the rules of civil society and insisting on occupying public space. Women, gays, racial minorities demanded literally the right to claim streets, squares, and other public spaces. Democratic politics was a politics of presence.

On the other hand, the concept of democracy grew more restrictive as a basis for economic policy. By the end of the 1960s Western political economies entered a long decade of inflation. After a decade of largely ineffectual corporatist bargaining for wage restraint, voters returned more confrontational conservatives, Margaret Thatcher and Ronald Reagan. Where Socialists still governed, they reversed their traditional priorities to extensive welfare and full employment. Democracy became more modest in its economic aspirations: social democrats claimed to be more efficient, not more reformist. In the United States the Democratic Party presidential candidate of 1988 went so far as to claim that the upcoming election was not about ideology, but competence.

In contrast to the inter-war era, economic claims and counter-claims produced no serious authoritarian claimants on the Right. None the less, as noted above, a crypto-antidemocratic discourse emerged around the management of the economy. Conservative economists and businessmen feared that inflation might be endemic under democratic regimes. A democracy could not impose the collective self-restraint to privilege investment for the future over consumption in the present. Only shielding key economic institutions—above all central banks, with their control of the money supply—from democratic majorities might reinvigorate stable growth. Control of the money supply, much as the basic liberties for religion and discussion, had to be placed beyond mass passions. By and large, Europe's socialists accepted these prescriptions in the 1980s. Certainly the French, West German, and Spanish socialists did. British Labour, which resisted the new gospel, remained in the political wilderness. Once again democracy was stabilized by limiting its claims. Another indication of the change was that whereas a major tract of the late 1970s rather typically criticized political pluralism for leaving the market economy a reservoir of non-democratic power (Lindblom 1977), by 1990, freely functioning markets were deemed to be a precondition of successful democracy. Democracy and capitalism were perceived as compatible after decades of mutual suspicion. Whether their honeymoon would outlast some of the economic difficulties that appeared to mount in the early 1990s remains a major question.

In any case the rapprochement between capitalism and democracy found no equivalent in issues outside the economic sphere. Issues of cultural conflict, migration, urban security, and the control of public space remained intensely charged. By the end of the 1980s anti-democratic potential emerged less from the older economic issues than from the politics of ethnic identity. Europe and North America faced the movement of peoples from periphery to core. Arabs and Africans lived in Paris, Africans and Asians in London, Latin Americans in Los Angeles, Turks in Frankfurt and Berlin. Just as the 'First World' earlier reinforced economic stratification in the 'Third World', so now the Third World recreated its deep social divisions in the First. At the very moment democrats enjoyed their greatest modern victories since 1945, in Eastern Europe, the potential for a populist authoritarianism grew threatening once again.

DEMOCRATIC VICTORIES: THE LESSONS OF 1989

Democratization has taken place in waves. The example of an influential country (or the pressure and sustenance it applies) seems to encourage emulation. Conversely clamorous failure (for example Germany in 1933) can set back progress elsewhere (Huntington 1991). The 'age of democratic revolution' encompassed the American and French revolutions, and efforts at democracy in Latin America and Europe. Most of these proved fragile and were reversed, although they contributed historical reference points for the future. The aftermath of the First World War brought a renewed thrust of democratization in Europe with some echoes in the so-called Third World. The inter-war democracies proved fragile; those in Central and Eastern Europe soon succumbed to authoritarian dictatorship. The 'regime transitions' that began in the 1970s have been more promising. Greece, Portugal, and Spain, then the reinstitution of civilian government in Latin America, tentative liberalization in South Korea and Taiwan, and even in Africa—and most dramatically the collapse of Communist single-party rule in the Soviet Union and Eastern Europe—have comprised the broadest advance of democracy to date.

Periods of democratic advance as well as of democratic stasis have traditionally stimulated thinking about the conditions favourable for democratic stability. During the 1950s and 1960s, when democracy seemed vigorous but largely confined to the Atlantic world, social scientists stressed its demanding prerequisites. When they examined the comparative history of regimes, it was plausible to propose that there had to be some original revolutionary rupture for democracy to take root on its own (Moore 1964). Some analysts suggested that successful democratic regimes rested on 'congruent' democratic arrangements in local government and associations (Eckstein 1961). Others (Dahl 1971) proposed that multiple and overlapping hierarchies of power ('polyarchy') ensured the maintenance of democracy since this pluralism allowed no single élite to monopolize political domination. Still other analysts proposed that economic and social development—literacy, a vigorous middle class, and the absence of stultifying poverty—was necessary if not sufficient (Rostow 1960). The last wave of democratization has similarly prodded reflection on the conditions for 'transition' to democracy (Schmitter et al. 1986). The thrust of these enquiries is different. They ask not about the conditions that are conducive to democratic breakdown, but those that facilitate the passage from authoritarian to liberal government. The question is still open whether the factors that help restore or inaugurate democracy (and undermine authoritarianism) are the same as those that help preserve it.

Both sets of theories emphasize the nature of the fit between state and society. Not surprisingly they focus on a theme central since Aristotle and continually renewed by every significant subsequent political thinker. Democracy, as Tocqueville stressed, derives from the tendencies of society as much as from the artifices of government. It is appropriate to return to the relationship of society and regime in light of the great democratic transformations of the last years.

A central theme of the democratic movement of 1989 was the appeal to 'civil society'. This fashionable term unfortunately remained an imprecise concept. Despite careless formulations, Communist regimes did have civil societies—that is, fabrics of associations and interest groups and organizations. But Communist civil society was patronized and controlled by the Party. The movements of the 1980s in Eastern Europe waged their revolution in the name of an autonomous civil society. We have noted that French conservatives in the nineteenth century had sought to construct a fabric of societal associations to dampen revolutionary politics. In the 1980s, in contrast, democrats in Eastern Europe sought to reconstruct civil society precisely to reconstruct democratic politics. Democracy required a level of autonomous association and sociability. The lessons of 1989 suggested that what was crucial for democratization .was less the 'congruence' between state and society than just the vigour and autonomy of associational life. The importance of individual resistance which seemed so important in the 1970s, when Westerners looked to heroic dissenters such as Solzhenitsyn and Sakharov, did not diminish in this perspective. But the civic infrastructure of collective ventures came to appear just as crucial. Hence one of the simple lessons from 1989: democracy required insisting on a social and not just a hermetic vision.

Not every important question about democracy involves the relationship between state and society. Democracy—its institution, its maintenance, its possibilities for self-destruction—demands reflection about politics in its own right. Such reflection has been the province more of political philosophy than political sociology, and the events of 1989 had lessons for it too. As the 2,500th anniversary of democracy approached, its ambiguities became notable once again. Democracy was a regime of number. It rested on majorities. If it set no limit on the scope of activity that numbers might legitimate, then democracy was subject to the degeneration that theorists from Plato and Aristotle to Walter Lippman or Leo Strauss predicted. If liberal ground rules were not protected by institutional safeguards, then unscrupulous demagogues could mobilize popular will for repressive ends. This had been the situation under Fascism and Communism. Could it again emerge as a result of rising ethnocentrism and xenophobia, as former national structures broke apart in Eastern Europe or migrants encroached on supposedly homogeneous societies? Majorities could become intolerant. On the other hand, the force of numbers, the appeal to public opinion, and the direct persuasiveness of gifted orators remained central to the underlying strength of democratic regimes. Woodrow Wilson and Lloyd George, Roosevelt and Churchill, and finally Boris Yeltsin, had reinvigorated democracy under siege through their tribune-like qualities.

And the advent of democracy in the Soviet Union, in Czechoslovakia, indeed in East Germany, did suggest that at crucial moments the major recourse of democratic initiatives remained as in 1789, the crowd. Sheer numbers provided the legitimation of democracy. In Western Europe and North America during the 1960s, younger 'radicals' had suggested that democracy had atrophied into bureaucratic decision rules. But the upheavals of 1989 (more than the revolts of 1968) confirmed the potential for participation.

Instituting democracy required, most problematically, the mobilization of the crowd. Mass protest remained irreplaceable—frightening occasionally, but also inspiring as in the Soviet defence of recent liberties during the uprising of August 1991. Even when repression succeeded, democracy presupposed the crowd as in Tiananmen Square. Britons and Americans, their revolutions long in the past, often neglected or drew back from this lesson. In an era when political oratory was mediated by television, they often forgot the magic of direct rhetoric. But without such interaction between orators and masses, might not political systems become stratified, élitist, with their members preoccupied by their private needs and consumption? Democracy in its earlier sense required a continuous public commitment, a willingness to discuss and think about what the populace wanted. Such an acceptance of crowd passions provided the dangers, but also the vitality.

Democracy was ending the century as the most demanding form of regime: it required continuous discussion, lest it degenerate into mere accolade. It did not make a good spectator sport, although television often threatened to transform it into one. It required restraint: majorities had to deny themselves total power. They had to place key resources of political and social pressure beyond their own control, lest civil war and repression result. But democracy also seemed to require some aspects of charisma—not to redress the bureaucratic encroachment that Max Weber believed to threaten political decision-making, but to engage mass opinion. Even when, perhaps especially when, democracy functioned well, as in the 1960s, it might appear to operate without life and soul and could alienate the young.

Hence democratic vitality was renewed through moments of high drama—even at the cost of stability. It involved great contests for public spaces. As one of democracy's fiercest critics, Vilfredo Pareto, had observed, democratic regimes (indeed all regimes) tended to operate cyclically. To remain vigorous, democracy required periodic efforts to include those hitherto left out of political and cultural and economic entitlement. These efforts at inclusion were traditionally the job of the Left, as in France and America in the 1930s, or throughout Western societies in the 1960s. They involved disorderly politics and fervid ideological claims. Their watchword was justice. The difficulty was that each effort at inclusion created new categories of those left out. In effect, democracies drew a larger perimeter of citizenship, but ultimately had to enforce this new perimeter. Administering these latter periods of consolidation fell to conservative majorities, as in the 1920s and the 1950s. These majorities broke with utopian expectations. They cut back economic redistribution and favoured social saving; they enforced social and territorial frontiers. They returned to normalcy. Their watchword was realism.

It was not clear what phase of the cycle was under way in 1992. Democracy in the 1980s had generally been entrusted to the conservatives or to social democrats who had behaved like conservatives. But in the Soviet Republics and Eastern Europe, the former dictatorships of Latin America, and the Republic of South Africa, governments were embarking on experiments in liberalization. At the same time, however, public pressure seemed to rise to limit experiments at inclusion, to firm up national boundaries and internal class frontiers. The great rhythm of Left and Right that had marked the history of modern democracies was difficult to discern. Democratic politics seemed in a state of curious fibrillation. Europeans and North Americans were rightly gratified by the success of democracy in 1989. Democracy had won remarkable victories, and without the excesses that had made those victories so brief and so sanguinary in the past. But there was no reason to believe that the exertions needed to make democracy both liberal and enduring would be any the easier in the millennium to come.

REFERENCES

Barry, Brian (1985), 'Does Democracy Cause Inflation? Political Ideas of some Economists', in Leon Lindberg and Charles S. Maier (eds.), *The Politics of Inflation and Economic Stagnation* (Washington, DC), 280–317.

Berlin, Sir Isaiah (1958), *Two Concepts of Liberty* (Oxford).

Brunner, Otto, Conze, Werner, and Koselleck, Reinhard (eds.) (1972), *Geschichtliche Grundbegriffe: Historisches Lexikon zur politisch-sozialen Sprache in Deutschland* (Stuttgart).

Calhoun, John C. (1854), *A Disquisition on Government*, in *Works of John C. Calhoun*, ed. Richard C. Cralle, 6 vols. (New York, 1854–5), vol. i.

Dahl, Robert A. (1971), *Polyarchy* (New Haven, Conn.).

—— and Lindblom, Charles E. (1973), *Politics, Economics and Welfare* (New York).

Donzelot, Jacques (1984), *L'invention du social: Essai sur le déclin des passions politiques* (Paris).

Eckstein, Harry (1961), *A Theory of Stable Democracy*, Woodrow Wilson School of Public and International Affairs Research Monograph 10 (Princeton, NJ).

Handlin, Lilian (1984), *George Bancroft: The Intellectual as Democrat* (New York).

Hofstadter, Richard (1969), *The Idea of a Party System* (Berkeley and Los Angeles, Calif.).

Holmes, Stephen (1984), *Benjamin Constant and the Making of Modern Liberalism* (New Haven, Conn.).

Huntington, Samuel P. (1991), *The Third Wave: Democratization in the Late Twentieth Century* (Norman, Okla.).

Kirchheimer, Otto (1957), 'The Waning of Opposition in Parliamentary Regimes', *Social Research* (summer), 128–56.

—— (1966), 'The Vanishing Opposition: The Case of Germany', in Robert A. Dahl (ed.), *Political Oppositions in Western Democracies* (New Haven, Conn.).

Kloppenberg, James T. (1986), *Uncertain Victory: Social Democracy and Progressivism in European and American Thought, 1870–1920* (New York and Oxford).

Koselleck, Reinhard, and Maier, Hans (1972), 'Demokratie', in Brunner *et al.* (1972).

Lindblom, Charles E. (1977), *Politics and Markets* (New York).

Madison, James (1788), *The Federalist: A Collection of Essays, written in favour of the new Constitution* . . . (New York).

Marshall, T. H. (1950), *Citizenship and Social Class* (Cambridge).

Mill, John Stuart (1910a), *On Liberty* [1859] Everyman edn. (London and New York).

—— (1910b), *Considerations on Representative Government* [1861] Everyman edn. (London and New York).

Moore, Barrington, jun. (1964), *Social Origins of Dictatorship and Democracy* (Boston).

Palmer, R. R. (1953), 'Notes on the Use of the Word "Democracy"', *Political Science Quarterly*, 68: 203 ff.

Rosanvallon, Pierre (1985), *Le moment Guizot* (Paris).

Rostow, Walt Whitman (1960), *The Stages of Economic Growth: A Non-Communist Manifesto* (Cambridge).

Sale, Kirkpatrick (1973), *SDS* (New York).

Schieder, Theodor (1962), 'The Theory of the Political Party', in *The State and Society in our Times* (Edinburgh and London).

Schmitter, Philippe C., O'Donnell, Guillermo, and Whitehead, Laurence (1986), *Transitions from Authoritarian Rule: Comparative Perspectives* (Baltimore).

Sorel, Georges (1917), *Matériaux d'une théorie du Proletariat* (Paris).

Sorlin, Pierre (1966), *Waldeck-Rousseau* (Paris).

Steel, Ronald (1980), *Walter Lippman and the American Century* (Boston).

Talmon, J. L. (1955), *The Origins of Totalitarian Democracy* (London).

Tocqueville, Alexis de (1951), *Democracy in America* [1835], trans. H. Reeve and P. Bowen, ed. P. Bradley (New York).

—— (1955), *The Old Regime and the French Revolution* [1856], trans. Stuart Gilbert (Garden City, NY).

—— (1959), *Recollections of Alexis de Tocqueville* [1853], trans. Alexander Teixeira de Mattos, ed. J. P. Mayer (Cleveland and New York).

NOTES

1. One harbinger of its re-emerging acceptability was George Bancroft's Northampton, Massachusetts, oration on 4 July 1826: 'The government is a democracy, a determined, uncompromising, democracy, administered by the people or by the people's responsible agents' (cited in Handlin 1984: 111). Jefferson and John Adams were both dying on the same day.
2. Restriction of the electorate has not been treated in a rigorous comparative fashion. It is a rich topic. Some ethnically divided societies such as post-1867 Hungary adopted informal measures of exclusion similar to that of Caucasian

American Southerners. Other regimes clung to open voting in which peasants or workers marked their ballots under the eyes of their employers' agents. (As late as 1987 private voting booths were optional in the German Democratic Republic: to have recourse to secrecy signalled opposition and only malcontents would do so.) Still others resorted to systematic altering of figures to get the desired result: the Spanish electoral regime of the Restoration after 1874 involved manufacturing majorities to achieve an alternation between Liberals and Conservatives (the *turno politico*). Urban political machines in the United States presumably could find their needed ballots at the end of a long election day. Occasionally even the dead performed a civic duty from which most of their fellow citizens might have deemed them finally exempt. Italo Calvino recorded how the good nuns brought the mentally ill and defective entrusted to their care to cast Christian Democratic ballots in post-war Turin. Finally, regimes with strong executives (Bonapartist, Gaullist, and, with the most abusive use, Fascist and Nazi) substituted yes or no plebiscites (with conspicuously marked ballots under public scrutiny) to demonstrate simple approval.

3. The underlying moral worth, at least of all white adult males, was not the only reason that justified electoral participation in politics. Champions of democracy could also argue not from worth, but from vulnerability. Since every individual adult might share the positive or negative impact, reward or pain, of a public decision, each deserved a voice. This view still presumed that each man's liability was roughly equal. But as long as property was seen as the crucial stake in politics, this assumption did not prevail.

CHAPTER 9

The Marxist-Leninist Detour

NEIL HARDING

I T is almost universally conceded that one of the principal factors leading to the discrediting of Communism was its neglect of meaningful democracy. As a result, all sorts of distortions of the system arose—irresponsible officials, remote politicians, economic shortcomings and corruption, legal abuse, and a general inability of the regime to respond to popular grievances. For a brief period the Soviet leadership believed that a renewal of democracy would actually serve to remedy the regime's deficiencies and deformities, expose the personnel and the policies that offended the popular will, and extend the social base of the regime. In the event the democracy movement proved to be the focus for those who sought not the renewal but the overthrow of the whole structure of power in the Soviet Union. In March 1989 the first properly democratic elections to be held in the Soviet Union since 1917 brought humiliation to the Communists. They were overwhelmed in their own urban strongholds and virtually eliminated in many of the Republics. Part of their catastrophic showing is, no doubt, explicable in terms of their evident failure to contain or arrest the growing economic crisis the Soviet Union faced, but the electorate undoubtedly also believed that the Communists just could not be trusted in their new-found advocacy of democracy. The attempted coup by the army and the KBG in August 1991 confirmed all these suspicions, for it soon became evident that barely a single important Communist Party spokesman or organization came out forcefully against it—on the contrary the Party hierarchy remained either silent or actively supportive. To the very last, it seemed, the Communist Party remained hostile to democracy and to the sort of politics from which it was bred.

There could, of course, be all sorts of reasons that might explain this hostility—jobs, perks, privileges, status, and power were clearly threatened and such things are never given up lightly. Some perhaps really did believe that the mounting economic, ethnic, and strategic crises the country had to face would be exacerbated rather than resolved by democracy. But all of this begs the larger question of whether Marxism-Leninism as a structure of ideas and as a structure of power actually could accommodate democracy in any meaningful sense. Is it, in short, merely accidental that Communists in power have everywhere been overwhelmingly hostile to Western democratic theory and practice? Is there, deep within the mind-set of Marxism-Leninism, a fundamental antagonism to democracy?

Ever since the first Communist revolution in October 1917 in Russia there has been a persistent debate about why Communist-dominated regimes proved to be so illiberal and antagonistic to representative democracy. There were, for instance, Marxist opponents of the Communists within Russia in 1917 who maintained that because the conditions set out by Marx for a successful advance to socialism were not present, any attempts to force the pace of history would necessarily lead to dictatorship. This group (the Mensheviks, as they were called) maintained that Marx in his economic writings such as *Capital* (vol. 1, 1867) had specified that industrial capitalism had to have run through all its possibilities for developing productive technique before there could be any prospect of a socialist revolution. Similarly they argued that Marx had in his historical and social writings specified that the working class (or proletariat) not only had to constitute a majority within society, it also had to be educated and mature. It had to be conscious of its goals and organized to fulfil them. Since these conditions had not been realized in backward Russia, the revolution, and socialism itself, would inevitably degenerate into dictatorship. The fault lay, in their view, not with Marx or Marxism but with his impatient 'disciples' who chose to ignore the preconditions he laid down. The Mensheviks were to have a very large influence on subsequent Western historiography and commentary that chose to emphasize the distinction between what John Plamenatz (1954) called *German Marxism and Russian Communism.*

There are, of course, others who maintain that the original Communist theoreticians were well aware of Marx's writings and honestly attempted to implement their spirit but were frustrated by unforeseen events. The attempts by armies of intervention organized or financed by hostile capitalist powers to overthrow Communism in Russia, the Civil War they fomented—all this brought unparalleled crisis which demanded decisive and authoritarian leadership. The Communists, this argument runs, had temporarily to suspend normal democratic practices because of the severity of the internal and international situations. Only later, it is maintained, was a virtue made of dictatorship by a psychopathic careerist who managed to usurp power within the Communist Party. Stalin, not Lenin, it is argued, is really responsible for the anti-democratic face of subsequent Communism. These attempts to salvage the reputations of both Marx and Lenin from responsibility for the anti-democratic ethos of modern Communism are unconvincing and misleading. Leninism was an authentic Marxism. As an ideology it faithfully reflected Marx's own impoverishment of the Western tradition of politics, limiting its scope, its permanence, and the richness of its vocabulary and distinctions. It also faithfully reflected Marx's own deep ambivalence towards and suspicion of democracy. The tragedy was, of course, that unlike Marx his Communist disciples were in the position not merely to theorize about these matters but to impose their views and structures of government upon hundreds of millions of people for several generations.

It cannot be denied that there are, in Marx's writings, scattered references that have been interpreted as supportive of democracy. In the *Manifesto of the Communist Party*, for instance, he asserted that 'the first step in the revolution by the working class is to raise the proletariat to the position of ruling class, to win the battle of democracy' (Marx and Engels 1848 *Works*, vi. 504). Moreover Marx and his supporters actively campaigned on behalf of those 'democrats' in Europe who were striving to realize the independence or unification of their own countries, in Germany, Poland, and Italy especially. And yet the overall sweep of the Marxist historical schema relegates democracy to a subsidiary role in the drama of human development, while politics as a whole is seen as the reflection of deeper and more basic forces within society. Every novice to Marxism is taught that the basic and determining factors of all human history are economic. History in this account is the history of how men are organized for the purposes of producing the goods they need and for distributing them. This ensemble of productive and distributive relations is said to constitute a mode of production and it is the mode of production that generates appropriate institutions for the management of public

affairs (government, in short) and bodies of ideas that support the continued operation of the productive system. Since throughout history successive modes of production had always been based upon unequal
allocations of power, status, and material reward, it followed that political
institutions and their supportive political ideas would defend and justify
these inequalities. Politics becomes the public face of economic interests.
In Lenin's view 'politics is the most concentrated expression of economics' (Lenin 1921 *Works*, xxxii. 32). If we want to understand politics,
therefore, we must first understand the class structures of society. In the
contemporary world this means understanding the interests and objectives
of those who owned the means of production and hired labour (the
capitalists) and those without their own productive resources who were
consequently obliged to sell their labour to others (the proletariat). For
Marx and the whole Marxist-Leninist tradition, it was evident that the
interests of these two basic classes of contemporary society were irrecon-
cilably opposed. The capitalists were obliged to attempt to maximize
their profits in order to stay in business. This meant that they had to
depress wages to the barest minimum. The proletarians, by contrast, naturally sought to maximize their wages, welfare, and security at the cost of
capitalist profits. The two groups were set in hostile opposition one to
the other. They were, Marx concluded, 'opposites' (Marx 1845 *Works*,
xli. 35). One sought to preserve existing power structures; the other to
overthrow them. As capitalism developed, this basic antagonism would
become increasingly organized, bitter, and irresolvable. Capitalism, as a
mode of production, would reveal the general truth of Marx's proposition that *all* history was the history of class struggle. The ever-increasing
hostility between capitalists and proletarians would further demonstrate
another of Marx's historical generalizations, namely that demands for the
radical restructuring of property, status, and power within society had
always been bitterly opposed by the dominant economic class. No class in
history had voluntarily relinquished, or peacefully negotiated away, their
powers—when the chips were down they had fought desperately to
retain them, using the power of the state they controlled to put down the
insurgents. No amount of talking, negotiation, or reasoned argument
would persuade them to abdicate. History demonstrated that only by
revolution could they be dislodged. Force was the midwife of history; it
alone enabled new, hitherto downtrodden classes to acquire the power to
introduce a new mode of production. Thus it had always been and thus it
would be in the coming confrontation between proletarians and capitalists. All the decisive issues in history—those that concerned the birth and

death of modes of production and the civilizations they gave rise to—had been decided by force. 'The necessity of systematically imbuing the masses with *this* and precisely this view of violent revolution lies at the root of the *entire* theory of Marx and Engels' (Lenin 1917 *Works*, xxv. 405).

In the Marxist-Leninist structure of ideas politics had no autonomy. It derived from economic interests. It was, moreover, an increasingly futile business, since the further a mode of production developed the more acute the antagonism between dominant and subordinate classes became, and the more obvious the irreconcilability of their interests. Politics would increasingly become a dialogue of the deaf. Politics, especially democratic politics, was founded upon an unwarranted utopianism, in the Marxist-Leninist account. It presupposed, in the first place, that men as creatures of reason were amenable to rational debate and would, once convinced, be swayed to act in conformity with their reason. In the second place democratic politics presupposed that all of the conflicts within society could be peacefully resolved through the processes of negotiation and compromise. Indeed it could not countenance the existence of a non-negotiable clash of interests escalating into armed confrontation between hostile groups. Democracy, from this point of view, was itself deaf to the lessons of history, and history would therefore necessarily have to pass it by.

All of this did not, of course, mean that politics and democracy had no functions or significance. The Marxist-Leninists were not anarchists, they did not abstain from the political process: on the contrary they were exhorted to use it to its fullest potential. The political phase of the struggle was crucial in preparing the proletariat for power, clarifying its awareness (or consciousness) of its goals and objectives, purging it of its illusions, teaching it who its friends and enemies were, and above all consolidating it organizationally as a cohesive and unified fighting force. The phase of politics, in a nutshell, prepared the proletariat for the time when the war of words would be displaced by actual civil war. Politics was always class politics. Its object was to make articulate and conscious the irreconcilability of the basic conflict within society—between possessors and the dispossessed. The Marxist-Leninist politician should therefore always promote those issues that exposed, revealed, and sharpened this antagonism. His style of politics ought always to be confrontational rather than accommodating, elevating conflict rather than consensus, militant opposition rather than compromise. His object, after all, was to prepare the proletariat organizationally, psychologically, and politically for the time when democratic politics would cease and the armed revolutionary assault would begin. That was the measure of a revolutionary politician and, quite clearly, his object was to expose the hypocrisy and ultimate futility of democracy.

It was an axiom of Marxism-Leninism that no bourgeois state form could be used to overthrow bourgeois dominance. So long as democracy provided an effective mask for the real power of capitalism over the state, it retained its utility. So long as the people believed they exercised control over 'their' government, they actually conspired to maintain their own subjugation. Government could claim a bogus legitimacy, isolate the few malcontents, and remain small, cheap, and non-intrusive. As the social base of the capitalists narrowed (as surely it would with the accumulation of capital into fewer and fewer hands) and as the proletariat became more organized, conscious of its goals, and militant, so the power of the state would have to grow. It would have to drop its pretended neutrality. It would be increasingly forced to intercede with army, police, and prison warders to defend the power and privilege of the dominant economic class. The greater the confrontation grew, the more extensive and intensive the class struggle within society, the more the state would reveal its essential nature as the punitive and coercive arm of the possessing classes. In proportion as it did so it would have to discard its democratic window-dressing. It would become a dictatorship. This was, according to Lenin, precisely what all bourgeois states became during the First World War and that was, moreover, the only form they could in future assume if the profits and power of the capitalists were to be maintained.

From 1914 onwards Lenin bolstered his case by pursuing the political implications of an economic theory of finance capitalism or imperialism that other Marxists had developed some years before. Basically the argument was that the competitive phase of classical capitalism had, by 1900, yielded place to monopoly capitalism. Competition between enterprises for a share of the internal national market had given way to a scramble for the economic territory of the whole world (imperialism) conducted by huge consolidated international corporations actively assisted by their governments. The export of finished goods gave way to the export of capital, and there followed the need to protect these global investments. Militarism, finance capitalism, and imperialism were, therefore, closely intertwined. Capitalism, in its final stage of monopoly capitalism, could now only live by extracting huge returns (or super-profits) from the exploitation of colonial labour, from setting monopoly prices for goods in

the protected home market, and from securing lucrative military contracts from government. Imperialism grew alongside monopoly capitalism
and alongside both grew the enormously expanded power of the state.
The logical end of this process was the recognition by the finance capitalists that their own survival intimately depended upon their control over
the state. It was the state that kept in check the pretensions of the home
and colonial labour force alike; it dictated tariffs to protect monopoly
prices; it awarded the fat contracts for arms and ships and materiel; and it
set the taxes to pay for them. The state and the state alone sustained the
economic, fiscal, coercive and ideological conditions for the very survival
of the capitalist mode of production in its monopoly phase. Unsurprisingly monopoly capitalism moved swiftly in to dominate it.
Monopoly capitalism became state monopoly capitalism, and with this
transition democracy withered away. Monopoly capitalism, or imperialism, according to Lenin 'logically contradicts *all* political democracy *in
general*' (Lenin 1916 *Works*, xxiii. 46). It had proclaimed itself the liberal
and liberatory ideal of bourgeois culture but had been unceremoniously
dumped whenever it threatened the maintenance of its cycle of exploitation. Even Britain and America, the bastions of Anglo-Saxon liberty, had
in Lenin's view 'completely sunk into the all-European filthy, bloody
morass of bureaucratic-military institutions which subordinate everything
to themselves and suppress everything' (Lenin 1917 *Works*, xxv. 420–1).

Lenin had, if anything, an even more jaundiced view of democracy
than Marx. Along with the other Russian Marxist orthodox he believed
that the Russian bourgeoisie was especially weak and supine. They might
through their journals and manifestos protest their attachment to liberal
and progressive values, but when it came to the issue, as it did in the
Russian Revolution of 1905 that all but toppled the tsar, they quickly
modified their position. They took fright at the radical proposals of peasants and workers alike and quickly made common cause with the big
landowners and the tsar to protect the sacred right of property. When the
tsar unilaterally dissolved their assembly and promulgated a new and
highly restrictive franchise, they raised barely a whimper of opposition.
At the first test they disgraced themselves and betrayed all their 'radical'
professions. The same had happened in the high citadels of democracy
with the outbreak of the First World War in August 1914, when the
European democracies abruptly renounced their democratic credentials.

It was in October 1917, with the success of the Bolshevik revolution
in Russia, that Marxism-Leninism first emerged as a potent force in
world politics. A large part of its appeal lay in its critique of bourgeois

democracy, bourgeois parliamentarianism, and the whole baggage of bourgeois politics. If, the Bolsheviks asserted, the world had been drawn over the brink of madness into a global blood-letting—on a scale unparalleled in history, by democracies and parliaments—then so much the worse for them. Their era was over. They had finally and irreversibly discredited themselves, and the world that was coming into being would find no place for them. They had actively and enthusiastically supported the war that had left Europe running with blood, brutalized, and stricken with famine. 'The war has exterminated millions of people, has drenched the world in blood, brought it to the brink of disaster' (Lenin 1917 *Works*, xxiv. 504). Capitalism and democracy had proved themselves impotent in bringing the war to an end, even when its prolongation spelt ruin and destruction for both sides to the conflict. Most damning of all, these selfsame democracies readily connived at the eclipse of democracy itself through the concentration of political and economic power into the hands of an irresponsible élite of bankers and military men. In the name of national security, basic liberties—freedom of movement and association, freedom of the press, and the right to strike—had been annulled or curtailed. Bourgeois democracy, they maintained, stood finally exposed for what it was—the threadbare disguise for the effective coercive and military power of those who profited from home and colonial exploitation.

Bourgeois, or parliamentary, democracy was, in the Marxist-Leninist analysis, only one of the constitutional forms in which the state power of capitalism chose to dress itself. In its heyday, during the epoch of genuinely competitive capitalism, it had proved its worth as an attractive and cost-effective device for masking the real power of capital. This was the period (up to 1900, according to Lenin) when the state had indeed been limited in scope and intrusiveness, when there had been a competition between ideas and élites, and when civil and political rights had, within limits, been meaningful. During this period capitalism had been (Lenin grudgingly conceded) progressive both in the economic and the political sphere, and competition was essential to both. So long as capitalism as an economic structure remained competitive it retained its progressive characteristics. The same went for its political superstructure. The great change in both respects came in the period 1900–16 when, with accelerating rapidity, capitalism became monopolistic and finally became state monopoly capitalism. Step by step with the change in the economic base the political superstructure also underwent a profound metamorphosis. In politics, too, pluralism and competition gave way to conformity and monolithism; the limited state of liberal democracy gave way to the massively intrusive bureaucratic-military power of the state capitalist trust. Democracy yielded place to dictatorship. As the competition between enterprises for a share of the national market was displaced by the competition between giant monopolist trusts for dominance in the world market, so the internal competition of political parties for national political power had given way to the struggle of mightily armed states for the economic territory of the whole world.

The political superstructure of this new economy, of monopoly capitalism (imperialism is monopoly capitalism) is the change *from* democracy *to* political reaction. Democracy corresponds to free competition. Political reaction corresponds to monopoly . . . Both in foreign and home policy imperialism strives towards violations of democracy, towards reaction. In this sense imperialism is indisputably the 'negation' of *democracy in general, of all democracy.* (Lenin 1916 *Works*, xxiii. 43)

It was absolutely central to Lenin's own thought, as it was to the whole subsequent history of Marxism-Leninism, that these changes in the economic and political life of society were not the result of temporary emergencies like the outbreak of war and the need to concentrate all resources on its successful prosecution. They were, rather, systemic and part of the necessary progression of capitalism itself. It was not, in short, the war that caused these changes but rather these changes that caused the war. And they would cause further wars of ever-greater dimensions unless capitalism and along with it classes, the nation-state, and politics as mankind had hitherto known them were all swept aside into the dustbin of history. Mankind was, in Lenin's view, confronted with two options. Either capitalism in its monopolistic form with all its trappings of the militarized power of the nation-state is allowed to continue or the whole web of uncontrollable power is subjected to direct popular control: either socialism or barbarism.

It is entirely evident that, in the Leninist account, Western-style representative democracy was no more than a sometimes convenient constitutional form through which the real economic dominance of the capitalist class was exercised. In the epoch of monopoly or finance capitalism it had become redundant and potentially destabilizing for the maintenance of the cycle of production and reproduction of capital. During the war it had finally become discredited and had been displaced by the direct rule of finance capital that unabashedly utilized the state to maintain and extend its own power. From all this it followed that representative democracy, with its elaborate division of powers and its attendant separate jurisdictions for legislative, executive, judiciary, army, and police, could not possibly serve as the political form for the realization of socialism. Liberal democracy had not merely preserved, it had refined and sanctified the age-old and basic division of society into governors and governed. Just as class society could only survive as long as the economic preroga- tives of the exploiter over the exploited were maintained, so its politics had to maintain the impossibility of the ruled ever ruling themselves. Lenin now came to the conclusion that as class society had reached its final impasse in the war, so too had class politics and the class-based state. The very content of socialism was the radical restructuring of politics, the revolutionary transformation of democracy, and the end of the state as conventionally understood. For a brief period of perhaps nine months after the October Revolution in 1917, the Bolsheviks committed them- selves to the most audacious attempt at transforming the vocabulary and the practice of politics since the French Revolution of 1789.

The project for socialism set out in *The State and Revolution* and 'Can the Bolsheviks Retain State Power?' (both written in August/September 1917) was, by any standards, extraordinary. It was a project that sought to eliminate the relations of power, of domination and subordination, that had always characterized society. Socialism was identified as self-govern- ment. All the powers hitherto arrogated to the state were to be reclaimed by the people in arms. The armed assemblies of the popular masses were to debate and decide upon public business (the legislative function); they were to implement measures for its realization (the executive function); they also adjudicated all disputes (the judicial function); and they exe- cuted punishments and provided for their own defence (the coercive functions of police and army). There were to be no more special powers attaching to separate groups of men. Division of powers and the complex checks and balances that had characterized liberal constitutions and made parliaments into ineffectual 'talking-shops' were to be swept away. They were now irrelevant and harmful, for their whole point and purpose had been to construct so many bulwarks and obstacles to the power of the people. They comprised the web of mediations through which popular power was purposely emasculated. Now, according to the Bolshevik pro- gramme, the power of the people was to be direct, immediate and unre- stricted. It was meant to be a clarion call to the people of the whole world to recover their potency as makers of their own politics and as par- ticipants in a transformed democracy.

The agencies through which all this was to be accomplished had been spontaneously created by the masses themselves in the course of their revolutionary struggle. The Russian soviets which had re-emerged in February 1917 were identified as the modern form of the Paris Commune of 1871 hailed by Marx as 'the political form at last discovered under which to work out the economic emancipation of labour' (Marx 1871a: 522–3). The first act of the Commune, in Marx's account, was to declare the abolition of the police, standing army, and bureaucracy. Separate bodies of armed men and of functionaries claiming exclusive rights attaching to their office were done away with. The people reclaimed the powers they had lost to the state and, in so doing, dissolved it. Marx was clear, the Commune was 'a Revolution against the State itself . . . a Revolution to break down this horrid machinery of class domination itself' (Marx 1871b: 152), regardless of the constitutional guise it from time to time assumed. Democracy was to be made a reality precisely through dissolving the bogus balance of powers of the liberal constitution. The Commune was to be at once a legislative, executive, judicial, and defensive body. It was to make a reality of democracy by involving all citizens in all aspects of the governmental process and it was to retain control over all its functionaries by electing them all, paying them workmen's wages, and keeping them subject to immediate recall by their constituents. This was, in the Bolshevik view, exactly the role of the soviets. They too would dissolve the state and make democracy real by directly involving the masses in the deliberation and administration of every aspect of public business. Democracy was to be direct, participatory, and transformative. Its purpose was to transform people from passive objects of the purposes of others into conscious and active subjects. It was to be measured, above all, in the ever-growing numbers who participated in the management of public affairs and the ever-increasing range of powers they assumed. This was Commune democracy and it was as proponents of this Commune idea that Lenin insisted that the Bolsheviks rename themselves Communists (Lenin April 1917 *Works*, xxiv. 24). For the same reason he insisted that their principal slogan should be 'All Power to the Soviets'.

The idea of soviet democracy was directly counterposed to that of 'bourgeois', 'liberal' or 'parliamentary' democracy. It signified the direct, unmediated participation of the people in the administration of all public affairs. The powers and prerogatives hitherto exercised exclusively by the licensed agents of the state were now to be exercised through a multitude of overlapping organizations—the people's militia, the soviets, the factory and regimental committees, communes, co-operatives and all manner of *ad hoc* committees for establishing canteens and kindergartens or for supervising the allocation of housing or fuel. Not only was division of powers to be done away with but the divide between state and civil society would also cease. According to the initial Communist programme this was not, in any way, a merely theorized projection or utopian aspiration. It was, on the contrary, the only way in which the people's energies could be released and harnessed to deal with the multitude of problems that finance capitalism and its war had bequeathed them. The collapse of industrial production, the crises in transportation of fuel and food supplies, famine, disease, and the disastrous consequences of war—these problems were too vast for small cohorts of functionaries to resolve. These pressing problems of life and death for whole societies could only be solved by galvanizing the entire population, by giving them the confidence and enthusiasm to resolve them. There was, in Lenin's view, no other way out of war and ruination. All other schemes, coalitions, and constitutions had been tried. None had been successful. Commune democracy, soviet democracy, was then presented as eminently practical and realistic. It was the positive alternative to the choking limitations of bourgeois parliamentarianism, it was actually being realized in the revolutionary organizations of the Russian people, and it was, finally, blessed with the warrant of Marx's approval. Soviet democracy was therefore the linchpin of the original project for socialism in Russia.

We cannot here explore the historical circumstances in which this original project was effectively abandoned. A brief examination of any of the texts on early Soviet history will disclose the catalogue of crises with which the Communists had to contend—war, armed intervention, civil war, peasant opposition, and increasing urban discontent. There were supply and production crises exacerbated by the collapse of communications. The problems of grain, fuel, and raw materials supply got worse rather than better. Above all the international revolution, upon which the whole revolutionary project had been predicated, failed to occur, and there was no immediate prospect of Russian backwardness being redeemed by the advanced West.

In order to deal with this succession of crises, from 1918 onwards, the Bolsheviks ever-increasingly relied upon highly centralized, indeed dictatorial, structures of power. The standing army was re-established and strict discipline reimposed. Factory and regimental committees were disbanded and replaced by the authority of managers and officers. The secret police (or Cheka) was greatly expanded to become (along with the army) the most important administrative agency of the new regime. The soviets virtually suspended their activities and political opposition was summarily put down. All this centralization of power into the hands of the Council of People's Commissars was justified by the Bolsheviks in the light of the extremity of the crises the Revolution confronted—especially the civil war that was at its most severe in the period from the end of 1918 to mid-1920. When the dangers from civil war began to abate, however, those groups that had grudgingly given up their autonomy for the duration of hostilities began to press for their powers and authority to be restored to them. They demanded an end to the Communist monopoly of power, the restitution of the soviets, workers' control of industry (and of their trade unions now dominated by Communist place-men). Some demanded freedom for other political parties and an end to the austerities that War Communism had introduced.

It was abundantly clear that, by mid-1920, the Communists were in a critical position. They were isolated both internationally and internally. The world revolution had not redeemed their backwardness. The social base of the regime had progressively narrowed. Initially all were to be involved in socialist self-activity and the building of a participatory democracy; then the peasantry had been found wanting; finally the remnants of the proletariat had rebelled, turning increasingly to the Mensheviks or the syndicalist-inspired Workers' Opposition. A huge gap had emerged between the original promises of the regime—to create a Commune democracy—and its actual practice. The Communists were now being challenged by those who demanded the restitution of precisely those values, practices, and institutions the Communists themselves had ardently promoted as the sum and substance of the revolution. The stark choice presented itself: either to change their practice to make it fit the initial theory, or discard the *initial* theory and create a new specification of socialist objectives and new institutions to realize them. The first option would, undoubtedly, have led to a rapid erosion of the monopoly of power the Communists had assumed during the civil war. The second option, however, would undoubtedly bring them into conflict with precisely those groups that had been in the forefront of the revolution and had been the regime's most ardent supporters. This was, perhaps, the single most important turning-point in the history of the Soviet Union, and one whose implications for the subsequent development of Communism as an ideology were to be no less profound. With hardly any hesitation or dissent, the leading Communists abruptly redefined the nature of socialism and democracy; they respecified the functions of the state, the Party, the proletariat, and politics. Simultaneously they began to rewrite the early history of the regime and to move with vengeance against those who reminded them of it. The Workers' Opposition was dissolved by administrative means and the rebellion at the naval base of Kronstadt in February 1921 for the restoration of power to the soviets and of rights to competing parties was put down by the army with massive loss of life. Trotsky led the campaign against the erstwhile darlings of the revolution. Lenin and the Council of People's Commissars applauded from the wings. The die was cast. The Party had only armed men and the state apparatus to rely upon for the maintenance of its power.

By mid-1920 the Party leaders had already frankly acknowledged that the social base of the regime had withered away. The industrial workers, they now declared, had become demoralized and disorientated. They had been seduced by petty bourgeois and semi-anarchist ideas. They had become infected by the political instability and petty trading habits of the peasantry that surrounded them. They lacked education and culture and were indelibly marked by the brutalization that their experience of capitalism, war, and civil war had stamped upon them. They had, in Lenin's account, suffered more than any class in history on the road to state power. Now even the 'proletarian vanguard' lay 'bleeding and in a state of prostration'. It was, he said, 'absurd and ridiculous to deny that the fact that the proletariat is declassed is a handicap' (Lenin 1921 *Works*, xxxii. 254 and 412). They were capable, in Bukharin's opinion, of destroying; but they could not build because they were unable to formulate a coherent plan of economic and political organization (Bukharin 1920).

At exactly this time, and with extraordinary consistency, the three most prominent Communist theorists set about the task of respecifying the nature of socialism, the goals of the regime, and the nature of the organizational means for their realization. Socialism, they unanimously agreed, could no longer be equated with the ever-broadening participation of the masses in managing their own affairs. It was emphatically not about the dissolution of the state and the supremacy of society. Those who continued to argue in that way were profoundly in error. They confused socialism with communism. Socialism was the necessary and prolonged phase preparatory to communism. Before the state could be abolished and communism achieved, the whole industrial and work process would have to be restructured on a technologically more advanced plane. Only on this basis could the needs of all be catered for and scarcity eliminated. Only on this basis could the slogan of communism 'From each according to his ability, to each according to his needs' be realized. It was clear that communism was a long way off. Its fruits would be enjoyed by future generations, not this one. In the mean while, the historical phase of socialism had as its objective the creation of the material base for the eventual advance to communism. Its tasks were principally economic and organizational. 'The creation of Socialist society means the organization of the workers on new foundations, and their labour re-education, with the one unchanging end of the increase in the productivity of labour' (Trotsky 1920: 146).

The vocabulary of the past was swiftly dropped. Commune, collegial administration, workers' control, industrial democracy yielded place to Taylorism, efficiency, discipline, responsibility, and planning. In particular the state emerged to centre stage as the co-ordinating agency of the whole economy and society. Far from withering away in the era of socialism, it would grow mightily. The road to socialism, according to Trotsky at the time, 'lies through a period of the highest possible intensification of the principle of the State' (Trotsky 1920: 170). According to Bukharin, '*revolutionary* state power is the mightiest lever of economic revolution' (Bukharin 1920: 151). Its tasks were to discipline and organize the working class, overcome its divisions and diversity, and to put an end to its prejudices about the authority of 'bourgeois' specialists. It would also, Bukharin, Trotsky, and Lenin agreed, have to develop a comprehensive national plan for the economy which would entail, first, state ownership and control of the major productive forces; secondly the authoritative direction of all capital and labour resources; and finally the allocation of the measure of labour and of consumption to the entire population.

Here, for the first time, an entirely novel state form was theorized. Its principles were to inform Soviet practice for the next seventy years. Nor were they merely abstract or academic principles. As we shall see, they led directly to structures of power that proved to be extraordinarily pervasive and durable, as well as very widely imitated in other countries.

The operative theory of the Soviet state, and of the regimes set up in imitation of it, remained unchanged from 1920 until the abrupt collapse of Communist state power in Eastern Europe in 1989 and in the Soviet Union in 1991. It was grounded in a view of man that was closely complemented by a conception of objective knowledge. Let us take the view of man to start with. It was a particular reading of Marx that was developed. We start with the seemingly uncontentious proposition that man, before all else, is a creature of physical needs that imperatively demand daily satisfaction. These material needs for food, shelter, and clothing are irreducibly given and compel man to be a productive or labouring being.

Very early on, however, the benefits of collaboration with others became apparent. Marx followed Aristotle in maintaining that the origins of human society lay in a shared interest in exchanging goods, services, and productive expertise so as to secure improved material well-being. The universal historiography, upon which societies of the Soviet type have since the 1920s relied, had it that the principal goal of human society was the maximization of production on the one hand, and the creation of a just system of distribution on the other. Socialism was, in this broad historical sweep, that epoch in the history of mankind in which all the latent potential of advanced technology is allowed its most rapid and fruitful development. This it would only be able to accomplish if the many barriers to unrestrained technological advance, created during the previous period of capitalism, were destroyed. Among these was, of course, the existence of great monopolies concerned solely with maximizing their profits—an objective that frequently ran counter to the massive capital investment that research and technological innovation demanded. More systematically, capitalism, by definition, had no consciously elaborated plan. Each enterprise ruthlessly pursued its narrow self-interest; no authoritative body was concerned to balance production against social demand; so inevitably booms were followed by slumps, periods of relative prosperity by times of austerity and unemployment. In the direction of resources—capital, land, and labour—there was no oversight or system of priorities apart from the market imperative to maximize profit. The elemental needs of the many were therefore sacrificed to satisfy the extravagance of the wealthy few. The first claim, therefore, that the Soviet version of socialism made was that it would introduce order and purposeful planning to make good the planless anarchy of the capitalist productive system. Its promise was that it would not only permit and encourage an unprecedented explosion of technological innovation, it would also, by scientifically setting priorities for the whole system of production, ensure a close correspondence between production and demand and maximize productive output. Its first promise, in short, was that it would outproduce all competitor economic systems.

Its second promise, no less important in legitimizing the regime, was that the system of distribution would be more just and more equitable than any competitor system. We have already seen that the objective of social organization was to maximize production. Men entered this society, therefore, as the bearers not of abstract or 'natural' rights, but as the bearers of productive powers—as labouring beings. A condition of full membership was preparedness to contribute to the social system of pro-

duction. Since the principal goal of society was the maximization of production, it followed that benefits within society ought to be distributed
according to the contribution of each towards the attainment of this goal.
People were to receive in proportion to their productive inputs. The slogan of socialism from Lenin to Gorbachev remained the same: 'From
each according to his ability, to each according to his work'. Reward was
to be made proportionate to the skill, intensity, and duration of work
performed. The socialist principle of distributive justice did not, evidently, make for equality. Marx, when he first propounded it, had been
quite clear that this could not be the case (Marx 1875: 24).

There was an implied social contract within this state form that was
never directly articulated, but which none the less constituted its inner
logic and helps us to explain its dramatic collapse in 1989 and in 1991.
We reconstruct it as follows: in return for sacrificing his autonomy as a
producer—his ownership of his own tools and instruments of production
as well as his freedom to dispose of his labour as he saw fit—the individual is admitted to a social system of production that plans what is to be
produced, by whom, in what location and quantity. In return for the
individual yielding to society the right of disposing of his labour (and the
aspiration to become an autonomous producer) society undertakes to
provide him with a greater range of material and cultural benefits than
would be available under any other system. It further guarantees that the
allocation of such benefits will be made according to the principle of the
greater the productive contribution the greater the reward. This was,
indeed, a wholly novel formulation of social contract theory. No other
state formation in history had contemplated, let alone attempted to
implement, a scheme of this sort. Like all social contract theories it carried a sting in its tail: namely, if the state transparently failed to live up to
its foundation promises, then the people's obligation to it therewith
ceased. Another way of putting this is to say that the state's real power to
sustain popular allegiance almost wholly coincided with its ability literally
to produce the goods. The mode of legitimation was expressly economic
rather than political. When, by the late 1970s and early 1980s, it became
entirely evident that the Soviet-type productive systems of Eastern
Europe and the Soviet Union were suffering from long-term systemic
decline and that the patterns of distribution were prone to massive abuse
and corruption—then by the system's own logic it followed that collapse
could not long be delayed.

One of the most striking features of the new state formation was that
its view of man, its foundation principles, its organizational structures,

and the promises it made, were alike almost wholly economic. It was not, in the conventional sense, political. Nor indeed was it supposed to be. According to the founding fathers of the new state form, who combined to theorize it in mid-1920, the era of politics, as conventionally understood, was now over. We should not, of course, forget that the Communists were, at the time, in a position of acute crisis. They were isolated internationally and within the Soviet Union. Their discovery that the era of conventional politics was at an end coincided exactly with a period when the resumption of politics as the free interplay of contested ideas, elections, and public debate would undoubtedly have swept them from power. Far from welcoming debate, publicity, elections, and controversy, Lenin, from 1920 onwards, became increasingly impatient with his colleagues for permitting such luxuries to continue. He made plain that he was personally sick and tired of the tendency 'to slide back to abstract theoretical propositions' (Lenin 1921 *Works*, xxxii. 41). At the Eighth Congress of Soviets in December 1920 Lenin looked forward to technical experts displacing politicians at the rostrum:

This marks the beginning of that very happy time when politics will recede into the background, when politics will be discussed less often and at shorter length, and when engineers and agronomists will do most of the talking . . . Henceforth, less politics will be the best politics. (Lenin 1921 *Works*, xxxii. 513–14)

Trotsky was of like opinion: 'Before the experts there opens a boundless field of activity.' The views of 'one expert who has passed through the technical school and who knows how to carry out the given technical work' were infinitely to be preferred, in Trotsky's view, to the decisions of elected boards of 'the best representatives of the working class' (Trotsky 1920: 120, 118). Bukharin, similarly, believed that the critically important task facing the Soviet government was the restoration of the linkage between the technical and professional intelligentsia and the workers. For the link to be restored the workers would imperatively have to be purged of their prejudices and active hostility to these *spetsii*, forced to acknowledge that they had little experience and less technical competence in the matter of efficiently running industry. The workers simply did not have the culture, education, or training to restructure economic relations on a new, more sophisticated, footing.

In the course of 1920, as we have seen, there entered into the writings of all the principal Communist theorists a wholly new and pessimistic note about the capacities of the Russian working class. Their limited and disjointed knowledge, derived from the accidental experience they had acquired, was contrasted to the properly systematic, integrated, and scientific knowledge of experts. Their knowledge was contentious and debatable, that of the experts demonstrable and therefore not amenable to improvement by debate but only by scientifically evaluated controlled experiment. The workers' knowledge was adventitious and subjective, that of the experts was objective and systematic. The distinction between subjective and objective knowledge was to become a central precept of the official, state-sponsored philosophical system known as dialectical materialism. This philosophy, it was consistently maintained for seventy years, was the world-view of the working class and of socialism. It maintained that the world and all that was in it was no more than matter, that matter conformed to laws, and that these laws were knowable. The route to knowledge of them lay, in turn, through correct application of dialectical thinking. The details and difficulties of the materialist metaphysic need not concern us here but the tenor of this philosophical stance was to have profound effects upon what passed for politics in these supposedly socialist regimes. The principal conclusion of dialectical materialism was that proper scientific method can and will disclose the real nature of *all* phenomena. It will penetrate the mere appearances of things to reveal their essential nature. This was true not only of its application to the natural world but also to society. The origins, evolution, and future of society could be established scientifically, as could the optimum solution to any problem related to the maximization of production. And this was, after all, the historical goal of social organization. The planners armed with science and the dialectic were, therefore, the paradigmatic personnel of socialist society. It was they who articulated the Plan for the whole system of production. In so doing, of course, they expressed social purpose—the concrete objectives of society.

It is clear that within this closed system there was little room for politics and still less for democracy. Indeed, as soon as the outlines of the new state formation began to be theorized all of the principal Communist leaders began, quite unambiguously, to decry not only bourgeois democracy but democracy in general. Lenin was quite clear 'that formal democracy must be subordinate to the revolutionary interest'. So long as the conflict between capitalism and socialism persisted, 'we do not promise any freedom or any democracy'. 'In the final analysis every kind of democracy, as political superstructure in general . . . serves production.' Finally he curtly reminded the romantics and dreamers in his Party, who wanted to go back to workers' control and industrial democracy, that 'Industry is indispensable, democracy is not' (Lenin 1921 *Works*, xxxii. 86, 495, 81, 27).

The distinction between objective and subjective knowledge, was a mirror of the Marxist-Leninist distinction between the real interests of the working class and its perception of them at any given time. Just as objective knowledge could not be uncovered by taking the lowest common denominator of consent, so too the objective interests of a class could never be arrived at from a straw vote. There was for Marx, as there was for Marxism-Leninism, always a gap between changes in actual life situation and perception of the implications of these changes in the consciousness of the mass of the people. The fundamental economic determinants of everyday life—the manner in which work was organized and power was distributed—might therefore undergo massive change considerably before they registered in the public consciousness. People might, and often did, continue to entertain conceptions of themselves and their situation that were fanciful, antiquated, or utopian. Marx put it in this way:

It is not a question of what this or that proletarian, or even the whole proletariat at the moment, *regards* as its aim. It is a question of *what the proletariat is*, and what, in accordance with this *being*, it will historically be compelled to do. Its aim and historical action is visibly and irrevocably foreshadowed in its own life situation as well as the whole organisation of bourgeois society today. (Marx and Engels 1845 *Works*, iv. 37)

For Marx, and subsequently for the Marxist-Leninists, the class only was a class to the extent that it displayed its essential characteristics. It had to be united on at least a national scale, politically organized and articulate, and speaking with just one voice. The process of class formation was the process through which all the divisions that had hitherto impeded the growth of solidarity and awareness of *common* purpose were progressively overcome. Historical experience in the struggle with a common enemy would teach the working class that its old divisions—regional, plant, craft, trade, gender, political, and so on—severely impeded its success in the struggle. Its progress was measured by its ability to transcend all these limitations and arrests. Under the interrelated impact of learning from its own errors and being guided by its theoretical and practical leaders, the workers purged themselves of all the divisions and utopian illusions characteristic of their early existence. They coalesced more and more around one militant centre—the Communist Party—that exemplified their singleness of purpose and of will. For Marx, Lenin, and the tradition they inspired, it was axiomatic that the proletariat (like science) spoke with but one voice. To put it another way, neither Marx nor Lenin ever acknowledged that variety of opinion or diversity of political standpoint was necessary, still less desirable, within the working class. For them both, the class only *is* a class properly so called when it is disciplined and organized on at least the national plane under the leadership of a single party that expresses and consolidates its unity of will.

It followed from all this that if the class was indeed to speak with one voice then it would have to develop those procedures and structures that ensured the public expression of unanimity. For the political leadership of the proletariat to be seen to be split and divided affronted the Marxist metaphysic of history that foresaw the ever-growing unity and solidarity of the class. Science too, according to the Marxist-Leninist theory of knowledge, had but one optimal solution to any given problem. It too spoke with a singleness of voice. Disputation over policy issues would, therefore, also diminish the authority of science and call into question the exactitude of dialectical method. For these reasons it was essential that organizational procedures and structures be developed that would ensure a single authoritative outcome. The Marxist-Leninist organizational precepts of democratic centralism were the practical means adopted to accomplish this. In its ideal form democratic centralism as it applied to the Communist Party stipulated that all major policy initiatives should be put up for discussion to the broad mass of the Party members. The lowest-level party organizations, having deliberated, would mandate their delegates to pursue decisions arrived at in the next-highest Party body which, in turn, would elect delegates to the next-highest Party body. When the supreme body of the Party—its Congress—had come to a final decision on any particular issue, then discussion and the canvassing of alternative views was to cease. The decisions of higher Party bodies were, in short, binding on all lower Party bodies. The disciplined acceptance of all higher Party decisions formed a large part of *partiinost* or party-mindedness. Failure to develop it was a certain route to censure and eventual expulsion. This system of effective accountability of lower organs to higher ones was accentuated with the establishment of a Party Secretariat and Orgburo (or Organizational Bureau) in 1922—with Stalin prominent in both. The central Party organs now insisted upon their right to nominate personnel to all branches and sections not only of the Party, but of both state and social bodies like the trade unions. By May 1920 Lenin admitted that, 'No important political or organisational question is decided by any state institution in our republic without the guidance of the Party's Central Committee.' Moreover all the competent leadership bodies of the trade unions were made up of Communist nominees (Lenin 1920 *Works*, xxx. 47–8). Obedience to the dictates of the Party applied, of course, to the Party cells that dominated the leadership bodies of all state and social organizations. They were bound by the dictates of democratic centralism. The boundary between Party, state, and social organizations became purposely blurred. It was made abundantly clear that under the dictatorship of the proletariat there could be no autonomous bodies. All would have to become adjuncts of the Party/State.

The severity of rigid centralization under the dictatorship of the proletariat was justified largely by pointing to the continuing threat of a hostile capitalist world. The social and economic systems of socialism and capitalism were in frank and open hostility one to the other. The permanent probability therefore existed of renewed military interventions; and to prepare for them the young Soviet Republic had no option but to emulate the determined centralism and dictatorial features of its opponents. All the capitalist states, regardless of constitutional disguise, were dictatorships. Given the world environment, it was inevitable that the Soviet Republic should become one also—the contemporary world allowed of no third way or middle course. One dictatorship or the other. That was the choice. For the next seventy years this remained the most insistent and plausible justification for authoritarian centralism within the Soviet system, and it produced a self-fulfilling cycle. The more the leaders of the Soviet Union proclaimed its hostility to capitalist regimes, the more they collaborated to defend themselves against this threat; and the more they did so, the more they justified more extreme Soviet responses. One of the other consequences of the Communist world-view was that it contributed to a deep-seated political relativism that blighted subsequent Soviet political thought and practice—and most of all in its attitude towards democracy.

As we have seen, in the Marxist analysis all states are class states. Their *raison d'être* is to defend the economic privileges of the dominant class within society. States, according to the Marxist-Leninist analysis, are to be judged for what they do, not what they say. The manner in which they justify themselves is a purely contingent consideration. The same class may, therefore, move with alacrity from justifying the power of the many to defending the power of the few or even of one man. They may prefer military to civilian or elective to imposed forms of government. What applies to the nature of bourgeois class power applies also to the class power of the proletariat. Its state power may, equally, be exercised by the many or the few. It may be elective and representative, or nominated and imposed. What matters is not the composition of governing bodies nor even their constitution. What matters is the essential class orientation of their policies. Democracy, in this notation, was just another form of class power—another state form that was perhaps more insidious and dangerous than openly avowed and undisguised dictatorship. It lulled people into the illusion that issues might be peacefully settled, that conciliation rather than conflict might solve basic social issues. Democracy in this guise was the stuff of idle dreamers or actual traitors to the proletariat like the leaders of European social democratic parties.

Relativism about political forms was complemented by relativism about the structures and procedures for managing other aspects of life. This was particularly so with regard to economic organization. The Communists, from 1920 onwards, consistently maintained the view that socialism wholly consisted in equality of ownership relations and not at all in equality in relations of power and authority. If the state owned all the property or means of production, then it followed that all members of the state were equal co-owners. If the state distributed the product of industry in an equitable way on the basis of labour input, then it followed that no one was any longer exploited. For production to be maximized so that all could benefit, it was now maintained that the authority of managers, experts, and the technical intelligentsia must be increased and protected. This was presented as the necessary means to realize the goal of maximizing production, which in turn was not identified as the goal of socialism and of society. Strict subordination to the authority of managers was therefore held to be imperative for the success of socialism. Henceforth, Trotsky insisted, specialists and managers were to be accountable not at all to the work-force but solely to the state.

The dictatorship of the proletariat is expressed in the abolition of private property in the means of production, in the supremacy over the whole Soviet mechanism of the collective will of the workers, and not at all in the manner in which individual economic enterprises are administered. (Trotsky 1920: 162)

There could be no place for democracy within the workplace. It became fashionable to recall Engels's words (in polemic with the anarchists) about the modern factory being a thoroughly authoritarian institution that, 'independent of all social organisation', subjugated man to 'a veritable despotism'. He concluded that there could be no freedom or individual autonomy within an industrial enterprise (Engels 1872: 639). The difference was that, within the labour state, all of society was to be turned into 'a single office and a single factory' (Lenin 1917 *Works*, xxv. 479). All labour was to be authoritatively allocated by the Plan and subject to a virtually military style of discipline.

Such a form of planned distribution pre-supposes the subordination of those distributed to the economic plan of the State. And this is the essence of *compulsory labor service*, which inevitably enters into the programme of the socialist organisation of labor, as its fundamental element. (Trotsky 1920: 142)

In this, as in so many other respects, the emergent labour state consciously mimicked the Communists' own theorized conception of the imperialist state formation. That was indeed the only model available to them that provided answers to their critical problems. It showed, in particular, how an isolated but disciplined and far-sighted minority had, against mounting odds, managed to sustain the reproducibility of their own power. They had done so by converting the state machine into the principal organizer of the productive system. Capitalism became state capitalism. The state moved in directly to control credit, resource allocation, whole sectors of industry, tariffs, taxes, and the allocation of labour. The proletarian state could do no other than follow its lead. The state was to be the principal active agent in the management and direction of the whole economy. Far from passively reflecting changes in the economic substructure, the state was to assume their direction. The erstwhile superstructure was now to determine the base. This was the historical originality of the imperialist state that would be carried over in the phase of socialism. It was to become *the* characteristic idea of the whole epoch of Soviet socialism, providing, for many decades, its strength and stability, but equally proving, at the last, its fatally vulnerable Achilles heel.

The basic ideas that were to dominate Soviet society until its recent demise were clearly established by the early 1920s. Socialism was conceived of as the maximization of production which could only be accomplished by state ownership of the means of production and the implementation of a national plan for the allocation of all resources and a pattern of distribution that directly related reward to productive contribution. Within this specification of socialism there was very little that might be termed political, still less democratic. This was a scheme of things that purposely masked the contentious matters of democratic politics beneath the veil of instrumental rationality. The trick it managed for so long to accomplish was to convince its adherents that the essential matters that concern society were not at all political matters that involved the power of some over others, rules governing the use of that power, its limitations and accountability, but that they were, rather, matters whose optimal resolution proceeded from the correct application of objective or scientific knowledge. It was pretended, against all evidence to the contrary, that resolutions arrived at in this way were not partial or accidental but demonstrable. Only the foolish or ignorant could dispute them.

If the ideas of this radically new form of administration were formulated in the early 1920s, it was only in the late 1920s and 1930s that they were brutally implemented by Stalin. Until then the Party/State was too weak to impose its vision upon society as a whole. It was forced into the 'temporary retreat' of the New Economic Policy, which was to last from 1921 until 1928.

It was with the launching of the First Five-Year Plan in 1928 that the labour state began in fact to be realized within the Soviet Union. Within five years the entire economy had been profoundly transformed. Prior to the first Five-Year Plan only some 5 per cent of the population had been employed by the state and they were almost wholly within the principal cities and industrial centres. To all intents and purposes the countryside and the peasantry had barely been affected by the revolution. Stalin was, with ruthless force and at the cost of millions of lives, to alter all that. By the time that the first Plan was completed almost all the peasants and their land had been amalgamated into huge state or collective farms. Populations had been moved (even eliminated) and labour armies had been organized for the creation of huge new industrial projects—steel complexes, dams, canals, and electricity stations. By the mid 1930s the state effectively governed all the productive forces within the country and controlled its entire work-force. The precondition for the creation of the labour state had been achieved.

From this time on the Party/State actually did become the sole employer and allocator of all scarce goods. Its power henceforth derived almost wholly from its exclusive jurisdiction over the allocation of both capital and labour resources, its sole control over what was produced—where, in what quantity, and at what price—and its control over who should have access to these goods. Politics did indeed dissolve into economics; it became almost wholly concerned with the administration of things. The original project for socialism in Russia had, as we have seen, been almost exclusively concerned with transforming the relationships of men to men—the power relations of governors and governed. The new formulation of socialism, cast as the dictatorship of the proletariat, consisted by contrast wholly in the attempt to transform the relationships of men to things. Socialism was identified as the institution of new property relations and the organization of new patterns of production and consumption.

Within the economic power structures that emerged and refined themselves in the course of Soviet development there was little space for democratic politics. There were, of course, elections; but it is evident that they were no more than an adjunct of economic management. It was far from accidental that, until 1989 at least, nation-wide elections were timed to coincide with the promulgation of a new Plan for the whole economy. Electors were not invited to deliberate on the merits of rival formulations of economic priorities: there was no question of them being offered alternative Plans from which to choose. Nor was there any choice of candidate. In almost all constituencies only one candidate stood and he or she was the nominee of those public organizations licensed by the state for the purpose. It goes without saying that the only organizations recognized by the state to nominate candidates were those dominated by the Communist Party of the Soviet Union. The actual content of election campaigns similarly demonstrated their functions. The principal objectives of the Plan were highlighted; the benefits and improvements in people's well-being that they would promote were advertised. Election campaigns throughout almost the whole history of the Soviet Union were concerted bouts of production propaganda and plan fulfilment. The act of voting was, similarly, not a properly political act. It signified, rather, the voter's commitment to accept the Plan and to work in his or her sphere of production to fulfil it. Voting was an affirmation of citizenship in so far as only those who contributed their labour power to the Soviet system of production were entitled to be citizens. The participation of all, of every citizen, in the process was therefore taken extremely seriously by the regime and enormous resources were devoted to ensuring it. The unanimity of the popular will had to be signified and recorded. Invariably the electoral returns displayed this unanimity of will. Always the results recorded at least 99 per cent in favour of the candidate and the Plan/Programme. One of the obvious results of electoral campaigns was the election of representatives to local, regional or all-Union deliberative bodies. It was, once again, the criterion of productivity that decided who would be a candidate and therefore a representative. Diligence and reliability at work was, for perhaps the majority of candidates, their one and only qualification. Again a process of signification was evident—the privileges, perks, and status that went with being a representative were seen to be earned only by exemplary workers. The representatives yielded by the electoral (or more properly the selectoral) system were exemplary in another sense too. Invariably it turned out that ethnic, gender, and occupational groups were represented almost precisely according to their presence in the population at large. This was a system of virtual representation in which nothing was left to the accident of volatile public choice.

It was in the workplace that each worker encountered not only the Plan but all the functionally distinct agencies of the state responsible for its formulation and implementation. All the primary organs of the Party—the single most important organization of the whole structure—were industrially or occupationally based. Their constituencies were functional and productive, not geographic. Each occupational group similarly had its single trade union whose primary organizations were within the workplace. The same applied to youth organizations—the Young Communist League, Octobrists, and Young Pioneers. Cultural, sporting, and social clubs and facilities were also almost always based within an enterprise. Finally, the manager was the agent of the national ministry of state. Within the workplace and only there did all the agencies of the state converge. Their role was to exhort and discipline the work-force and to socialize them into those values and practices that would sustain the socialist system of production. They guaranteed the conditions that ensured the reproducibility of the whole system of power; and the resources at their disposition were commensurate with the importance of their task.

The enterprise was the real locus of power within the Soviet system. It was here that the worker/citizen encountered the state, the Plan, and their overlapping agencies. It was here too that the worker quite literally made his or her life, living in its accommodation, sending children to its kindergarten, going on holidays to its sanatoria and holiday homes, attending its social and recreational clubs, and looking forward to its promotional or retirement benefits. Through the enterprise the citizen as consumer enjoyed the prospect (often remote) of obtaining highly scarce commodities. The key to unravelling the Soviet system of power is to understand that all these goods were in scarce supply—flats, promotions, bonuses, holidays, colour televisions, access to higher education or foreign travel. All of these goods were, unsurprisingly, earnestly sought and, as is universally the case, the great majority of people quickly adapted themselves to those outward patterns of behaviour and signification that would gain (or at least not deny) access to them. For the great majority of the people this did not mean that they enrolled in classes on Marxism-Leninism or even joined the Party—it meant adopting a diligent and responsible attitude to one's work. That was the lesson they learnt and that was the lesson it was intended that they should learn, for it was that that sustained the whole power structure. The more man worked the more he received but, equally, the more he contributed to the social surplus extracted by the state. The greater the social surplus the more resources available to the state (its agencies or enterprises) to grant to or withhold from every individual within the state. The continuous rise in labour productivity, or at least the continued rise in the surplus available to the state, was the condition of its stability and survival.

Soviet society developed a sophisticated hierarchy of welfare benefits and welfare sanctions that permeated all of society. At the lowest level, as we have seen, ordinary workers were socialized into patterns of behaviour that would enable them to have access to all those benefits that most nearly affected their lifestyle and were therefore most keenly desired. A comprehensive range of inducements and possible sanctions became available to the regime. Shows of political dissent or restiveness, anti-social behaviour or a lax attitude towards work could now be dealt with by withdrawal of promotion or holiday entitlement, loss of bonus, or demotion to a lower-paid job. More serious or repeated infractions might result in eviction from accommodation, the loss of access to higher educational opportunities, or, finally, dismissal from work with no social security or unemployment benefit. All those sanctions were available and were employed. People learnt from the experience of others what it was necessary to do to gain access, or at the minimum to avoid sanction. This was true, equally, for the complex hierarchy of special benefits differentially enjoyed by the élite of Soviet society comprising the *nomenklatura*.

To obtain access to these highly valued goods involved, at each level, patterns of behaviour, loyalty to the system, and commitment to its maintenance. It was equally obvious, at every stage, that the more one enjoyed the more one had to lose and the higher one stood the further the fall. What was in the gift of the Party/State to grant was also its to withdraw. Each was entrapped by his or her own success. Even the unsuccessful almost always had something to lose. Prudence was the mark of civility within this regime. Its stability was not in any way founded upon properly political procedures but rather upon the recognition that very few, in any society, are prepared to sacrifice not only all their own but all their family's well-being for a principled stand against it. We should remember, too, that no regime in history has ever directly and indirectly disposed of so broad a range of welfare inducements and welfare sanctions to socialize its people into acceptance of its principles and practices.

This is in no sense to ignore, or by silence condone, the awesome forces of physical coercion that the Soviet Union built up. From Lenin's time onwards the secret police, under its various acronyms and leaders, built up a vast network of informers, special forces, labour camps, and special jurisdictions that became infamous throughout the world. Under Stalin they were turned not only against millions of ordinary workers but against the entire old guard of the Communist Party itself. Even after Stalin they continued to act as the eyes, ears, and fist of the regime. The point to be made, however, is that with the implementation of the labour state under Stalin the need for mass coercion steadily declined and became, to a degree, a hindrance to the maintenance of the system. Welfare benefit and welfare sanction could now be used in a much more sophisticated way to put down the first glimmerings of dissent or opposition. All this rested, of course, on the regime's ability to meet rising expectations from the social surplus available to it. When that declined and then catastrophically plummeted in the late 1970s and early 1980s, it was evident that the regime was facing a systemic crisis. When, additionally, the failure to meet even the most elementary expectations of its people was combined with widespread and officially reported evidence of corruption on a vast scale (suitably embellished in popular rumour), the crisis began to grow to threatening proportions. By the late 1980s the regime had demonstrably and lamentably failed to fulfil the two basic promises by means of which it had legitimized itself. It had broken its part of the bargain implied in its social contract with the people. In the light of acute shortages of basic commodities, it had become laughable to suggest that the system of production outperformed all available competitor systems. In the light of the observable privations ordinary workers had to suffer and general knowledge of the luxurious lifestyle of the *nomenklatura*, it became impossible to maintain that reward within the society was made solely on the basis of productive endeavour. The promises to realize a more efficient productive system and a juster distributive system had become thoroughly discredited in the popular mind long before the end of the 1980s.

With the accession of Gorbachev to power and his subsequent licensing of *glasnost*, public disillusion was allowed open expression. Abuses of power, corruption, and reports of inefficiency and waste on all sides, acute shortages and environmental devastation, scandalous health provision and increasing mortality, national, ethnic, and religious oppression, were all highlighted. The plan to use the media to undermine the conservative reactionaries in Party and state turned into the reality of a full and comprehensive critique of almost every aspect of the Communists' tenure of power. The Party was forced to concede that it did not any longer dispose of a monopoly of appropriate knowledge and that grave errors of policy and inadequacy of personnel had marred its work. The arrogant metaphysic of objective knowledge and science upon which it had based itself was abruptly shattered. Almost at the same time the Party was forced to retreat from its constitutionally guaranteed position as the guiding and leading force of all state and social organizations. Article 6 of the Constitution was repealed; and it was clear that disintegration was fast approaching. Democracy now, at last, became the watchword of the opposition both in Eastern Europe and in the Soviet Union. As in the revolution of October 1917, the people in their tens of thousands took to the streets to demand a restructuring of the power relationships within society. Gorbachev had himself authorized this explosion of people's power not only by providing *glasnost* but also by promoting *demokratizatsia*—democratization. This was the less noticed complement to *perestroika*, which formed the third element of his strategy. In its initial form it was, like *glasnost*, supposed to act as a cleansing and revitalizing means to regenerate the existing regime. By exposing the venal and authoritarian Party and state bosses to the test of public choice, Gorbachev hoped to rid himself of those who were flatly opposed to the radical economic restructuring that he had in mind. In a dangerous gamble he attempted to mobilize the people against the opposition to his policies within the state and Party apparatus. For the first time since 1917 genuinely contested elections were held in the Soviet Union in March 1989 (although a third of the seats in the Congress of People's Deputies were still reserved for Communists and their supporters). The results produced spectacular defeats for the Communists in almost all the major industrial and urban centres, and their eclipse by nationalist popular fronts in some of the Republics. They also demonstrated the overwhelming Russian support for Gorbachev's principal political antagonist, Boris Yeltsin, who went on to get himself elected President of the Russian Republic.

The regime was comprehensively outflanked in March 1989. The democrats refused to be confined to the narrow agenda Gorbachev had set for them—the very logic of winning a constituency and obtaining a popular mandate required them to articulate and represent their constituents' economic and political grievances. It also demanded that these grievances be allowed free public expression through public meetings and demonstrations, an independent press, TV, and radio, and the emergence of interest groups, clubs, associations, and political groupings. Civil society began to emerge, reflecting and strengthening the public mood for freedom.

By this time the Soviet regime had already frankly acknowledged that the economy was in crisis. It accepted that the planners had failed and that market rather than plan would increasingly dictate allocations of resources, and the nature, volume, and quality of goods produced. The Soviet Union, it was openly acknowledged, had lagged lamentably behind the rest of the developed world in the modernization of its production and distributive processes. This was, of course, hardly news to the population at large. Empty shelves, acute shortages of basic commodities, and the virtual impossibility of obtaining consumer durables had long made them painfully aware of the great chasm between the regime's promises and its actual performance. It was risible, indeed insulting, for the Party/State to maintain the superiority of its mode of production over all competitors when elementary needs could not be satisfied. The regime had broken its part of the social contract. It had, quite literally, failed to produce the goods. The metaphysic of science and objective knowledge so jealously guarded by the Party, upon which the whole vast planning system was grounded, was demonstrably bogus.

Marxism-Leninism from the outset openly declared its contempt for 'bourgeois', 'parliamentary', or 'formal' democracy, and set out to destroy it. Small wonder that, for the whole period from the Bolshevik Revolution of October 1917 until the effective collapse of Communism in 1991, Western democratic societies viewed Marxism-Leninism as their principal ideological enemy. Small wonder either that they enthusiastically greeted the emergence of pro-democracy movements in Eastern Europe, China, and the Soviet Union, giving them the confidence and the daring to sap the legitimacy of these regimes, sure in the knowledge that the eyes of the world were focused upon them. One by one, with astonishing rapidity, the Communist regimes of Eastern Europe and the Soviet Union crumbled before the assertion of people's power, whose common watchword was the realization of a genuinely representative and responsible democratic form of government. In the last decade of the twentieth century democracy rediscovered its optimism and universality. In the wake of its meteoric reassertion Marxism-Leninism was devastated. It clung on brutally in China only by massacring its own people: otherwise it was only in such backwaters as Cuba, North Korea, and Vietnam that it retained its grip. With its principal ideological opponent effectively defeated, democracy exultantly proclaimed itself the political form of the future. It has now become the preponderant idea of the modern world and has done so by vanquishing its only substantial opponent. Communism is dead! Long live democracy!

It may well be that this mood of triumphalism will be jolted in the years ahead which cannot but pose huge social, economic, and political problems for the fledgling democracies that are striving to emerge. Virulent nationalism already threatens to usurp democracy by imposing a new intolerance. Ethnic and religious animosities, buried for the past seventy years, have already erupted with vengeance and have found fertile ground in the economic austerity, unemployment, and dislocation that mark almost all the ex-Communist regimes. These are hardly auspicious circumstances in which to initiate democracy in countries which have had, almost without exception, no experience of either the institutions and procedural rules or the attitudes of mind and forbearances that make democracy workable. There can be no guarantees that in the post-Communist world democracy will always be a benign, humanitarian, and tolerant structure of ideas or of institutions. The history of our own century is cautionary note enough to the fragility of democracy when it demonstrably fails to attend to acute social and economic dislocation, or fails to answer the frustrated aspirations of national groups. As Communism has lately foundered largely because of *its* evident failure to resolve such problems, we would do well to remember that Marxism-Leninism first rose to prominence in the world precisely through the force of its critique of democracy's incapacity to satisfy the minimum expectations of ordinary people. There is, in short, a sort of dramatic flux in the turbulent relationship between democracy and Marxism-Leninism. Marxism-Leninism presented itself to the world as both a critique and an alternative to the theory and the practice of Western democracy that proved attractive in the acute crisis of the First World War. It was to rise to renewed prominence and power only during the crises of the Second World War and its aftermath. Only when it, in turn, displayed its incapacity to realize the economic (and national) aspirations of its people did Communism itself become vulnerable to the democratic critique. The question now is whether democracy (and its implicit twin, the market economy) can succeed where Marxism-Leninism has obviously failed and discredited itself.

REFERENCES

In this chapter, in order to give the reader a clearer idea of chronological progression, I have made reference to the date of writing or of first publication of primary sources. Page numbers given refer, however, to the editions below:

Bukharin (1920) N. I. Bukharin, *Economics of the Transition Period* (New York, 1971).

Engels (1872) F. Engels, 'On Authority', in K. Marx and F. Engels, *Selected Works*, 2 vols. (Moscow, 1962), vol. i.

Lenin, *Works* V. I. Lenin, *Collected Works*, 45 vols. (Moscow 1960–70).

Marx and Engels, *Works* K. Marx and F. Engels, *Collected Works* (London, 1975–).

Marx (1871a) 'The Civil War in France' in K. Marx and F. Engels, *Selected Works*, 2 vols. (Moscow, 1962), vol. i.

—— (1871b) *Karl Marx and Frederick Engels on the Paris Commune* (Moscow, 1971).

—— (1875) 'The Critique of the Gotha Programme', in K. Marx and F. Engels *Selected Works*, 2 vols. (Moscow, 1962), vol. ii.

Trotsky (1920) L. Trotsky, *Terrorism and Communism* (Ann Arbor, Mich., 1961).

Plamenatz, J. (1954), *German Marxism and Russian Communism* (London).

CHAPTER 10

India's Democratic Career

SUNIL KHILNANI

I

INDIA is a political exception. An immense, imperially seamed territory, where over 800 million mainly poor and socially very diverse
people live, it has political structures that have remained recogniz-
ably democratic for over four decades now. Why? India unsettles
comfortable political assumptions: it is in many respects the most important arena for thinking about what democratic politics under modern
conditions might actually mean today. Its political history reveals both the
fierce attachment of modern populations to the ideal of democracy, and
the sheer risks and raw dangers, the disappointments, of practising this
form of politics. How did it become a democracy? And how long can it
be reasonably expected to remain one?

In interpreting India's political history since 1947, it is important to
distinguish two perspectives. From the first, India appears as a particular
example of a general category: the sovereign entities which emerged
from the most recent wave of nation–state formation, created by the
global ebb of European empire after 1945. This essentially external perspective seeks to assess and explain the capacities of new states to preserve
their territorial boundaries within an international state system; to maintain the security of those who live within their boundaries; to institutionalize, regulate, and adjudicate domestic conflicts (through the operations
of, among other things, political parties, elections, and unconstrained
public debate); to make themselves politically accountable to their

members; and finally, to develop their societies, to achieve levels of economic performance within a competitive international system which enhance the living conditions of their populations. This set of instrumental criteria of explanation and evaluation only gradually and within historically very specific circumstances emerged as realistic standards for states to aim at, but they presented themselves and were taken as universal and immediately relevant standards of performance. Those who adopt this perspective have volunteered over the past forty years to instruct new states on exactly how they might improve their performance by bringing such criteria to bear. This is the idiom of political science and development economics, in its liberal or (now dying) socialist tones.

But India's political trajectory since 1947 may also be considered more specifically in terms of its own history, as a passage of human experience. Seen from this angle, the past forty-five years represent a sharp intensification of a long-running confrontation between, on the one hand, one of the world's 'Great Traditions', a society and culture possessing enormous historical depth and elaborately designed with the express purpose of reproducing itself as a society (a community with a shared moral order), and, ranged against it, the conceptually alien model of commercial society. This model, premissed on a proclaimed link between an economic system of private property and market exchange and a political structure that enshrines individual rights and representation (and which assumes a global expansion of its domain), exists under permanent threat of being unable to reproduce itself. In this perspective India has faced an uncomfortable but unavoidable encounter with modernity, that enticingly packaged if internally inconsistent combination of instrumental rationality, utilitarianism, and respect for individual autonomy and choice. It focuses on the capacity of a culture and its members to maintain their identity, once they entrust their destiny (as they must) to a modern state, subject to all the exigencies of modern politics. Despite their differing orientation, these two ways of considering India's modern political history are far from mutually exclusive: after all, for Indians themselves, the experience of the past half-century and more has in part involved coming to understand and describe their own identities in the terms provided by the first, external perspective. Yet the profound irony is that the political identities created by the agencies and structures of political and economic transformation have proved to be corrosive of those very agencies and structures, exposing with some poignancy the self-devouring capacities of modern democratic politics.

The single most remarkable fact about India's political history since

1947, one which sets it apart from the great majority of other new states which have come to be collectively labelled the 'developing world' (or—and now inaccurately—the 'Third World'), is the continuity of its political regime. Still more unusually, it has (except for a twenty-month interlude between June 1975 and March 1977) maintained a political structure of constitutional representative democracy: competitive elections have been held regularly, a register of civil and political liberties formally maintained, and power peacefully transferred between political parties. The persistence of political structures is inevitably open to deeply contrasting evaluations. But the main result of a stable regime is that it enables a modern state to pursue a coherent economic policy; and for those states which are able to protect the security of their populations against internal and external threat, the most important way in which they can affect the everyday lives of their populations is through the formulation, choice, and conduct of economic policy. (Needless to say, the conduct of effective economic policy is—and with unavoidable circularity—an essential precondition of states being able to protect their populations.) In this respect India is again atypical. Besides maintaining its democratic political identity, it has followed a relatively constant pattern of economic development, unmarked by dramatic shifts: despite rhetorical poses, macroeconomic and fiscal policies have been markedly conservative in character, resulting in a stable economy, with low inflation and steady (if only moderate) growth, but very little success in improving the quality of life of the country's 400 million poor.

Although the conduct of economic policy is clearly the most crucial continuous political activity in which most modern states engage, understanding and explaining the dynamics of this form of state agency—identifying the consequences of economic policies, or ascribing responsibility for these—remains an obscure business. If one of the important purposes of the reforms set in motion by Kleisthenes in 508 BC was to establish an effective 'civic presence' at the centre of the *polis*—that is, to make the Athenian citizenry the sole legitimate political agency within the territory of the *polis*—it is hard for anything of the kind to be sustained within a modern state and a global system of production and exchange. This has little to do with the no doubt real practical difficulties of summing the expressed preferences of, in India's case, some 500 million electors. It is because there is no available way of conceiving how such a civic presence—which moderns have sought to achieve variously, through a benign far-seeing Party or, less trustingly, through the institutions of representative politics—can be reliably connected with an effective economic policy, one which allows a state to create conditions of economic stability, growth, and distribution within its territory. The idea that the desire for greater democratization and the pursuit of coherent economic policy are happily and fully compatible hardly looks plausible today: indeed they often appear to be in direct conflict with one another. Liberal and socialist political theory confidently promised to deliver such compatibility: through rational state planning, or through markets and the institutions of representative politics. The socialist answer has caved in, but it would be a mistake to believe that the liberal response—which remains the most elaborate theoretical and practical one available today— can really deliver any such guarantee.

How did the political ideas and institutions of constitutional representative democracy appear in India? Where did they come from, and why were they adopted? After all, these forms were—at least initially— spurned by many other new states emerging from under the shadow of colonial power, in favour of the political forms of revolutionary socialism or authoritarian populism. Why did the Indian state steer away from these alternatives? What problems were its institutions devised to address? Was representative democracy constructed in India because of the presence of a distinctive social structure? What was it that enabled constitutional representative democracy in India to survive? No full answer to any of these questions can be given here; but we can at least clarify what such an answer must depend upon.

II

Representative politics was instituted in India under circumstances drastically divergent from those which prevailed in the territories where such institutions first came into existence. No doubt there did exist deliberative and dialogic forms of politics within the diverse regional variations of Hindu and Muslim patterns of governance. (Perhaps they were not exactly in the form of 'village republics' as some—particularly nationalist historians—enthusiastically claimed; but it is clear that as a whole pre-colonial India was very unlike the static 'oriental despotism' so favoured by colonial and some Marxist historians.) But in India there was no protracted history of representative institutions emerging in opposition to unified State and Church powers, a history which crucially delimited the boundaries between Church and State; nor (despite a by no means politically unselfconscious or passive rural and urban poor) were there large-scale popular movements which could act decisively to curb the capacities of rulers. Economic prosperity was sporadic, and society itself varied across the subcontinent, with great differentiation alongside a complex hierarchical order. It is hard to capture both the differentiation and the hierarchy; but it is helpful, for example, to see in caste (a term which enters ubiquitously into all discussions of India's politics and society) as much a means of political agency as a structure of constraint; it would be quite impossible otherwise to understand contemporary Indian politics. Political authority was more a matter of paramountcy than one of sovereignty: kingship was exercised through overlapping circuits of rights and obligations, linking together local societies but also sheltering them from wider changes.

Wherever constitutional representative democracy has emerged, it has done so within the territorial boundaries of a nation-state. The single most decisive moment in the formation of such an entity was of course the entry into the subcontinent of European traders and commercial agencies, encountering a lively indigenous commercialism. Of these trading agencies, the English East India Company emerged as most successful at acquiring and defending commercial privileges, and by the late eighteenth century these were gradually being converted into imperial power, as the Company became further drawn into the political, economic, and military administration of certain regions. The Company's subjugation and uneven exploitation of the subcontinent established in early and stark relief what was to become an enduring bond between the globally expanding economies of northern Europe and non-European societies. India, like Ireland in the seventeenth and eighteenth centuries, became an object around which the English state developed its own distinctive conception of *raison d'état*.

By the nineteenth century the British were fully committed to constructing a system of administration in India, a state. The mechanics of this system varied in line with changing British conceptions of Indian society (for example, the view of India as a 'feudal' society, with its natural ordering of lords, chiefs, and yeomen, had by the 1870s come into conflict with a conception that saw Indian society as composed of changing 'communities' which had to be actively 'represented'); the one constant was that India incarnated anarchic diversity, so that only the integral carapace of British imperial rule could give it any coherence or stable identity. But the basic ideological impetus for the design of this state had a steady and clear enough source: utilitarianism, especially the authoritarian strains of Jeremy Bentham's philosophy. For James Mill, and yet more unambiguously for James Fitzjames Stephen, India marked the perfect site upon which a system of (relatively minimally defined) 'good government' might be erected, unhindered by the constraints of representational politics present in England. The great justifying claim of imperial power was the simple Hobbesian claim to have established social peace, through military might and law. The realities were often less cheery than the initial injunction to 'Settle the country; make the people happy; and take care there are no rows!' (*Memorials of Herbert Edwardes*, i. 58, cited in Stokes 1959: 245).

The state that was constructed linked selected regions through a network of channels of coercion, extraction, and information. It developed its own distinctive language and world-view, contraposing state or government with society or community in terms of development and control, leaving to its post-colonial inheritors a quite alien vision of the relations between state and society, and of the purposes and agencies which sustained these. Its very alienness was the condition of its success: there was no shared, common terrain upon which to oppose it. But the imperial state, like its successor, could not maintain itself simply by coercion, or even by the successful manipulation of interests. (The point as usual had been neatly put by Hume (1875; 125): 'though men be much governed by interest, yet even interest itself, and all human affairs, are entirely governed by opinion'.) It could justify itself in the eyes of those over whom it ruled either by translating its power into local and locally recognized forms of authority; or by adopting the determinedly external *de haut en bas* voice of utilitarian rationality. It developed considerable dexterity at operating both forms, switching between them to its advantage. Alongside Victorian enactments of the durbar, it held its ground by the construction and strict enforcement of an impersonal legal system.

With the creation of a unitary judicial–administrative authority based upon ostentatiously rational principles and laws, political power was made (at least partially) visible and predictable. It was publicly displayed, most spectacularly at ceremonies like that held in Delhi in 1876 to confer on Queen Victoria her imperial title as 'Kaiser-i-Hind'. As an imperial state it kept its subjects under close surveillance, and was itself permanently on open view. It was this dual, or split, character—at once a relay of information about the indigenous inhabitants (enabling them to perceive themselves as communities, with collective identities and powers of agency: a process crucially helped by, for example, the institution in 1871 of a decennial government census), and a network of governance and adjudication over them—which first made it possible to imagine a self-governing national community.

Interpreters of the mechanics and political effects of imperial rule differ sharply, particularly when they come to explain the forms of opposition it engendered. Why did this take the forms it did? Why, for example, was there no mass revolutionary opposition to the imperial state? At the centre of these disagreements stands the question of nationalism. Here, the role of the Indian National Congress must be confronted. Created in 1885 (two decades before the British Labour Party, and thirty-two years before the Russian Revolution, which was to inspire so many subsequent movements against colonial rule), its presence looms, massive and dominating over India's modern politics. Its identity and political choices, unsurprisingly, are still a subject of intensive political controversy. One ready explanation for the choice of representative democracy depended on taking at face value the Congress Party's dominant self-image: that of an enlightened, high-minded urban middle-class élite, which learnt its politics through practical engagement over more than half a century with rationally designed British institutions (bureaucratic and judicial procedures, common law, and, beginning in 1909, elections). This élite acted as an integrative presence, seeking to mobilize the urban and rural masses through political instruction. The Congress here appeared as an ideologically coherent organization, committed to the procedures of constitutional and representative politics in its own internal operations, and determined to extend these to the state when it came into possession.

This is by no means an empty explanation, but it is misleading. It assumes continuity when, after all, the direct legacy of British rule was not parliamentary government and self-representation, but an authoritarian state and sectarian (or, as it came to be called in India, communal) politics. And it remains possible, while maintaining this focus on the urban élite, to view it in a more Machiavellian light: the Congress Party then appears as a league of aspiring groups and power-broking individuals, initially created by the 'collaborative' strategy of British rule. The political dynamism of the movement owed little to ideological conviction: rather, driven by internal jostling and competition into faction-building, it was pushed into the grubby world of local politics in order to enlist support from the inert urban and rural populations.

But, whether a devoted élite or a gaggle of power-hungry aspirants, the Congress Party had to draw in the political support of the culturally very distant Indian countryside (in 1901, less than 10 per cent of the population lived in towns, though this had risen to 17 per cent by 1951). The imaginative link needed to span this huge gap between the urban and rural bases of nationalist support was found in the extraordinary person of

Mahatma Gandhi. More practically, the link was also forged by the resolution of the Congress Party to compete in the elections to the provincial
assemblies in 1937 that had been announced two years earlier by the
Government of India Act; their entry, in this manner, into large-scale
representative politics was to involve the Congress in alliances and commitments which came to dominate India's politics for the first two
decades after independence. There were at least two components of this
rural support. Recent historians have emphasized the insurrectionary
activities and potential of the 'subaltern classes' (artisans, poor peasants,
landless labourers), who, it is claimed, possessed a self-conscious and
coherent conception of resistance (whether directed against rich peasant,
urban merchant, or colonial Collector). But why was this revolutionary
potential dissipated so effectively? (To stress the conservative bent of the
Congress leadership is simply to restore an exclusive focus on the character of the élite). Here it is important to emphasize the political
significance of India's 'rich peasants', upper-caste men who—as a recog-
nizably rational response to immediate economic crises—gave their support to the Congress Party. Their presence conferred on the Congress
movement much of its peculiar identity (so markedly at odds with, for
example, that of the Chinese Communist Party): a Party with a mass
base, yet politically far from revolutionary, and committed over many
decades to parliamentary procedures. It also identifies what was to
become, after 1947, an often decisive constraint on the policies of the
Congress and indeed of any national political party.

There is no simple and conclusive way of accounting either for the
bases of India's constitutional representative democracy since 1947, or
their extended survival in this form. While these bases must be emphatically political in character, much of their complexity stems from the sheer
heterogeneity of Indian society: the availability of many different forms of
self-organization, and the absence of any single unifying organizing principle. (As in many other post-colonial territories, politics in modern India
is marked by the intermittent and unreliable presence of any shared cultural frame of reference between rulers and ruled, and often even
between the ruled themselves.) The Congress Party, for instance, has
never possessed a clear class profile, and does not represent any distinct
social class: an enduring condition of its success. Many social identities
can become politically significant (religion, rural or urban location, caste,
language, class, ethnic origin), and many potential agencies for political
representation can make their mark (parties, trade unions, religious and
caste associations, business associations, women's and 'grass-roots' social

movements). The organizational bases of Indian political parties are a good index of this diversity: there have been parties based on religious nationalism (the Bharatiya Janata Party, BJP); on caste and class (the Lok Dal); on class alone (the Communist Party of India); on caste (the All India Scheduled Caste Federation); on religious separatism (the Akali Dal); on tribe (the Jharkhand movement); on cultural identity (the Dravida parties of Tamil Nadu); on nativism (the Shiv Sena).

India has no clearly defined ruling class, with the capacity to impose its own vision and interests decisively on the society at large. The precarious and insubstantial character of India's social classes meant that its belated entry into capitalist production and economy had to be accomplished for it, by a state bureaucracy rather than a hegemonic class. Since no one social group has been powerful enough to establish dominance, the state itself has been left to stand in lonely eminence. But in a society of weak classes, there may well be a violent equilibrium of social power. And this may induce social groups and classes to form alliances which successfully 'recapture' the state, transforming its identity from an agent of development to a selective disburser of public resources. Economists like Pranab Bardhan have traced the persistence of democratic politics in India to a form of coalition between India's 'dominant-proprietary' groups (industrialists, rich farmers, and professional administrators and bureaucrats). Rational agents in pursuit of scarce resources, equally matched in strength, these groups enter into a Humean compact, drawing very concrete practical gains from the procedures of democratic politics. But there is a paradox here. The economic costs of maintaining this system of proliferating subsidies and hand-outs make it inherently unstable and collectively irrational. Yet each of the individual players, trapped by the structures of intense political and economic competition, can do nothing to alter it.

But it was not just the structural configurations of society which encouraged the emergence of representative democracy in India: equally significant were intellectual choices. Intellectual responses to the British presence in India centred initially on the obvious puzzle of why the subcontinent had come to be subjugated by a nation of traders (there were no indigenous conceptual schemes for connecting commercial prowess and political power or capacities). What did this subjugation mean for Indian—and, as it was most usually asked, Hindu—culture and society, and how might this be galvanized into a culturally regenerate and self-governing society? The responses varied: some, like Bankim Chandra Chattopadhyay (1838–94), urged revolutionary cultural transformation;

others, the adoption of Western institutions and rational procedures (most famously, Jawaharlal Nehru (1889–1964), and, in a different sense, Subhas Chandra Bose (1897–1945)); some, an outright rejection of the West (men like Bipin Chandra Pal (1858–1932), Bal Gangadhar Tilak (1856–1920), and Aurobindo Ghose (1872–1950)). But the typical reaction was ambivalence, veering between chauvinism and admiring acceptance of the West. There was always an unease about accepting institutions which had stood as instruments of domination; yet what alternatives were there to fight back with? Even Gandhi's success with methods such as *satyagraha*, peaceful non-cooperation, and processional marches depended on his own mastery of British law: it was precisely this which enabled him to flout it so deftly. But, if Gandhi showed himself adept at manipulating the instruments of the imperial state, he displayed little attachment to its public institutions, nor did he propose to try to match Western commercial societies in terms of their productive capacities. Unlike Nehru, he was convinced of the need to dismantle the colonial state: he did not see it as an agency necessary for the conduct of economic policy, charged with responsibility for acting in a global economy in order to secure the welfare of its population.

But it is the history of the Indian state, even more decisively than the distinctive configuration of Indian society, which is of fundamental importance in explaining India's relatively durable political stability. Here the crucial point is that, since the suppression of the rebellion of 1857, the Indian state has never stood in serious danger of being domestically rivalled in its coercive capacities (in considering the recent bloody history of Punjab, Assam, Nagaland, and Kashmir, it is important to remember that the Indian state has had long historical practice in suppressing local and regional insurgency). The withdrawal of colonial power in 1947 was not the result of a war which weakened the state, as was, for example, the case for many states created by French and Dutch decolonization (although there did occur on the Indian subcontinent a violent rearrangement of the balance of forces within society, through the mass migration and displacement of religious communities which followed the partition of the territory into India and Pakistan).

The intact state over which the Congress Party gained control in 1947 had been created by an alien power for its own extractive purposes; now, it had somehow to be made legitimate, it had to be able to require obligations of its population. The state's harming capacities would have to be seen to be restrained in favour of its benevolent attributes. In Nehru's response to this task, what was required was a transformation of the state's formal identity, not merely a change in the colour of its administration: he mocked those for whom '*Swaraj* [self-government] means that everything continues as before, only with a darker shade' (Nehru 1936: 417). The means for such a transformation lay in the concepts of constitutionalism and legality: a constitution, Nehru insisted, 'controls the making of the laws . . . protects liberties . . . checks the executive [and] provides democratic methods of bringing about changes in the political and economic structure' (ibid. 422–3). The colonial state nowhere approximated to these four criteria: under colonial rule, the term 'constitutional' was used mainly 'in support of the executive's more or less arbitrary actions' (ibid. 423). For Nehru, the commitment to constitutionalism was to be the distinctive trait of the new Indian state, marking its break with the old political order (though he candidly admitted that to invoke constitutionalism and legality was after all to remain 'within the orbit of their [the colonial power's] ideology' (ibid. 427)). It allowed the state to make legitimate claims upon its citizens.

In many respects the Constitution promulgated in 1950 did mark a departure from inherited forms. The product of over two years' deliberation by a Constituent Assembly carefully chosen by Congress leaders so as to appear representative of the social and religious composition of the new nation-state (but given a somewhat spurious cohesiveness by the absence of any organized representation of India's 100 million Muslims, a result of the Muslim League's pre-1947 boycott of the Assembly), the 1935 Government of India Act was clearly used as a basic point of reference. But significant changes were made. The princely states (with jurisdiction over a third of the land area, and a quarter of the population) were assimilated and the sovereign power of parliament affirmed. Fundamental rights were declared (most significantly the right to private property: this was later curtailed by the 44th Amendment, allowing the state to acquire property compulsorily), as well as (often incompatible) directive principles of state policy, and a Supreme Court with powers of judicial review established. A federal structure was instituted, giving many powers concerning governance of the rural population to the states of the Union (the states were also allowed to determine politically significant caste categories), but retaining important fiscal powers for the Centre, as it came to be called. Universal suffrage was introduced (with some success in bringing women into the electoral process: by 1977, for instance, 55 per cent of enfranchised women voted, compared with 65 per cent of their male counterparts, and this has moved towards parity). Communal or group representation was set aside in favour of the representation of individual interests, as part of the commitment to secular, rational politics (but the first Constitutional Amendment in 1951 'reserved' a fifth of all parliamentary, administrative, and educational places for 'backward castes'). The document was set squarely in the best Western liberal tradition: no real trace of Gandhi's views could be found, and little was done to dismantle the centralizing and authoritarian powers of the state (the emergency provisions inserted by the British remained in place, conveniently available for future draconian use). As one mortified member of the Assembly put it, 'we wanted music of Veena and Sitar, but here we have the music of an English band' (Austin 1966: 325).

Genuine respect for the institutional design set out at Independence lasted for about one generation, after which it began to fade. The late 1960s are usually taken to mark a pivotal moment in India's political history, brought about by a blurring of the hitherto clear national support for the Congress Party and an internal battle for the Party leadership. It is certainly true that until the mid-1960s, particularly while Nehru was alive, the special intimacy created by the collective struggles of the National movement lingered on, sustaining a measure of loyalty to the externalities of modern state routines and rule. The ruling élite held to a conception of the state as a guardian or protector, and members of the upper echelons of the state and civil service could (wherever necessary) still be embarrassed into maintaining a Gandhian austerity when it came to their political and financial ambitions. Yet, as Upendra Baxi (1990) has pointed out, it is worth remembering that even Nehru himself was not at times averse to avoiding the norms of constitutional legality, in favour of other ways of justifying the actions of those responsible for the state's doings. Take for instance Nehru's handling of the matter of the 'privy purses'. Even though he opposed the practice, he refused to abolish the anomaly of a republican state continuing to grant pensions to the princely families, because in his opinion this would have meant breaking the 'government's word and [the] government's honour' (Nehru to Patel, in Gopal 1979: 79): he turned here to the discourse of *rajdharma*, an appeal by a modern prince to the medieval Hindu codes of royal honour. So too he could invoke his compelling charismatic qualities to deflect—through paternalistic reasoning—enquiries about the illegalities of his associates (most notoriously in trying to protect ministers like Krishna Menon and Pratap Singh Kairon). But here one must also acknowledge that, amongst the political leaders of the new states created after 1945, Nehru was distinguished by his quite exceptional probity. Yet the fact remains that the constitutional ground rules were generally observed during this period, though this was not purely the result of unusual normative commitment: sticking to them served as an efficient way of spreading risks and of enhancing trust within a political system operated by one electorally dominant but internally very discordant party.

Until the mid-1960s, India enjoyed what was in many respects quite good government; but things were to become much less clear over the next two decades. In trying to account for the increasingly palpable strains on constitutional democracy in India over the past two decades, the finger is usually pointed at the Congress Party, and specifically at its leader from 1967 until her assassination in 1984, Indira Gandhi. What in 1947 had been a skilful initial choice from available forms of political legitimacy began, by the early 1970s, to be wielded in quite different ways. Under Indira Gandhi, the authoritarian aspect of the state's identity was vividly displayed, underlining the extent to which the quality of government achieved in a state like India depends upon the contingencies of political leadership.

Insecure in her power, Mrs Gandhi tightened the chains of command (after 1972, no intra-party elections were held), and adopted populist electioneering strategies designed to evade the power brokerages of the regional party leadership. She moved away from the forms of governance established by the imperial state and maintained by the Congress under Nehru. Tempted into a twenty-month suspension of constitutional legality in June 1975 (she gave political and economic reasons for her assumption of emergency dictatorial powers: a popular strike—which she described as a threat to the country's unity—and inflationary pressures), she finally relented, restoring procedures of political accountability. But by the early 1980s, as it became clear that the established arenas of public deliberation and decision-making were being increasingly ignored, regional and central leaderships in the federation entered into sour confrontation, each heightening their claims. Regional parties and governments, seeking to bolster political support, invoked vernacular and ethnic forms of identity; Indira Gandhi, meanwhile, flirted with religious sentiments and appeals, hinting at an overlap between the descriptions 'non-Hindu' and 'anti-national'. Corruption increasingly became a fixed feature of government functioning, provoking successive waves of public indignation and amnesia. With political procedures and institutions falling into disregard, the effects of several decades of unevenly directed economic development (overlaid upon the inherited colonial pattern of local economic imbalances) began to matter politically. As elsewhere, competitive electoral politics became an available instrument for focusing resentment at such skewed economic benefits. It served the politically ambitious well to press forms of social identity, once locally contained, into national politics, thereby transforming the state into an arena of combat populated by indivisible and non-negotiable identities. Faith replaced trust, creating its own lethal obligations.

To some, this signals civil society's 'revenge' upon the state. The Indian nation was of course created in the midst of terrible aggression between Hindus and Muslims (half a million people are estimated to have been killed at the time of Partition): this remains a fearful memory for many of either faith, an abiding source of mutual resentment. Yet religious and caste identities began only relatively recently to figure in national politics. Over the past decade they have invaded with a ferocious energy, testing to the limit the compatibility between political violence and democratic procedures. Why has this happened now? How is it that a Hindu nationalist party (the BJP) could, in the elections of 1991, collect 20 per cent of the votes cast (during the previous four decades, it could only manage well below 10 per cent)? The historical antecedents of this particularly potent form of political identity go back at least to the nineteenth century, to the Brahminic Hindu 'renaissance' which was such an important component of Indian nationalism. Nationalism in India did not displace the numerous varieties of Hinduism, but skilfully incorporated them: it is worth recalling that the Congress Party never really held the allegiance of Muslims; in 1938, for instance, out of 3 million party members, only around 100,000 were Muslims. But the appeal of Hindu nationalism has now come to extend well beyond its original upper-caste, urban constituency, taking in the 'middle' and 'backward' castes of the countryside: it threatens to achieve a scale which could redefine the identity of the Indian nation. This surge of religious identities into national politics is directly linked to the intensification of political competition, to the need—on the part of both leaders and led—to offer and find a view of group interest that possesses some recognizable substance. The activities of the Indian state over the past four decades have obviously done much to aggravate these frictions, helping to produce a domestic landscape riven by paths of opportunity as well as troughs of desperation. Differential policies aimed at regional groups, selective and often haphazard recognition of the claims of certain groups at the expense of others, and (often in consequence) intensive internal migration (particularly into the great conurbations) have all fomented this vicious competition. And the stakes are obstinately real. Cleaving to religious identities becomes in these circumstances not simply a case of external manipulation of the innocent by the entrepreneurial, but rather a self-conscious effort on the part of vulnerable human beings at creating and sustaining a sense of community, at identifying who is threatening and who really is trustworthy in very uncertain conditions. But it is a form of political representation which has little tolerance for extant liberal models of democracy.

How much responsibility for the way in which India has been governed since 1947 can be ascribed to the structures of constitutional representative democracy? Clearly the Constitution has played an important role. Economic stability, for example, owes much to the Constitutional allocation of fiscal powers, which disallows states of the federation from printing money or borrowing from commercial markets in order to fund deficits, thus retaining vital economic controls in the hands of the central government. The (sometimes precariously maintained) principle of judicial review has also been important, and the fortunes of political justice have been tied to the varying vigour with which the register of civil and political liberties has been upheld or defended; in recent years, the presence of such liberties has provided the impetus for 'public interest litigation', conducted in the Supreme Court. So too, as Amartya Sen (1989: 387) has suggested, an uncensored press has probably helped to concentrate the government's mind towards pre-empting that recurring spectre of pre-independence India, famine; China is here an instructive comparison. Constitutional political conduct has suffered moments of oblivion; but there have also been periods of general (if for many, passive) endorsement of India's political identity as it is articulated in the Constitution: the flicker of optimism which followed the elections of 1984, and the grim seriousness which has inflected national politics since the 1991 elections are recent examples of such commitment, and they provide something on which to pin hopes for the future. Elections have had an effect upon the conduct of professional politicians, particularly at local constituency levels. A voluble and by no means recalcitrant electorate (turnout at elections has ranged between 45 per cent in 1952 and 64 per cent in 1984) has regularly chastised elected representatives for poor performance, and in a country where the incomes of the poor are unindexed, the need to muster support democratically has encouraged governments to avoid inflationary policies. But there is little to sustain the conclusion that elections have left any decisive imprint on the conduct of governmental economic policy (the electoral expediency of adopting certain rhetorical postures is another matter). In fact, the formulation and choice of macroeconomic and fiscal policy in India seem to have been largely insulated from the workings of representative politics. In this respect, the Indian state has been relatively lucky in having had continuous access to the skills of a competent intelligentsia and bureaucracy.

III

All states that are latecomers to the feast have committed themselves to the economic development of their societies, but the perception of economic backwardness has produced very disparate political responses. Among those post-colonial states which secured their political independence after the Second World War, India is almost unique in having maintained, alongside this commitment, a commitment to achieve economic development through a regime of representative democracy. (This has resulted in a remarkable simultaneity of political forms: in a highly compressed period of time, people have had to learn to move skilfully between exploiting to their benefit old relations of deference and discovering and asserting individual rights.) To evaluate the performance of the Indian state as an agency of development is a complicated matter, involving counterfactual logic and the comparison of dissimilar entities. But it is this economic performance, seen in terms of stability, growth, and distribution, which will to all intents decide the future of constitutional representative democracy in India. In itself, this is hardly a novel point. Yet, and this must be insisted upon, this performance will depend upon the practical capacities and agency of both politicians and those over whom they rule: it will depend on how effectively they can together respond to the threats and opportunities of the international market-place. This, for India, is a new kind of challenge. Almost alone among non-Communist states, it managed to prolong until the 1980s a quite exceptional insulation from the vagaries of the global economy; what will be required now are new skills, quickly learnt and deployed.

The 'crisis of governability' which many claim to detect in India, as elsewhere, points to a real conflict between the democratic character of a state and its effective capacities: between a respect for subjective evaluations, and the pursuit of causal strategies designed to procure goods and entitlements over which such evaluations may be exercised. There will always be claims, made by individuals or individuals on behalf of traditions of thought, to resolve this conflict. The last decade has seen the at least temporary breaking of the socialist promise that planning is the most effective resolution to the problem. This thinning in the range of options available to states is already reflected in the policy shifts of the Indian state (as the Indian government's 1991 Budget and new economic policy, with its modish stress on liberalization and deregulation, manifests). But in these matters, it is not necessarily through elimination that viable answers are arrived at.

The politics of India since 1947 makes incomparably clear the deficiencies of the most commonly available understandings of representative democracy. According to such understandings, political parties are agencies rationally chosen by individuals as instruments for the pursuit of their interests; yet this is a poor description of the operation of such politics in India (or anywhere). The relation between representative and represented is never simply an instrumental one: it presupposes a cultural, felt sense of identification, a relation of trust between politicians and their supporters. Successful representative politics appears to require a stability of identities, and of perceptions of interest. But political identities and interests have to be created; they do not exist outside of politics. And politics as a process of identity formation is a dangerous business—a process more akin to conflict than competition. This is the situation which obtains in India today. Constitutional representative democracy there does not mean that the *demos* have in their own hands those powers of agency which modern states in fact do possess; nor even that the *demos* have much choice over who exercises these powers of agency, or how exactly they do this. What it does mean is that they are free to engage in the creation of collective identities, an activity which in a democracy will always partly escape the powers of the state to define and coerce. That freedom has its risks; but it remains, for all those risks, a value to moderns.

For their help in connection with this essay, I am very grateful to John Dunn, Roy Foster, Geoffrey Hawthorn, Vijay Joshi, and Asha Sarabhai.

REFERENCES

Austin, Granville (1966), *The Indian Constitution: Cornerstone of a Nation* (Oxford).
Baxi, Upendra (1990), 'The Recovery of Fire: Nehru and the Legitimation of Power in India', *Economic and Political Weekly* (Jan. 13), 107–12.
Gopal, S. (1979), *Jawaharlal Nehru: A Biography, 1947–1956*, ii (London).
Hume, David (1875), *Essays Moral, Political and Literary*, ed. T. H. Green and T. H. Grose, i (London).
Nehru, Jawaharlal (1936), *Autobiography* (London).
Sen, Amartya (1989), 'Indian Development: Lessons and Non-Lessons', *Daedalus*, 118: 367–92.
Stokes, Eric (1959), *The English Utilitarians and India* (Oxford).

CHAPTER 11

Losing the Faith

Feminism and Democracy

SUSAN MENDUS

Since Mary Wollstonecraft, generations of women and some men wove painstaking arguments to demonstrate that excluding women from modern public and political life contradicts the liberal democratic promise of universal emancipation and equality. They identified the liberation of women with expanding civil and political rights to include women on the same terms as men, and with the entrance of women into the public life dominated by men on an equal basis with them. After two centuries of faith that the ideal of equality and fraternity included women have still not brought emancipation for women, contemporary feminists have begun to question the faith itself.

(Young 1990: 93)

A T a time when the Berlin Wall has been dismantled and Eastern Europe is embracing the values of Western liberal democracy, when an attempted coup in Moscow has been overthrown, and the republics of the former USSR have claimed independence and democratic freedoms, it may seem churlish to criticize democracy or to doubt its ability to live up to its own ideals. Democracy may indeed be an imperfect form of government, but all the others are far worse and this, surely, is a moment for recognizing the benefits which democracy brings, not a moment for drawing attention to its shortcomings. It is a moment for confirming our faith, not a moment for doubting it.

And yet, some feminists do doubt it. Moreover, the doubts run deep, and constitute an attack not only on the achievements of modern democratic states, but also on the underlying ideals of democratic theory itself. Feminists have long drawn attention to the facts of women's under-representation in political life, and of their over-representation amongst the unemployed, the low-paid, and the part-time work-force. They now suspect that these features, common to all modern democratic states, are not merely unfortunate contingencies, or remediable imperfections of specific states. Rather, they are an indication of deep gender bias in democratic theory itself. For feminists, democracy is not something which, as a matter of unfortunate fact, has failed to deliver on its promises to women. It embodies ideals which guarantee that it will never deliver unless it embarks upon extensive critical examination of its own philosophical assumptions. In brief, the charge made against democracy is that, for women, it was never more than an article of faith, and when two hundred years of democratization have failed (and are still failing) to deliver equality for women, even faith is giving out.

The uncharitable may interpret these remarks as nothing more than evidence of feminist paranoia and of women's general inability to recognize when they are well off. It is therefore important to stress that the charge is not simply that democratic *states* are, as a matter of fact, ones in which women are disadvantaged (though they are), but rather that democratic *theory* is, as a matter of principle, committed to ideals which guarantee that that will remain so. As a faith, democracy was always a false faith, and its prophets (including nearly all the major political philosophers of the past two hundred years) are now exposed as false prophets.

These are serious, depressing, and even dangerous charges. The more so if we have no preferred alternative to democracy, and no revised interpretation of its central ideals. The tasks for contemporary feminism are therefore twofold: first, to justify the claim that traditional democratic theory leads to undemocratic practice; secondly, to identify the ways in which that theory might be reinterpreted so as to come closer to democratic ideals. The former is feminism's critique of the faith; the latter is feminism's revision of the faith.

A CRITIQUE OF THE FAITH

The belief that democratic theory condones undemocratic practice is not confined to feminist theorists. John Dunn has argued that there are 'two distinct and developed democratic theories loose in the world today— one dismally ideological and the other fairly blatantly utopian'. On the dismally ideological account democracy is simply the least bad mechanism for securing a measure of responsibility on the part of the governors to the governed. By contrast, the blatantly utopian account envisages a society in which all social arrangements represent the interests of all people.

The former constitutes a practical proposal, but hardly an inspiring one; the latter may be inspiring, but is hardly practical. Despairing of finding anything which can reflect democracy's status as both a high ideal and a practical proposal, Dunn concludes that 'today, in politics, democracy is the *name* for what we cannot have—yet cannot cease to want' (Dunn 1979: 26–7). On Dunn's analysis the grounds for scepticism about democracy lie largely in the circumstances of modern life: the social and economic differentiation which are characteristic of the modern world necessarily generate inequalities which fit ill with the democratic ideal of political equality. Connectedly, the sheer size of modern states creates a rift between the individual and the community which makes it impossible for individuals to perceive the state as a focus of common good. Thus, democracy is not attainable in large, modern, postindustrial societies: as an ideal, it promises human fulfilment and human freedom, but in the modern world this promise cannot be met and democracy has therefore become at best a method of curbing the excesses of rulers, and at worst an idle, or even a utopian dream.

But if Dunn fears that democracy cannot exist, given the nature of modern states, feminists note with some chagrin that democracy never did exist even prior to the growth of modern states: Carole Pateman briskly dismisses the subject, claiming that 'for feminists, democracy has never existed; women never have been and still are not admitted as full and equal members in any country known as a "democracy"' (Pateman 1989: 210). Put together, the two accounts are deeply unsettling: Dunn tells us that without small states and an undifferentiated public there cannot be democracy. Feminists tell us that even when there were small states and an undifferentiated public, still there never was democracy. For feminists, the facts of history—the denial of the vote to women, their historical confinement to a domestic realm, their incorporation within the interests of their husbands—prove beyond doubt that for women democracy has never existed. For them, therefore, Dunn's lament is not even a lament for times past, but only a reflection on what might have been but in fact never was.

Why was there never democracy for women, and why is there still no democracy for women? A number of modern writers implicitly assume that it is because women have historically been denied equality under the law and the formal, political right to vote. For example, Robert Dahl recognizes that almost all the major writers in the democratic tradition excluded women from their theories, but he implies that this is merely evidence of the fact that philosophers are children of their time, and that the problem may be solved simply by rewriting references to 'all men' as 'all men and women' or 'all adults'. Thus, indicating that all is now well, he writes: 'In most countries women gained the suffrage only in this century, and in a few only after the Second World War. In fact, not until our own century did democratic theory and practice begin to reflect a belief that all (or virtually all) adults should be included in the demos as a matter of right' (Dahl 1989: 115–16). And this completes his discussion of the role of women in modern democratic states.

Dahl's optimism is grounded in his recognition that women are now formally equal citizens, and in his belief that this formal equality need not be fatally undermined by social and economic inequalities. He accepts the general claim that political equality is compromised by lack of economic power, but argues that this should not lead to the pessimistic conclusion that democracy is 'something we cannot have yet cannot cease to want'. Rather, it suggests the more robust conclusion that the pursuit of democracy includes the removal of social and economic inequalities. He writes:

Though the idea of equal opportunity is often so weakly interpreted that it is rightly dismissed as too undemanding, when it is taken in its fullest sense it is extraordinarily demanding—so demanding, indeed, that the criteria for the democratic process would require a people committed to it to institute measures well beyond those that even the most democratic states have hitherto brought about. (Dahl 1989: 115)

For Dahl, therefore, inequality is a practical problem which admits of practical solutions. Since it is a widespread and intransigent problem, there will be no 'quick fix', but there can be progress, and in tracing that progress Dahl does not see the need to make reference to any special feature of women's position beyond the recognition that they are, in general, amongst those who suffer from a lack of social and economic power. By implication, he denies that women constitute a special and intransigent problem for democratic theory. They are simply a specific example of a quite general, but remediable, problem, the problem of how to ensure that social and economic inequalities do not undermine the formal equality of the vote.

Many feminists dissent: although agreeing that there are practical problems, they also insist that, in the case of women, the problems have a theoretical origin which goes beyond mere social and economic inequality. Women, they argue, are different not simply because they lack economic and social power, but because historically they have been explicitly excluded from the category of citizen in the democratic state. So we might agree that democracy depends upon enlarging the economic power of those who are citizens, but so long as women (along with children, animals, and the insane) were excluded from that category, the question of enlarging their economic and social power frequently failed to arise. Indeed, women's economic power was normally identified with the economic power of their husbands, and the fact that wives themselves owned nothing was (and often still is) conveniently forgotten. Again, it is important to be clear about the status of this objection: usually, it is taken as simply a reflection on the historical facts of democratic societies, but it also contains the seeds of a criticism of democratic theory itself. The criticism may be made explicit by considering Dahl's two interpretations of what he calls 'the principle of inclusion' in democratic theory. This principle is the principle which dictates who shall count as a citizen in the democratic state, and therefore who shall have a say in determining the laws of the state.

Dahl notes that historically philosophers have vacillated between a contingent and a categorical principle of inclusion: thus, some urge that all adult members of a state are also, and thereby, citizens (the categorical criterion); others claim that only those who are qualified to rule may be citizens (the contingent claim). He concedes that the contingent criterion has been the most popular in the history of political philosophy, but urges that the categorical criterion is the appropriate one for modern democratic states. There should be no question of individuals having to prove their fitness to rule. The criterion for being a full citizen is simply that one is an adult member of the state in question. This, and this alone, justifies according rights of citizenship.

There is, however, a worrying tension between the assumptions inherent in the demand for increased social and economic equality and the assumptions inherent in the demand for a categorical criterion of citizenship. For the former recognizes that if citizenship is to be meaningful, more than formal equality is required, whereas the latter is content with a formal criterion for being or becoming a citizen. The danger is that acceptance of the categorical principle of inclusion, with its requirement that we ignore differences between people at the formal level, may lead to minimizing differences between people in framing social policy. Most importantly, it may lead to an understanding of difference, specifically women's differences, as disadvantage, disability, or deviance. If difference is the problem at the level of inclusion, then the removal of difference may be thought to be the solution at the level of social policy.

Thus, to provide a concrete example, pregnancy is often treated as akin to illness, and maternity leave as a special case of sick-leave. Pregnant women are then equated with men who are ill or temporarily disabled, and the attempt to attain 'equality' for them rests on the assumption that they are, in effect, disabled men. By this strategy, inequalities are certainly reduced because women attain something by way of maternity benefit, and something is surely better than nothing. But the importance of the practical benefits should not disguise the fact that the theoretical assumptions of the strategy are assimilationist and patriarchal. Women attain a degree of equality only by conceding that the differences between themselves and men are differences which carry the implication of female inferiority. Moreover, this is not simply a complaint about the practical arrangements governing pregnancy and childbirth; it is a more general concern about the unspoken assumptions of many democratic theorists, specifically their assumption that equality is to be attained via the removal or minimization of disadvantage, where what counts as disadvantage is held to be clear and uncontroversial, but is in fact determined by reference to a model which is intrinsically male.

Considerations of this sort highlight the fact that for women lack of social and economic power is only half the story: it is not simply bad luck that women, in general, lack economic power. It is the male model of normality which *guarantees* that that will be so. Iris Marion Young expresses the point forcefully:

In my view an equal treatment approach to pregnancy and childbirth is inadequate because it either implies that women do not have any right to leave and job security when having babies, or assimilates such guarantees under the supposedly gender-neutral category of 'disability' . . . Assimilating pregnancy and disability tends to stigmatize these processes as 'unhealthy'. (Young 1990: 176)

It is for this reason that many feminists have found it difficult to retain faith in democracy and democratic theory. And, as we have seen, the loss of faith occurs at several levels: historically, feminists are aware that the denial of difference at the level of inclusion has rarely been observed. Most philosophers have noted differences between men and women, and have argued that these differences support the exclusion of women from even the rights of formal political equality. More recently, feminists have drawn attention to the fact that even where the categorical criterion has been employed, it has not been accompanied by any strenuous efforts to remove the social and economic disadvantages suffered by women, and therefore formal political equality has been undermined by practical social and economic inequality. Finally, and most importantly, many feminists now doubt whether the denial or removal of difference is even an acceptable aim for political theory and practice. Again, the doubts arise on two levels. Anne Phillips has argued that the individualistic character of modern philosophy makes it inadequate for feminist purposes. She notes:

The anti-discrimination that informs much contemporary liberalism implies removing obstacles that block an individual's path and then applauding when that individual succeeds. The problem is still perceived in terms of previous *mis*treatment, which judged and dismissed people because they had deviated from some prejudiced norm. The answer is presented in terms of treating them just as people instead. (Phillips 1991: 150)

Where difference is interpreted as deviance or disadvantage, the response to it is to implement social policy which will minimize the effects of that disadvantage *in the specific case*. This individualistic response has been countered by the demand that what is required is recognition of *group* disadvantage. Far from asserting that it should not matter whether we are men or women, this strategy insists that men and women do have different degrees of power and that therefore policies should be implemented which take account of this fact and guarantee increased power to women as a group.

The second response is rather different. It denies that difference is always to be construed as disadvantage and, in the case of women, urges a restructuring of both political theory and political practice in such a way as to celebrate at least some differences. In other words, it denies that all difference is disability, and it objects to the strategy whereby the 'disadvantages' of pregnancy and childbirth are mitigated by assimilating them to male illness. So, where democratic theory characteristically urges that we should assume that everyone is the same, feminists urge a recognition that men and women are different. Similarly, where democratic theorists have urged that, in decisions about social policy, we should aim to minimize the disadvantages which spring from difference, feminists ask why such normal states as pregnancy should be categorized as disadvantages at all.

For feminists, therefore, losing the faith has been losing faith in the ability of doctrines of equality, understood as doctrines which advocate the minimization of difference, to deliver a political theory which will be sensitive to the realities of women's lives. The solution to this problem lies in a rewriting of democratic theory in such a way as to ensure that it acknowledges and incorporates difference. Most importantly, it lies in a recognition that, in the case of women, the disadvantages which spring from difference are themselves politically significant. They are disadvantages inherent in not being male. So democratic theory falls at the first hurdle because it in fact employs a male, rather than a gender-neutral, standard by which to decide what counts as disadvantage.

The proposed solution is not without its dangers: oppressed and disadvantaged groups have long used a doctrine of equality as their most important single weapon, and have appealed to such concepts as 'common humanity' in their attempts to attain political and legal rights. Moreover, they have vigorously denied the significance of difference in political contexts, and urged that differences between them and other, more advantaged, groups should be ignored in the distribution of political rights. It is therefore a discomfiting about-face for feminist theorists now to insist on a politics of difference, and to pin their faith in the possibility that difference may be acknowledged, not construed as disadvantage.

To what extent do feminists wish to attack democratic ideals, and to what extent do they wish to reconstruct them? Is their argument that we should substitute an acceptance of difference for the demand for equality, or that the demand for equality itself requires a full and sensitive recognition of the practical significance of difference?

REVISING THE FAITH

Some critics have argued that feminists do indeed reject the ideal of equality, and that they do so because they wrongly assume that equality is at odds with the recognition of difference. Thus, Richard Norman writes: 'Equality does not require the elimination of difference. Sexual equality, in particular, does not require a denial of the inescapable biological facts of sexual difference, and leaves open what further differences might follow from these' (Osborne 1991: 122). Certainly some feminists have spoken of equality in dismissive terms, and have urged that we should pay less attention to it. Virginia Held, for example says:

Occasionally, for those who give birth, equality will be an important concept as we strive to treat children fairly and have them treat each other with respect. But it is normally greatly overshadowed by such other concerns as that the relationship between ourselves and our children and each other be trusting and considerate. (Held 1989: 225)

But this is simply the point that equality is not the only concept in moral and political life. It is not the complaint that equality necessarily conflicts with difference. And more generally, when feminists express reservations about equality, it is because they recognize that democratic theory itself has interpreted it as requiring the elimination or minimization of difference. In general, it is not feminists who urge that equality and difference are incompatible concepts; it is democratic theory which does that by its insistence on a specific understanding of equality—as something to be attained by the minimization of difference. The crucial debate in contemporary feminism is the debate between those who urge that sex should become irrelevant and those who believe that sex should not provide the basis for inequality. Neither of these strategies involves rejecting equality. Rather, the dispute is about how equality is to be attained.

However, the strategic problem is acute in the case of women for the simple reason that, unlike social and economic differences, sexual difference cannot be removed by social policy in quite the simple way which the theory requires. Where inequalities of power spring simply from social and economic inequalities, there is some hope of removing them by seeking to minimize them—though the task would be difficult. But where inequalities of power spring from sex, it may be morally undesirable, or even impossible, to attempt to remove them by this approach. Of course, such strategies have been used, and with great success, by early feminists in their attempt to secure equal legal and political rights for women. But feminists are now sceptical about such attempts, fearing that ultimately they leave for women only the possibility of assimilation into a male world. Speaking about her own 'assimilation' feminism, Simone de Beauvoir said: 'the modern woman accepts masculine values: she prides herself on thinking, taking action, working, creating, on the same terms as men; instead of seeking to disparage them, she declares herself their equal' (Walzer 1989: 164). But the price of this form of feminism is high for, as Simone de Beauvoir herself concedes, it is incompatible with child care and mothering. This not only means that, for many women, it will be difficult, if not impossible, to 'win the game', it also means accepting the rules of the game—where those rules dictate that pregnancy is an illness and child care a disadvantage.

What is needed, therefore, is a way of conceptualizing difference which renders it compatible with equality, but also, and crucially, does not simply increase social differentiation. Yet more radically, what is needed is a recognition that in much traditional democratic theory the concepts of equality, difference, and disadvantage are themselves gender-biased: they assume a standard of normality which is inherently male.

What are the possibilities of re-conceptualizing in this way? How can democratic states revise the ideal in a way which acknowledges difference as both ineliminable and valuable? At this stage, it is worth emphasizing that it is not only feminists who should have a strong interest in this question. Modern states are characterized by the heterogeneity of the people who inhabit them. Unlike fifth-century Athens, or Rousseau's ideal state, they are not gatherings of the like-minded, gentlemen's clubs writ large, where those who deviate may be excluded or required to conform. The denial of citizenship to all but white males is no longer an option, nor is the easy assumption that newcomers must earn their right to citizenship by becoming 'like us'. Difference is not going to go away, nor is it something for which those who are different feel disposed to apologize. Against this background, the insistence that equality is to be preserved via the minimization of difference, or via assimilation itself appears utopian and the complaint that the differentiation of modern life militates against democracy may elicit the response: 'so much the worse for democracy'.

However, before moving too rapidly to that pessimistic conclusion, I want to explore the possibility that such a re-conceptualization is possible, and that it is compatible with the democratic ideal of equality. One part of the answer lies in distinguishing between two levels of democratic interest: these answer to Dahl's two principles mentioned earlier—the principle of inclusion and the principle of equality. At the former level, difference is properly to be ignored, but at the latter level, it is to be recognized and accommodated. Thus, for purposes of deciding who is to count as a citizen of a democratic state, differences of class, race, and gender should not matter. But in adhering to a strong principle of equality, we are obliged to acknowledge these differences—to acknowledge them, but not thereby to eliminate them. For whereas traditional democratic theory tends to construe difference as an obstacle to the attainment of a truly democratic state, feminist theory should alert us to the possibility that difference is rather what necessitates the pursuit of democracy. Since it is the fact that we are not all the same which requires democracy, attempting to make us all the same will not deliver democracy. On the contrary, it will remove the rationale for democracy.

Perhaps this point can be made clearer by drawing attention to one very important rationale for a democratic order—its ability to accommodate variety and criticism. Famously, E. M. Forster once called for 'two cheers for democracy' and he explained 'one because it admits variety and two because it permits criticism' (Forster 1951: 79). This argument is often interpreted as a claim about the ability of democracy, in the long run, to deliver truth: the free market-place of ideas will, it is claimed, ensure that truth triumphs over error. But there may also be a different interpretation, which is that democratic societies are superior not because they deliver unity out of diversity, but simply because and in so far as they acknowledge diversity. The most famous exponent of this view is, of course, John Stuart Mill, whose political theory began from the premiss that 'human beings are not like sheep, and even sheep are not indistinguishably alike' (Mill 1975: 83). Mill's ideal political future was not one in which disagreement and difference are eradicated, for he did not believe that any such future was possible. Rather, his claim was that the existence of difference, and the recognition that difference was ineradicable, itself provided a major argument for democracy. Connectedly, Mill understood democracy not as a state, but rather as a process. There would be no end to disagreement, but this fact provided the reason for adopting a democratic order rather than a reason for doubting its practicality. Therefore, where some modern democratic theorists begin from a principle of equality, Mill begins from a recognition of difference. And where modern democratic theorists see their main aim as being to create equality by removing difference, Mill recognizes that it is difference which must be preserved lest the pursuit of equality simply degenerate into the imposition of uniformity. In brief, then, the significance of Mill's account is that he recognizes, and emphasizes, the priority of difference over equality and urges that equality must be pursued via the recognition of difference.

Historically, democratic theory guaranteed equality by according the rights of citizenship only to those who were already equal. Later, as in the philosophy of Kant, citizenship rights were theoretically allowed to those who were able to 'improve' themselves and thus earn the title 'citizen'. Recently, hope of equality (or despair about it) has rested upon the chances of employing social policy to obliterate the effects of arbitrary inequalities. In all these cases, difference has been perceived as an obstacle to equality, and the democratic aspiration has been to ignore or remove it. In so far, therefore, as the democratic faith has been a faith that difference may be ignored or removed, feminists have lost that faith.

But feminist concerns about democratic theory go beyond the insistence that equality must be attained without the elimination of difference. Feminists also highlight the extent to which difference itself is a value-laden concept, which takes male experience as the norm and interprets female experience as disadvantaged by comparison with it. If we view matters in this way, then we will see that what is asked for is not special treatment for women, but rather an end to the existing system of special treatment for men. Catharine MacKinnon writes:

In reality . . . virtually every quality that distinguishes men from women is already affirmatively compensated in this society. Men's physiology defines most sports, their needs define auto and health insurance coverage, their socially defined biographies define workplace expectations and successful career patterns, their perspectives and concerns define quality in scholarship . . . For each of their differences from women, what amounts to an affirmative action plan is in effect, otherwise known as the structure and values of American society. (MacKinnon 1987: 36)

In Britain too, existing structures favour men's lifestyles. Thus, the demand that Parliamentary hours be changed in order to take account of women's domestic responsibilities is not a request for preferential treatment for women. It is simply a recognition that what already exists is a case of preferential treatment for men. In cases such as this there is often no happy medium, or mutually convenient compromise. But that fact should not lead us to the conclusion that what currently exists is neutral between men and women, or that when women ask for arrangements more suitable to them, they are asking for special favours.

The contribution which feminist theory makes to democratic theory is therefore twofold: by asserting that some differences are ineliminable, feminism searches for an understanding of democracy as something to be aimed at *through* difference, not something to be attained via the *removal* of difference. Specifically, it indicates that the pursuit of equality via the elimination of difference is not the route to a democratic society, but the route to an oppressive and exclusive society. Historically, societies which have claimed to 'represent the people' have in fact represented only that portion of the people which displays homogeneity. In modern theory 'representing the people' must not be interpreted as representing that portion of the people who can be forced into the appropriate mould. If there is to be any hope for democracy, it must therefore cease to pursue equality by trying to eliminate difference and instead concentrate on pursuing it by recognizing difference more adequately.

This last claim, however, signals feminism's second contribution to the debate, which is that in modern democratic societies the concept of difference, and the connected concept of disadvantage, are themselves male-centred. To be different is to deviate from some norm and, in democratic societies, that norm is invariably a male norm. Debates about the need to encourage women to participate more fully in political life tend to take the form of requests for assistance for women who have child-care and domestic responsibilities. But, as we have seen, even this approach assumes not only that women are different, but that they require 'help' if they are to attain male standards. It assumes both that the male standard is correct, and that something more than justice is required if women are to attain it. Therefore, if democratic theory is to be sustained and improved, it must recognize not only that difference is sometimes ineliminable, but also that what counts as difference is not value-neutral. It must recognize its own gender-bias even (indeed especially) in cases where it seeks to 'assist' women. The faith that democracy can be transformed in this way is the faith to which feminists now cling.

REFERENCES

Dahl, Robert A. (1989), *Democracy and its Critics* (New Haven, Conn., and London).
Dunn, John (1979), *Western Political Theory in the Face of the Future* (Cambridge).
Forster, E. M. (1951), *Two Cheers for Democracy* (London).
Held, Virginia (1989), 'Liberty and Equality from a Feminist Perspective', in N. MacCormick and Z. Bankowski (eds.), *Enlightenment, Rights and Revolution: Essays in Legal and Social Philosophy* (Aberdeen), 214–29.
MacKinnon, Catharine A. (1987), *Feminism Unmodified* (Cambridge, Mass., and London).
Mill, J. S. (1975), *On Liberty*, in J. S. Mill, *Three Essays*, ed. R. Wollheim (Oxford).
Osborne, Peter (1991), *Socialism and the Limits of Liberalism* (London and New York).
Pateman, Carole (1989), *The Disorder of Women* (Cambridge).
Phillips, Anne (1991), *Engendering Democracy* (Cambridge).
Walzer, Michael (1989), *The Company of Critics* (London).
Young, Iris Marion (1990), *Throwing Like a Girl and Other Essays in Feminist Philosophy and Social Theory* (Bloomington, Ind.).

CHAPTER 12

1989 in Eastern Europe

Constitutional Representative Democracy as a 'Return to Normality'?

NEAL ASCHERSON

BIRTH is also a disintegration. Between 1989 and late 1992, the Soviet imperium disintegrated in three stages: in the world of overseas influence and global armed strength, in Eastern and Central Europe, and finally in the Soviet Union itself, which formally ceased to exist in the last days of 1991. The world order of the Cold War, originally highly dangerous but (after about 1960) increasingly stable, fell apart after lasting for just over forty years.

Out of this disintegration was born a large number of nation-states and nationalities. As a proliferation and reassertion of 'the national idea', this was a far bigger event than either the 1848 'Springtime of Nations' or the consequences of the disintegration of four Eurasian empires between 1917 and 1920.

At the same time, these nations—with the possible exceptions of Croatia and Slovenia within the collapsing Yugoslav federation—could not claim the main credit for their own liberation. Poland could not have regained independence in 1918 by her own efforts, through the struggles of Pilsudski's legions, but required the miracle of the simultaneous collapse of the three partitioning powers. In the same way, spontaneous acts of self-liberation like the Romanian revolution, the great popular demonstrations in Prague and Leipzig in late 1989 or even the over-whelming anti-Communist vote returned by the Poles in the semi-free elections that June, were made possible by events and pronouncements in Moscow. Mikhail Gorbachev made it obvious, if not exactly clear, that there would be no further use of Soviet armed force to protect the exist-ing Communist regimes in eastern and central Europe. By the end of 1988, at the latest, it was evident that domestic politics in Warsaw or Budapest really were domestic.

The consequences of this were mostly good. Except for Romania, the revolutions were almost bloodless. The crowds and their leaders were none the less afforded the enormous pride of sensing that their own deci-sion to come out into the street had won them freedom: a pride which was to provide moral capital for subsequent governments. At the same time, there was an underlying confidence that—while police and security forces might open fire—there would be no Soviet intervention, and that whatever was done would not put national survival in peril.

In many cases, birth meant rebirth. For the East Europeans, 1989 trans-formed sham nation-state independence within the Soviet empire into something much more 'real': approximating to popular memory of what independence had meant in the post-Versailles period. For the three Baltic republics within the USSR, the events of 1990–1 restored state-hood formally lost in 1940. Byelorussia, on the other hand, has never had an identifiable independent state existence before (unless we agree with 'Belarus' nationalist intellectuals that the old Grand Duchy of Lithuania before the union with Poland was the medieval Byelorussian state). Ukraine was dubiously independent, under heavy Polish pressure, for a year or so before the Polish–Soviet war of 1920. Croatia had not been independent since the late eleventh century; Slovenia, never. These were genuinely new babies.

What, then, could be meant by 'a return to normality'? Here con-sciousness did not always reflect history, and often distorted it. To gener-alize: there was an almost universal feeling that the revolutions meant a 'return' to 'European standards' (or European culture or civilization), and therefore to broad democratic values to which every single one of these nations or nationalities had aspired—and which had been repressed or denied by Communism. On the other hand, democratic systems (as opposed to aspirations) were certainly not 'normality' in the region before the Communist period. By the late 1930s, Czechoslovakia was almost the only state maintaining a functioning parliamentary democracy, and that operated with restrictions under a strong presidential regime.

This combination of a sense of familiarity with democratic institutions with widespread lack of experience in their operation was to dominate political developments after 1989.

'FORUM POLITICS'

In the immediate aftermath of the revolutions, two contrasting views emerged in the West about the political values of the groups which had made them. One view argued that, broadly speaking, these groups had developed an original approach to politics and social organization during the later years of opposition to Communism, and that they would offer a novel and invigorating contribution to European democratic thinking. The other view, eloquently represented by Timothy Garton Ash of St Antony's College, Oxford, held that there was no novelty here. Instead, the revolutions stood for a simple wish to have what the West was perceived to have already: plural political systems, open societies, and market economies.

Neither view was entirely right. On the one hand, the wish to 'join the West' soon obliterated the chances of new political experiments based on old opposition ideas. The most vivid example of that process was the tidal wave of popular feeling in East Germany which—between the breaching of the Wall in November 1989 and unification in the following year—swamped the small group of reformers who were proposing a 'Third Way' in the form of a cleansed and democratized East German state. On the other hand, the originality of those opposition ideas, and their distinctness from orthodox Western approaches to politics, remain (to this author, at least) undeniable. The word 'forum' was often chosen by such groups to describe themselves. Allowing for differences, I would describe the common elements in their thinking as 'Forum politics'.

This was a creature which first evolved in the 1970s. It arose because of the failure of previous forms of opposition to be effective. Those previous forms included:

- armed struggle (not only insurrections like the Hungarian Revolution of 1956, but the guerrilla fighting which survived in Poland, Ukraine, and the Baltic states into the early 1950s);
- the persistence of wartime underground organizations which were civil as well as military;
- clandestine survivals of pre-war political parties and banned religious groups;

- 'illegal' cells of dissident Party members working for a reformed Communism which would respect 'democratic norms' (variously defined, but seldom including plural party competition which might actually evict a ruling Communist Party from its monopoly of political power).

'Forum politics' was to emerge in several different contexts of opposition. The foundation of KOR (Committee for Workers' Defence) in Poland in 1976 established the most prolific and inventive centre of new ideas. KOR was the intellectual progenitor of the Solidarity trade union and movement which burst into the world in August 1980, and bequeathed to it many of the union's central ideas. In Hungary, selective blows against dissident intellectuals in Budapest in the early 1970s ultimately led to 'Szeta', an independent body ostensibly devoted to the relief of poverty which became a focus of moral and political opposition. Out of the wholesale repressions and purges which followed the tragedy of 1968 in Czechoslovakia evolved Charter 77, a democratic manifesto which collected around it a dauntless, brutally persecuted handful of men and women whose backgrounds ran across a spectrum from neo-Marxism to Catholic orthodoxy. Here too, meetings, debates, and controversies in the underground press produced original ideas. In the German Democratic Republic, very small circles of opposition debate (mostly sheltering in the chinks of the Lutheran Church) came together in the 1980s and finally gave birth to formations like Neues Forum, which briefly took the political initiative as the Honecker regime began to come apart.

Broadly speaking, the Forum people were to lead the revolutionary movements of 1989 throughout central and north-eastern Europe, and to form the first post-revolutionary governments. As they approached that supreme moment (for which 1980–1 in Poland had been the dress rehearsal), they naturally displayed great differences. The Polish opposition, for example, was far the largest, reaching—after the first Solidarity experience—deep into the industrial working class, and inspiring the 'second circulation', an illegal press and publication industry with thousands of titles and hundreds of thousands of readers. The Hungarian groups were relatively tiny, and the openness of Communist administration in the last years of the János Kádár regime posed them difficult moral problems about collaboration and independence.

Other distinctions between 'Forum' movements, some based on the political environment and others more to do with national traditions, could be listed. But the similarities were more striking. Eight of these shared characteristics can be identified:

1. Emphasis on human rights. This related both to President Carter's foreign policy ideology and to the pronouncements at the Vatican II Council of the Catholic Church.

2. Insistence on non-violent methods.

3. A vision of a new type of 'self-managing' society, based on independent social organizations ('civil society') with democratic internal procedures which would arise and operate without reference to the state. Solidarity in Poland emerged from such a project, for 'independent self-managing trade unions'. With this went interest in workers' self-management: a society composed of independent enterprises owned and managed by their own workers.

4. Belief that elements of a self-managing and free society could be built before the overthrow of Communist governments (assumed to be a still remote event), and within the existing system. A free society could gradually grow up within an unfree polity, which would slowly be reduced to a mere husk around a living and expanding bud. The usual model here was the Communist-inspired *comisiones obreras* in Spain: the 'workers' commissions' which were authentic elected bodies growing within the framework of Franco's official trade union structure.

5. Internationalism. The Forum groups were sophisticated and knowledgeable about the outside world. They were antagonistic to raw nationalism of the xenophobic kind, which they distinguished from the healthy will to national independence as a condition for social decency and reform.

6. Liberalism. Attitudes which (in that part of Europe) were once associated with pre-war anticlericals and Jewish intellectuals: support for the rights to abortion, contraception, and divorce, choice of the lay state, support for prison reform, opposition to capital punishment (prevalent throughout the Soviet dominions). But these liberal positions did not prevent alliances of convenience with the Catholic Church to defend the rights of the individual and the independence of the nation. The churches—especially the Catholic Church—were sometimes identified as a variety of the ideal 'self-managing social organization'.

7. Origins. The backgrounds of Forum members were heterogeneous. But certain characteristics turn up very frequently. Many, especially in the early years, came from Communist backgrounds: pre-war Party families of high idealism and sometimes a parent prominent in the Stalinist

bureaucracy. Many had been members of Party youth movements, and had passed through phases of intense belief in the ideology ending in equally intense disillusion. In turn, this disillusion had often led on to ultra-left positions (Trotskyite or semi-Maoist and often related to New Left attitudes in the 1968 upheavals in the West), so that the Communist regimes were under attack at first from the left rather than the right. Forum members tended to be urban—from capital cities rather than provincial centres—and a high proportion of them came from assimilated Jewish families.

8. 'Third Way' ideals. Forum people were not uncritical of the West, which they often described as naïve, crassly materialistic, and plagued by self-doubt about its own achievements and liberties. It was assumed that something better than either the Soviet or Western systems was possible. Workers' self-management was perceived as a concept of property which was neither private nor state but 'public' in the sense that it was directly owned and run by the community.

Many of these ideals clearly had their roots in dissident Marxist thought: the interest in workers' control goes back to the radical Communism of the 1920s. This raises the question whether the Forum people wanted capitalism at all.

There is no easy answer, except to recall that the prospect seemed so remote in the 1970s and even in most of the 1980s that little thought was given to it. Had those groups been asked whether they wanted for their own countries the introduction of mass unemployment, asset strippers, foreign carpet-baggers, stock exchanges, privatization of industry, and heavy falls in living standards, they would of course have rejected them. However, all these opposition movements emerged at a time when economic reform in the direction of market forces was on the agenda of almost all Communist states. Within each Party, the repressive 'old guard' were opposed to reform while the 'liberals' who wanted a more tolerant society favoured it.

Thus the oppositions, in spite of intellectual roots which connected them to fundamentalist Marxism, assumed from the outset that there was a necessary connection between a market economy and greater democracy, and they therefore supported reform. It was evident (as Leszek Kolakowski had demonstrated in Warsaw in the late 1960s) that a reformed economy posited an end to censorship, because a market based on false or restricted information could not function. But it had also emerged from debates among liberal Communist economists that such reforms would cost a painful social price—unemployment and insecurity in the industrial working class. In Czechoslovakia, the consequences of this were being worked out in bargains between the Dubček regime and organized labour at the time of the Soviet-led invasion of August 1968.

The Forum answer to the dilemma was to insist on market reforms, but to argue that empowering the working class through self-management of enterprises would be the appropriate compensation for falling living standards. Writers in the Polish opposition, however, were already beginning to reverse the traditional justification for the nationalization of the means of production. It was now the Communist *nomenklatura*, they suggested, who represented the greedy, selfish clique who would exploit social resources in order to satisfy their own short-term interests at the expense of the community. A private owner might, in contrast, be an authentic representative of that community with a direct interest in serving its needs. This was at first an ironic flourish. As time passed, however, it came to correspond to the instincts of very large numbers of ordinary people—to many more than those who were attracted by experiments in industrial democracy through workers' control.

In the event, Forum policies were never applied with any consequence after the 1989 revolutions. Their proponents were either blown off course by the storm of events and economic pressures, or removed from power by other political rivals, or kept in impotent opposition even after the collapse of Communism. But the 'if'—the question of what democratic innovations might have been made if the Forum people had been allowed their head—remains worth asking.

In the first place, there would certainly have been multi-party systems and constitutional republics: in that, they agreed with all other anti-Communist forces. The emphasis would, however, have lain more heavily on the parliamentary element of democracy and less on the presidential side. The trend towards presidential rule which is now (in early 1992) developing in Poland, Lithuania, south-eastern Europe, and the republics of the Commonwealth of Independent Nations is the antithesis of Forum tradition, which was always anti-authoritarian.

There might well have been experiments in representation. These could have taken the form of parliamentary chambers or upper houses filled wholly or in part of representatives by social or geographical interest groups. There were also highly elaborate practices of election, some of which have survived. (Solidarity, for example, was induced in 1980 to accept a balloting system in which no candidate for office could be elected unless he or she had taken 51 per cent of the votes in the hall.

This noble mechanism turned out to be disastrous. Allowing any remotely well-known candidate to be easily knocked out by his or her opponents, it almost guaranteed the return of individuals so obscure and pallid that the voters could not even identify them.)

Less hypothetical was the general failure of the Forum groups to consider the issue of party formation. This failure has consequences today in the vagueness and looseness of larger parties and the frantic proliferation of smaller ones. Perhaps the 1970s oppositions were not very interested in parties—an indirect hangover from the Marxist element in their genes. But, as in the case of capitalism, they never suspected that an open multi-party system might be functioning within a few years.

A minority in the various Forum groups were in fact members of old, pre-Communist political parties (in Poland, there was an element of the Polish Socialist Party—PPS—in KOR), and the rare discussions about party formation after liberation almost always assumed that some of these traditional movements would revive. But this did not happen—one of the most startling and significant aspects of the post-1989 democracies.

It was supposed that those traditional mass parties which were not tainted by collaboration with either Stalinism or Fascism would emerge again as soon as repression ended: especially the social-democrat parties and the huge peasant movements. Both had usually preserved some kind of continuity through leaderships in Western exile. Both still corresponded in theory to enormous constituencies in Eastern Europe: to the non-Communist industrial proletariat and to the peasantry—collectivized or still (as in the Polish case) largely private smallholders. But their strength in the 1990s has turned out negligible. Instead, power has gone to parties which are not class- or section-based, but ramshackle coalitions united around some general principle: 'national revival' or 'rejoining Europe'.

Especially in the West, modern understanding of political parties remains affected by Marxist thinking about base and superstructure. Well after the 1989 revolutions, it was assumed that party formation would rapidly revert to an essentially class basis. But there is so far little sign that this is taking place, and many signs that the vote of the industrial working classes, for example, is fragmented between numerous medium-sized and small parties. There is a slight but evident preference for nationalist rhetoric (on the grounds that several of the nationalist movements or coalitions are less ruthless and radical about the process of economic transformation), and workers also often show suspicion of Forum politicians on the grounds that they are privileged, intellectual, possibly still guilty of hankering for a purified Marxism, and remote from the arduous daily lives of working people. If any movement can claim to stand for what used to be known as the proletariat, it is the reassembled and sanitized successor parties of Communism. But even they, small as they now are, draw their support at least as much from the jobless ex-members of the Party bureaucracy and their families as from older manual workers.

WHY DID FORUM POLITICS FAIL?

The leading part played by Forum people in the overthrow of the Communist regimes is a matter of history. In Poland, Solidarity's campaign in the June elections of 1989 broke the will of the Polish United Workers' Party. Within a few weeks a Solidarity-led government was in power in which a number of KOR veterans (like Jacek Kuron) were ministers, while many others sat as deputies or senators. However, at the first fully free elections held in October 1991 the successor-groups and associates of Solidarity were badly reduced, and the government coalition which they supported fell.

In Czechoslovakia, Chartists and their allies joined in Civic Forum to provide the revolutionary initiative and leadership in November 1989 and, again, they and their sympathizers dominated the post-revolutionary governments. The playwright Václav Havel became president, Jiri Dienstbier became foreign minister, Petr Uhl—an indomitable figure who had been imprisoned by the Communists as a Trotskyite—became first inspector of prisons and then head of the national news agency, and so on. At the time of writing, political power is still held by a coalition government based upon Civic Forum and its Slovak equivalent, People against Violence. But the unity of Civic Forum is now little more than a memory: new political parties of old complexions are appearing from left to ultra-right; the crisis over Slovak wishes for greater autonomy or secession dominates politics; and the moral authority of President Havel has been badly abraded.

In East Germany, the New Forum group (whose original leaders were mostly modest and politically inexperienced teachers and artists) seemed to acquire the political initiative as the Communist state apparatus began to break up in the autumn and winter of 1989. As late as January 1990, New Forum was still the biggest single political force in the country and at its Leipzig congress claimed some 200,000 members. But from that peak the movement's influence declined steeply and rapidly. At the first and last free GDR elections in March 1990, Alliance 90 (of which New Forum was the largest component) won only 12 out of 400 seats. The pro-unification bloc dominated by the Christian Democrats took 193 seats; even the reformed Communists renamed the Party for Democratic Socialism, took 65.

In Hungary, events went rather differently. Most of the great 1989 demonstrations which heralded the approaching end of Communist power were organized by co-operation between several opposition groups and the reformist wing of the Communists led by Imre Pozsgay. Of those groups, the most vigorous was the Free Democrats, a political party formed mostly from Forum dissidents who had been operating illegally or semi-legally in some cases since the early 1970s. At the centre of this experienced core of oppositionists were Miklos Haraszti and János Kis and their circle, gathered since 1981 around the illegal journal *Beszelö*. In the late 1980s, they had been joined by environmentalists and by Fidesz, an unofficial youth movement which was later to become another political party in close alliance with the Free Democrats. However, the transfer of power was a gradual, relatively undramatic process in Hungary. The Communist reformers retained the initiative and dismantled their own power: a democratic republic was proclaimed on 23 October, and the first free elections took place in the spring of 1990. These elections showed that a tide had already started to turn against Forum politics. After the second round, the Free Democrats emerged with only 24 per cent of the seats, and the government was formed by a coalition led by the Democratic Forum, which won 42.5 per cent of the seats. (In spite of the 'forum' title, the Democratic Forum was in fact a much more conservative and nationalist opposition movement which had been founded only two years before.)

These declines of Forum groups from influence or power had four general reasons:

1. The dilution of original Forum thinking. In several countries of this region of Europe, neo-conservative thinking had begun to influence the opposition in the early 1980s. This was far from traditional nationalism, which was also to make its own revival, but equally remote from the socially conscious Christian Democrat political family on the right in Western Europe. It was vigorously anti-Communist but equally vigorously pro-capitalist: its cult figures were Reagan and Thatcher, Roger Scruton and Irving Kristol. Intolerant of detente, which was seen as a weak-kneed Western temporizing with unreformable Communism, this school of thought strongly influenced the generation which was in its twenties in the early 1980s. Neo-conservative opposition groups were

rare on the ground, so that most of these young people who became politically active were working (printing and distributing clandestine publications, or courier work to the underground) for leaderships with a more leftist, 'Forum'-like ideology. But their ideas, especially the dream of the free-market economy, spread widely.

By contrast, national-conservative politics of the old-fashioned kind, which spread rapidly in the north-western part of 'ex-Soviet Europe' after the 1989 revolutions, were not common in underground opposition. A few such groups (Confederation for an Independent Poland—KPN, for instance) made their appearance in Poland in the late 1970s.

There are several plausible explanations for this lateness. One was a preference for old-fashioned political-party structure, which was obviously almost impossible to construct and operate in conditions of clandestine resistance and illegality. KPN, which surfaced on the streets at the end of 1980 and, by the time that martial law was imposed in December 1981, had acquired a substantial following, was the first entirely new and authentic political party to appear in Poland for over forty years. A second explanation is the way in which, especially after 1956 and the end of Stalinism, many Communist regimes adopted and refashioned traditional nationalism for their own purposes. There would have been little chance for an anti-Communist, anti-Semitic, and ultra-patriotic opposition group to compete successfully with the racialist and chauvinist demagogy of the Polish regime in the late 1960s, when General Moczar made his bid for power. The same was true of Ceausescu's Romania, on a grand scale. In the GDR an artificial cult of Prussia and Prussian authoritarianism was established in the late 1970s. In Czechoslovakia, after 1968, the Husak regime adopted a highly 'patriotic' and xenophobic rhetoric to justify its programme of cutting the country off from contact with the West and suppressing all criticism. This ability of post-Stalinist Communist parties to mimic authoritarian nationalism was to have astonishing consequences in south-eastern Europe after the 1989 revolutions, to which I will return. The point here is to suggest that the ground on which unreconstructed nationalism used to stand was occupied by ruling Communist parties in the decades after 1956, with the incidental effect of further discrediting nationalism in the eyes of the intellectual opposition.

2. Economic circumstances were a second factor in the failure of Forum politics to put down roots. The post-revolutionary governments found themselves in a world tormented by recession and burdened by debt. Their traditional Soviet market was collapsing. The new economic

orthodoxy in the West, as interpreted by President Reagan and Mrs Thatcher, made a second Marshall Plan on the model of the 1947 European Recovery Programme unthinkable. In these circumstances, the International Monetary Fund and to a lesser extent the private banks were able to lay down the policy guidelines they required. These left almost no room for experiments in 'Third Way' patterns of social ownership or workers' self-management. The odd trace of Forum thinking survived, as in the early versions of the Polish privatization programme which gave the workers in privatized enterprises a large slice of the initial share-cake. But in general the Forum people found themselves beggars who could not be choosers, even in countries like Czechoslovakia whose hard-currency debt was relatively slight.

3. Public opinion was not really prepared to support Forum politics. Events in Germany showed this reluctance all too plainly. Alliance 90 and New Forum offered the voters a purified and transfigured East German Utopia. But the citizenry took the view that they had been suffering as subjects of one grand social experiment ever since 1945, and they had no intention of volunteering as laboratory rats for another. Across the border was another Germany which worked, and which invited them to join it. They joined, first by mass flight as the borders weakened and then, in the early spring of 1990, by voting overwhelmingly for the unification of Germany.

4. There were also popular doubts about the Forum people themselves. After the revolutions, they were accused of remoteness from the concerns of ordinary people, attributed to their intellectual origins. (There were few grounds for this. They had shared the common experience, with the exception that almost all of them had stood up for their opinions in public and been imprisoned for it. Remoteness was a matter of personality: Tadeusz Mazowiecki, Poland's first non-Communist prime minister, was a shy Catholic journal editor with no taste for publicity, whereas President Havel of Czechoslovakia—no less intellectual—turned out to have a popular touch.) They were from time to time criticized for Jewishness, even when they were not Jewish, and—more subtly—identified as people whose minds had been formed by variants of Marxism rather than by the Western type of society which the population usually wanted to emulate.

As time passed, these makers of the revolution began to pay a political penalty for the economic reforms they were carrying out. The first euphoria of the revolution ebbed slowly away, and the population became less ready to suffer frozen wages, soaring prices, and collapsing employment in order to pay the entrance fee to capitalist prosperity. Moreover, the makers of government economic policy—Leszek Balcerowicz in Poland, or Václav Klaus in Czechoslovakia—adopted a particularly ruthless approach, based on what they imagined (wrongly) to be the practice of Thatcherism or Reaganism in Britain and the United States. This fanatical faith in the free market worked reasonably well as a means of stabilizing the currency at its 'real' exchange value, encouraging private small trading, bringing supply into balance with demand by the abolition of retail subsidies, and reducing budget deficits. It was to be much less successful as an approach to reforming the industrial economy, and its political cost was extremely high. By 1992, the experience of liberation from Communism followed by an apparently endless plunge of living standards was producing widespread political disillusion and cynicism about the democratic process. Participation in elections began to fall away steeply, and the political balance began to move towards the more traditional Right, towards leaders less inclined to radical reform at the cost of popularity and more inclined to symbolic politics (the 'outing' of ex-Communists still in public service, and rhetoric which made foreigners, immigrant refugees, and sometimes 'the Jews' responsible for the nation's problems).

'NATIONAL-COMMUNISM'

Forum politics was much less in evidence, before and after 1989, in the southern and eastern parts of the old Soviet imperium. In that zone, roughly speaking, little organized opposition had existed beyond a few handfuls of exceedingly brave individuals whose names were almost entirely unknown to their fellow citizens (unless they listened to Western broadcasts in their own language). This was due partly to the ferocity of repression but also to the relative underdevelopment of those nations as political societies.

It is possible to draw a line starting at Dubrovnik on the Adriatic, and running roughly north-east between Montenegro and Serbia on one side and Bosnia and Croatia on the other, up along the border between Romania and Hungary, into Ruthenia and up in a direction which would divide the western Ukraine (Lvov), from the Ukraine of Kiev and Donbas. On the southern side of that line, ruling Communist parties have generally contrived to pass through a process of rapid repentance and respraying and to emerge as freely elected but authoritarian nationalist parties still in control of their states. The Ramiz Alia regime in Albania, the Milosevic regime in Serbia and the Iliescu regime in Romania all followed this model, and so did Bulgaria until the elections in October 1991. Leonid Kravchuk, President of Ukraine, is another ex-Communist nationalist: elected by the central and eastern parts of his country, but not by that western region whose political history and allegiance has been very different.

This line corresponds quite closely to the eastern boundary of the old Habsburg Empire, and to the dividing line between Orthodox Christianity and the other churches. It offers a temptation to shallow geopolitical chatter about the link between the Orthodox Churches and autocracy or—even shallower—between the Catholic Church and democracy. The correspondence cannot be a simple one; after all, as I have already pointed out, ruling Communist parties north of the line (Poland, Czechoslovakia, East Germany) have also found it easy to play the patriotic-authoritarian card. All the same, the line is there, and its relationship to those historical lines of demarcation cannot be entirely accidental.

THE COMMUNIST LEGACY

The Bolshevik Revolution is over. When it ended can be debated: in the narrow sense, perhaps, in 1928 when Stalin finally made himself dictator; in the broader sense, when the Soviet system in what had been the Russian empire collapsed in the course of 1991. The French Revolution ended narrowly in 1794, broadly with the defeat of Napoleon in 1815. Both, however, left Europe changed: transiently and permanently. Three post-Communist effects seem especially significant for the future of democracy:

1. Damaged societies. Many of the nations emerging from up to fifty years of Soviet control show widespread societal damage. Little of the traditional, informal fabric remains. The totalitarian claim of the Party means that authentic, self-managing civil society scarcely survived at all. In consequence, there were few intermediate nodes of loyalty between the basic level of the family and the abstract level of the nation (a value usually immune to Communist interpretations and appropriations). The exceptions were—in some countries—the Christian churches. In regions where a strong socialist movement had existed before 1939 (Saxony, Bohemia, parts of industrial Silesia) the Communist Party also acted as such a node at the outset, but rapidly discredited itself after the onset of 'Stalinization' in 1948.

In these impoverished societies, stripped of their traditional sources of energy and spontaneity, it has been difficult to construct durable political movements which are not built round either 'the nation' or the personality of one ambitious individual. Equally, it has been hard to restore an environment in which the small entrepreneur can be seen as a normal member of a rich and varied society, rather than as a swindler profiting from shortages.

2. The dream of development. Pre-war Communists in Eastern Europe hoped to fuse an enlightened nationalism with an imitation of Stalin's industrialization programme in the Soviet Union. They perceived Europe between the world wars as a continent divided along colonial lines: an industrialized and wealthy West dominating a beggarly East confined to the role of provider of cheap raw materials, food, and labour-power. Socialism, they reasoned, could overcome this dependency and all its ills (rural overpopulation, lack of industry) by constructing a national industrial base in conditions of autarky and protection. The outcome would be not only a strong nation-state whose independence had economic reality, but eventually a new, educated, Communist industrial proletariat to take its place in the world revolution.

It would be dangerous to think that this sort of vision has been forgotten. Eastern Europe is again threatened by deindustrialization, as the 'socialist sectors' of the economies are privatized and exposed to open competition, and the possibility of almost colonial degrees of dependence on Western demand is all too real again. The temptation of combining nationalism, protectionism, and autocracy (the myth of the Man on the White Horse) is still there, waiting off-stage for its chance.

3. The deep-freeze. Eastern and Central Europe in 1939 contained numerous disputes: national hatreds, minority problems, challenged frontiers, racial discriminations against Jews and gypsies. The advent of Soviet Communism had the effect of throwing these disputes into a sort of deep-freeze. They had not been solved or even talked through, but it was agreed that in this new type of society they no longer existed. The revolutions of 1989, and indeed the political relaxation which had taken place in Poland and Hungary before then, began to thaw them all out again. They proved to retain much of their venom and their power to contaminate the political environment, even after nearly fifty years of enforced concealment. In addition, the Soviet colonial system kept the members of the 'socialist community' in extraordinary national isolation, in spite of its propaganda about fraternity and solidarity. Compared to the volume of

Western travel, the number of Poles or Czechs who had visited one another's countries or spent any time there was infinitesimal.

The strength of this preserved toxin is shown with terrible clarity by the Serb–Croat conflict, with its retinue of atrocities and propaganda lies. Apart from the Yugoslav tragedy, however, the new governments of Eastern and Central Europe have insisted that they do not wish to revive obsolete national exclusivity, and are anxious to form alliances, customs unions, and ultimately political mergers. The dispute between Romania and Hungary over the Magyar minority has not, after all, escalated into violence, as was predicted a few years ago. The inflammatory problem of Polish minorities in Lithuania and Byelorussia has so far been handled carefully and without demagogy on the Polish side. But the toxin is none the less present again in the ground-water of society. The transmission of prejudice and ignorance to yet another generation must remain a danger-ous liability for the survival of democracy.

THE OUTLOOK FOR POLITICAL DEMOCRACY

The will to constitutional democracy is almost universally present, in the nations emancipated in 1989–90. At the time of writing, almost all of them have regimes whose form is constitutional and democratic: popular sovereignty, elected parliaments, plural political systems, the rule of law under written constitutions. Undeniably, democracy is less of a reality in some states (Romania, for example) than in others. But none has yet suc-cumbed to dictatorship, although the trend towards stronger presidential powers is unmistakable.

The period of 'Forum politics' is almost over, and with it the last con-tinuity with the period of Communism and of opposition to Communism. At the same time, the process of reconstructing the webs of informal association which make up civil society has gone powerfully forward. But the demolition and replacement of the Communist eco-nomic structures are setting up great social tensions, and these tensions—acting upon the inheritance of untreated prejudices and fears from the distant past and upon the dangers of gross international exploitation in the future—form the central threat to democratic development.

A race is in progress. This race is between the attainment of at least the first tokens of new prosperity and the exhaustion of public patience with deprivation and poverty. If patience runs out first, the chances for vigor-ous democracy are poor. The consequence—already visible in Russia—will be political apathy and cynicism on the part of the vast majority, and the uncontrolled growth of fanatical *groupuscules* in the resulting vacuum. That would be a course set towards disaster.

It is unreasonable to expect a future of calm, stable parliamentarism in this part of Europe. Politics will be turbulent, and at times authoritarian, and the Man on the White Horse will probably ride again. At the same time, this is not pre-1939 Eastern Europe revived for another season. The mass of educated, capable, sophisticated citizens—which scarcely existed in those distant years—will defend its basic liberties and its own opportunities. It would be wise to hope for a rather 'Italian' future for the region. I mean countries in which a quarrelsome and unreliable parliamentary surface conceals a hard-working citizenry. They seldom pay taxes or obey a law unquestioningly, but they are constructing a general prosperity without reference to politicians. They are both democrats and patriots, but they have no illusions about prime ministers or fellow countrymen. With them, a good and lasting European peace can be built.

CHAPTER 13

Conclusion

JOHN DUNN

W HY is democracy today the overwhelmingly dominant, and increasingly the well-nigh exclusive, claimant to set the standard for legitimate political authority? It takes some imaginative concentration to register quite what an extraordinary fact this really is. Nothing else in the history of the world which had, as far as we can tell, quite such local, casual, and concrete origins enjoys the same untrammelled authority for ordinary human beings today, and does so virtually across the globe. Each of the great world religions, to be sure, began from highly specific and local stories, and continues to exert a profound authority for at least some of its own worshippers. But despite the insistent hopes of hundreds of millions of the devotees of these drastic movements of thought and sentiment, the religious history of the world has remained intractably plural throughout. In contrast with this enduring plurality, the sciences of nature, since the seventeenth century, have had considerably greater success in establishing a unified and cosmopolitan standard of practical truth. But the authority of scientific claims has never gone uncontested. It is probably fair to say that we have a far less clear conception today of just why scientific enquiry has proved so effective than we supposed that we possessed thirty years ago, and, in part in consequence, that we are now altogether more hesitant to presume that current scientific findings are either as clearly valid or as universal in their validity as then seemed evident. In the case of democracy, moreover, the completeness of its triumph is in some respects remarkably recent. Even a dozen years ago its claims to furnish a common standard for modern political legitimacy had more the air of a shared verbal talisman than of a real agreement in practical judgement on any concrete topic—and least of all on its ostensible and urgent subject-matter of how power should be allocated and exercised in contemporary political communities.

Today, at least for the present, things look very different. We may well doubt that they really *are* quite so different; and I shall argue in conclusion that we are certainly well advised to do so. But to argue this with any cogency, we must first at least try to give some real explanation of why they have come to seem as they do today.

Let me begin with the bizarreness of the fact itself. Democracy, we must remember, was the name of a type of political regime first durably established in the Greek city-state of Athens by the aristocrat Kleisthenes in 508/507 BC. We do not in fact know that it was the term which Kleisthenes himself employed to describe this regime (or even that it was so applied by anyone at all at the time, or perhaps for some decades later). We can be quite certain that it was *not* the name of a type of regime already confidently regarded by anyone as especially just, or especially effective, or peaceful, or deserving of obedience and loyalty, and advocated to his fellow citizens by Kleisthenes precisely because it was so regarded—commended, that is, for its proven ideological potency or its evident rational force.

The social and political relations amongst the Athenians had, of course, been sharply modified almost a century earlier by the reforms of Solon. But the only role model for Kleisthenes mentioned by the historian Herodotus was his namesake and maternal grandfather Kleisthenes, tyrant of the smaller Greek city-state of Sicyon; and the lesson so imbibed was one of factional vindictiveness rather than democratic generosity (Herodotus 5. 67–9). This is of considerable importance, since what we know of Kleisthenes' own past and political intentions makes it evident that he adopted the political programme now indelibly associated with his name, for the first time, in circumstances of personal political defeat in bitter factional struggle with his fellow aristocrats; that in this struggle what he did was to take the people at large, the massively unaristocratic majority of the male Athenians, into his own faction; and that to consolidate the new political regime he found it necessary to reorganize the social units of Athenian society and the political geography of Attica with some thoroughness. No one in Athens at the time could have begun to imagine that what they were doing, in this hazardous and anxious flurry of political innovation, was to inaugurate a genuinely cosmopolitan criterion for political legitimacy for all human beings two and a half millennia later.

Democracy for the Athenians, from the days of Pericles to those of

Demosthenes a full century later, was a system of citizen self-rule. The balance of political power and influence within Athens shifted at intervals over the century and three-quarters of the democracy's history; and the institutions themselves changed quite extensively (Hansen 1991). But for at least a century, with only the briefest of extra-constitutional interruptions, it was literally true that the citizens of Athens ruled themselves. Any citizen of Athens who lived out a normal adult life was likely, sooner or later, to find himself acting for a day as head of the official executive body of the Athenian state, the council, receiving and conferring with foreign envoys as the representative of Athens, or preparing the agenda for formal meetings of the council or assembly (Hansen 1991: 141, 250–3). No citizen of Athens could occupy this role for more than a day in his entire life. Every citizen of Athens was equally entitled to attend, vote, and speak at meetings of the assembly, which decided all the great issues of state: the making of war or peace, the passing of laws, and the political exile or death of individual leaders; and did so by simple majority vote. Every Athenian citizen who reached the age of 30 was eligible (and expected) to staff one of the multitude of official positions, and to sit and decide in the courts which adjudicated on the outcome of individual disputes and criminal or political prosecutions, or confirmed or overruled novel items of legislation passed by the assembly. By the fourth century, moreover, the most important of these activities were paid for at a daily rate which ensured that no Athenians would be precluded from engaging in them by the economic cost of doing so, and may well have given some Athenians a direct economic incentive to take part in public affairs.

Athens did, of course, have political leaders, men usually from aristocratic or wealthy backgrounds, or with professional rhetorical skills, who devoted much of their lives to political persuasion, diplomatic strategy, or military command. It was even possible for some of these leaders to live in part off, as well as for, politics. In the second half of the fourth century the city had acquired a small number of more permanent public officials, whose expertise gave them a measure of real political influence and who were elected rather than chosen by lot (Hansen 1991: 149, 160). But all of these comparatively professional features of Athenian politics and public administration were seen (and distrusted) as encroachments on the authentically democratic structure of the great bulk of Athenian political life. Political leaders might sway the assembly by special oratorical gifts or carefully honed rhetorical skills. Sometimes, naturally, such leaders also had more or less committed followers. But none of them could ever confidently rely on the disciplined political retinue of a modern political party to secure their ascendancy for them on a regular basis. Athenian military leaders were elected, since Athens was often at war, and its citizens understandably preferred to follow into battle individual generals in whom they had some confidence. But they fully recognized that election was an aristocratic method, which favoured the well-born, the prominent, and the wealthy, and they went to startling lengths to ensure that the great bulk of Athenian public roles were allocated instead by the incontestably democratic procedure of the casting of lots—by random selection from all eligible citizens rather than by the natural workings of social influence.

What was the point of this extraordinary invention? The main Athenian answer to this question was clear and relatively constant over time. The point of democracy was the freedom which it made possible. It, and it alone, could and did enable the citizens of Athens to live in freedom: not simply to be their own rulers on a remarkably full-time basis, but also to live as they collectively and individually chose for themselves, and to protect that personal opportunity unstintingly against any forces, either from inside Athens itself or from elsewhere, which appeared to them to threaten it. In thinking of freedom every citizen of Athens had a harsh and vivid contrast permanently in mind: the condition of slavery. Very many of them had slaves themselves; and those who did not, as Aristotle sneered, often treated their own wives and children virtually as slaves to make up for the deficit (*Politics* 1323^a, Aristotle 1977: 528).

What Kleisthenes did was to turn the relatively unorganized majority of the free male inhabitants of Attica for the first time into an entity capable of systematic political agency over time (Manville 1990), and capable, as it proved, of protecting its own freedom for well over a century by this new mode of acting. He turned a motley, insecure, and essentially powerless aggregation of residents in a vaguely demarcated territory into a proud and self-confident sovereign people. For Athenian democrats, the citizens of Athens, the *demos*, constituted a single community of free men (with their legally dependent women and children—Manville 1990: 13). The public political life of those citizens, the endless seething activity, the myriad independent and unconcerted decisions of its courts and magistrates and public assembly, served not merely as external protection or guarantee for that freedom; it also exemplified both their own individual freedom and their collective solidarity in the most graphic fashion every day of every year of the democracy's history.

Both then and now critics of the democracy saw its realities very differently. For Aristotle, and still more for his teacher Plato, the systematic emphasis on citizen equality was itself a repudiation of the force and authority of the real qualities of human beings, a dishonest or absurd denial of the practical importance of genuine excellences or true depravities, and a denial with predictably disastrous consequences. At least for Plato—Aristotle on this point was more equivocal—the political processes of democracy were intrinsically corrupting; and the effective freedom to do as one likes, which in Athens in his view extended even to the female, slave, and animal populations (*Republic* 562b–563c, Plato 1987: 2. 304–10), was inherently destructive even for its supposed beneficiaries.

For the Swiss political theorist Benjamin Constant over two thousand years later (Constant 1988: 313–28), the freedom which ancient democracies sought (and which Athens very largely achieved) was the collective solidarity in public agency of the citizenry as a body. This freedom, the liberty of the ancients, had little or nothing to do with the privileges valued by modern populations, 'the liberty of the moderns', to do as they severally feel inclined, a liberty which rested principally on secure institutional guarantees of individual rights. Even Constant acknowledged, however, that there was greater concern in practice for personal rights in Athens, most populous, wealthiest, and most commercial of the Greek city-states. But in the great teeming revolutionary metropolis of Paris, and in face of the grim recent trauma of the Terror, he insisted vehemently on the blunt impossibility of re-establishing in a modern territorial commercial society the same rapt, indefatigable, and almost universally shared popular commitment to political agency at the centre of the state, and on the fearsome costs to individual freedoms and rights that the futile quest to re-establish it must necessarily inflict. For its Greek participants ancient liberty, in his eyes, was more rewarding in what it provided and less punitive in what it took away than any attempt to revive it would inevitably prove. In the modern commercial societies of late eighteenth- and early nineteenth-century Western Europe, the purely protective contribution of ancient democratic institutions was less urgently needed; and when and where it was needed (as, for example, in the face of Napoleon Bonaparte and his armies) it was overwhelmingly less likely to prove effective. For Constant, therefore, the mirage of ancient liberty—participatory democracy as the ceaseless exemplification of community in collective public action—was a malign survival in the politics of the modern commercial West, an ideological residue of a very distant world and one which could now do nothing but harm. Constant's contrast between ancient and modern liberty was less a detached demonstration of the existence of a firm and reliable fissure between ancient and modern politics than a purposeful attempt to domesticate the imaginative legacy of ancient democracy for the world of the modern state and the market economy: an effort to establish just such a barrier. The prospects for complete success in such domestication were never very high. But it is, for the present, Constant's severely domesticated interpretation, the democracy of the moderns, which has won such a remarkable victory.

What ended democracy in Athens, however, was not the criticism of philosophers but the military power of the kingdom of Macedon, and what ended independent democratic rule throughout the Mediterranean world over the next two centuries was the far greater and more enduring military power of Rome. The historian Herodotus may have exaggerated the impact of democratic freedom on Athenian fighting capacities, whether against the Persians or against their fellow Greeks (Herodotus 5. 78). But what is certain is that for a century and three-quarters the democratic citizenry of Athens proved as well able to take care of themselves in land and naval warfare as they did in establishing and maintaining their common political life. It was not the distinctive military vulnerability of ancient democracy which eliminated it so durably from the subsequent political history of the European world, but simply the distinctive military potency of Macedon and Rome.

Some historians of Rome have recently argued that it too was really a democracy, since the pursuit of a career of public office and political leadership within the ranks of the Roman aristocracy required them at regular intervals to secure election by the popular assemblies of Roman citizens. But the parallel in this respect with the residually aristocratic political and military leadership of Athens' democracy is weak and misleading. Until the Roman armies chose to follow their generals and destroy the political authority of the republic, the consuls and lesser magistrates of Rome may have required a degree of intermittent popularity to pursue their lofty careers successfully. But once they had secured their offices in each instance, they were able to wield the authority which these conferred with massive self-assurance; and they did so, for the most part, with wary attention to the susceptibilities of their fellow members of the senatorial nobility, but with relative indifference to those of the great plebeian majority of Rome's citizens.

By Athenian standards Rome was far from being a democracy. But for most of its history, from the death of its last king up to the triumph of Octavian, it was indisputably a republic. The role of the people in choosing their own rulers was an enduring theme in the tradition of republican government, a democratic element in what was often an overbearing and markedly undemocratic system of authority. (We have seen that even the judgement that this was indeed a democratic element was not one which the Greeks of the fourth century really shared.) After the fall of imperial Rome, the theme of popular choice of magistrates (the special merits of elections as a means of selecting rulers or public officials) resurfaced recurrently, wherever social and political circumstances rendered it practically attractive, most notably in the cities of medieval Italy and in the victorious Parliamentary armies at the close of the English Civil War. But it had to do so, in most settings, in the teeth of a devastatingly inegalitarian social order, founded on the brutal extraction of agrarian surplus from a huge and heavily dependent rural labour force. (It was no accident that the setting in which the rich democratic life of the Greek *polis* was reinvented most evocatively in medieval or early modern Europe was in the units closest to them in socio-economic and political character, the independent city-republics of Italy, with their thriving commerce and prosperous rural hinterlands: the territories epitomized in Ambrogio Lorenzetti's great fresco of the blessings of good government on the walls of the Council Chamber in the Palazzo Communale in Siena.)

But although the distinctive appeal and dignity of republican government remained a vivid presence in the ideological history of Western Europe, it was not on the whole a presence conspicuous for its political effectiveness. By the middle of the eighteenth century none of the most dynamic and militarily powerful states of Europe was still a republic, let alone a democratic republic. But a mere half-century later, bemusingly and erratically, the tide had plainly begun to turn. It turned first, of course, not in Western Europe itself but amongst elements of the European diaspora, scattered up and down the eastern seaboard of North America. (Even here the victorious colonial war of independence produced as its enduring political legacy a state form which its most influential shaper and interpreter, James Madison, was at pains to insist was in no sense a democracy (Ball 1988: 59–60, 76–8).) But the tide turned too, quite soon afterwards, in the most sophisticated and urbane metropolis of any of Europe's absolute monarchies, in the great teeming city of Paris, the very epicentre of aristocratic *douceur de vivre*.

To understand why democracy today has won such a comprehensive ideological triumph, we need to separate two components which have recently come together with considerable momentum, but which may well prove less adhesive to one another in the longer run. The first is the imaginative appeal and the sheer human force of democracy as an idea. The second is the severely practical viability of a particular compound of economic, social, and political arrangements. If we look back to the second half of the eighteenth century and ask why it is that a political conception that seemed so comprehensively crushed by historical experience could revive so dramatically and begin to turn the tables so thoroughly on its adversaries, the contrast between appeal and viability gives a decisive clue to the answer. What was new in the eighteenth century was certainly not the appeal of the idea of citizen self-rule, and least of all so to the more drastically subjugated elements of European populations. What was new was the relative fragility of the system of subjugation. In the long term, a good half-century and more later, the same economic and social factors which made the system of subjugation fragile had begun to establish conditions in which democratic republican rule was not merely vividly appealing in comparison with dynastic monarchy but also far more sturdily viable.

Sophisticated modern historians, with their emphasis on the history of language, and on the shifts in conceiving and imagining political possibility which language carries within it, may offer acute guidance on the intense political process through which the imaginative appeal of democracy resurfaced so prominently in France and elsewhere, and the conditions of its practical viability came to be explored so arrestingly. But there is some danger of their distracting us from the attempt to grasp those conditions of practical viability themselves, an issue not helpfully explored through the history of words and their use. What has led—and led so recently—to the triumph of modern representative constitutional democracy over such a large proportion of the globe is not a sudden surge in the intrinsic imaginative appeal of its constitutive ideas, but a fresh and increasingly undeniable lesson about the practical viability of its only significant surviving cosmopolitan competitor as a theory of legitimate rule, the self-conscious legacy of Russia's Bolshevik Revolution. (The intractable plurality of the world's religious history will continue to mean that what still remain some of the most dynamic competitors as theories of legitimate rule or dissidence in particular territories (Islamic, Christian, Buddhist, Hindu) have no hope whatever of winning a genuinely cosmopolitan imaginative authority.)

For the moment, therefore, one particular model of democratic rule, the modern secular constitutional representative democracy firmly founded on an essentially market economy, dominates the political life of the modern world. How should we understand the nature of that state and the circumstances that have brought it to this dizzy (and perhaps precarious) pre-eminence? We must focus first on the fact that it is a modern state, a legal order of political authority as much at home on the scale of a vast land mass like the United States of America or Canada or India as on that of a tiny city-republic like Singapore. The democracy of Athens was made possible by the creation of the Athenian *demos* as an effective political agent. It was preserved militarily, for as long as it lasted, by the military and naval efficacy of the *demos* in arms; and its day-to-day political life continuously displayed the intimacy and intensity (if by no means always the harmony) of its common commitments.

Modern states are not at all like this. The idea of the modern state is a key, if somewhat treacherous, element in the practical reality of every modern state. That idea was first painfully constructed in Western Europe, above all in France and Britain, between the mid-sixteenth and mid-seventeenth centuries (Skinner 1989), in face of the cumulative horrors of religious warfare. It saw the political core of a given society's life as lying in a common structure of authority which incorporated all the rightful denizens of a given territory but which was quite distinct in character from either subjects or rulers, from the people or the government or the lands over which the latter exerted control. Greek political thinkers sometimes contrasted the authority of the laws (the *nomoi*) with that of the less trustworthy human agents (*demos*, oligarchs, or tyrants) who held temporary dominance in a particular community; and fourth-century Athenians might on occasion claim that it was the laws (rather than the *demos*) which held ultimate sway in Athens itself (Hansen 1991: 303). But what they meant by this claim was in each instance something quite specific and simple about the continuity and dependability of political life in a particular locality, not something dramatically abstract about the very nature of that political life. It is important to recognize that the idea of the modern state was constructed, painstakingly and purposefully, above all by Jean Bodin and Thomas Hobbes, for the express purpose of denying that any given population, any people, had either the capacity or the right to act together for themselves, either independently of or against their sovereign. The central point of the concept was to deny the very possibility that any *demos* (let alone one on the demographic scale of a European territorial monarchy) could be a genuine political agent, could *act* at all, let alone act with sufficiently continuous identity and practical coherence for it to be able to rule itself. In Hobbes's eyes the imaginative legacy of the ancient world, even that of Roman republicanism and of Aristotle's severely qualified enthusiasm for democracy, was just as intensely and inherently subversive and anarchic as the legacy of an activist Christianity in a society in which broad masses of the population now had both the elementary skills and the effective opportunity to read and interpret the Word of God for themselves. The idea of the modern state was invented precisely to repudiate the possible coherence of democratic claims to rule or even take genuinely political action, whether these claims were advanced under secular or religious inspiration.

But if that was the task for which it was invented, that has hardly been a full description of the purpose which it has since served. Even a dozen years ago, the claim that it was the *demos* which held political authority, the people who was sovereign, was a shibboleth virtually throughout the world. Yet if the people are almost everywhere the supposed sovereign, it is palpably not anywhere the people who are in fact ruling. If an accredited diplomat goes to pay a formal call on the American or Russian or Egyptian, or even the Swiss, state, it is not a randomly selected (and day by day invariably a different) member of the population at large whom they can expect to encounter. In the guise in which it has triumphed as a state form for any length of time in any setting since 1776, democracy has been very evidently representative rather than participatory. More participatory institutions of collective decision-making still persist in some of the Swiss cantons; and most existing representative democracies have appreciably more participatory institutions for taking public decisions on far more local questions.

But since at least the middle of the seventeenth century it has been the practical character of the state which has increasingly set the terms for institutional candidates for legitimate political authority the world over. It is its authority which is to be judged legitimate or to be denied legitimacy. The *demos* has sometimes erupted dramatically into its comfortable routines; individual interest groups and bodies of opinion amongst the *demos* have challenged its entitlement to rule, more or less without interruption and in every sovereign political community over a large part of that time. But once the eruptions have come to an end, it is always somehow the state that continues to rule.

Representative democracy is democracy made safe for the modern state: democracy converted from unruly and incoherent master to docile and dependable servant. To an Athenian eye this version of democracy would seem not so much tamed (as Aristotle, and his subsequent admirers and followers amongst the advocates of a mixed constitution, hoped to tame it), as *neutered*—denatured, and deprived of all generative energy and force of its own. But this is a little too brisk, since representative democracy has proved with some pertinacity to be well able to combine the practical viability of a relatively coherent system of political authority (a modern state) with the more insinuating appeals of the idea of popular self-rule. To its critics, this deftly synthetic capacity has always seemed a monstrous conjuring trick. It certainly has its illusionist elements. But, *faute de mieux*, it may well still be a conjuring trick which any sober and honourable judge can only hope will continue to work. What we know now is how easy it is to do unimaginably and durably much worse.

To understand the success of such a practical conjuring trick, it is essential to assess just what sorts of disbelief have had to be suspended. Modern constitutional representative democracy, where it has worked effectively for any length of time, has on the whole secured three separate and humanly compelling political goods. In the first place it has provided moderate government, a system of rule which minimizes the direct risks which governmental power poses to the physical security of individual subjects and groups of subjects. (This was a service for which the first great theorists of the modern state massively underestimated the need, and which the history of twentieth century state power on other constitutional models has amplified appallingly.) A more expansive description of this service, signalled in the American Bill of Rights or the French Declaration of the Rights of Man and the Citizen, would be that modern representative democracy had guaranteed to its citizens the effective protection of their human rights. But this is both a more exaggerated and a far less clear claim; and it is also less obvious that it has been realized anything like as extensively in practice.

The second major political service which modern representative democracy has furnished to its citizens is a modest measure of governmental responsibility to the governed. Even Aristotle could readily see the point of such responsibility. But that point is at its most searingly obvious when the service is most crisply and arrogantly withheld. In the face of the sheer domestic power of the modern state, its ability to intrude into and devastate the lives of all its citizens, this is a very considerable service indeed. It cannot ensure prosperity or popular contentment. But what it can guarantee, for as long as the immediate civil and military servants of the state sustain and protect its constitutional order, is a collective security against a notably disagreeable common risk, the risk of permanent subjection to a keenly resented apparatus of rule. (Even within a working constitutional order, of course, it can only do even this where the resentment in question runs persistently across a clear majority of the electing body. Representative democracy as such is no sure protection for the common interests of either Catholics or Protestants in Northern Ireland, Catalans or Basques in Spain, Tamils in Sri Lanka,

Muslims in India.) But this second form of protection against the risks of governmental harm has been one of the major goals of political action across the world in the twentieth century—the main ideological premiss of the collapse of alien rule in the great European empires, in Eastern Europe, and the Soviet Union itself, and a permanent basis for challenge to the existing territorial integrity of most of even the advanced states in the world.

The third major political service which modern representative democracy has rendered to its citizens is slyer and less explicit than the first two, and probably also somewhat less secure. Representative democracy is definitely democracy made safe for the modern state. But it is also, as these first two services indicate, an appreciable modification of the character of that state, and one which renders the state itself, whose core justification is to enhance the security of its individual members, far less of a real threat over time to precisely that security. But the third political service which representative democracy has provided is one which modifies both democracy and state: which draws the sting of two extreme and potentially perilous ideas. In brief, it makes democracy safe for a modern capitalist economy; but it also makes a modern state distinctly safer for a modern capitalist economy.

This would have come as a very considerable surprise to the Greeks. Even moderate critics of ancient democracy, like Aristotle, saw unmodified democracy as the direct rule of the poorer and less well-born majority of citizens over the wealthier and more aristocratic, and conspicuously failed to applaud it for being such. The political war cry of the democratic party across the Greek city-states was the demand for division of lands and the abolition of debts: a direct and vehement threat to the property rights which had emerged from the economic and social history of individual Greek communities. In Athens itself, following the reforms of Solon, this threat was kept firmly off the political agenda, with virtually no interruption, for a good two and half centuries, and despite the bitter domestic political conflict unleashed by the disasters of the Peloponnesian War. But from the time of Kleisthenes onwards this determined exclusion was in effect a deliberate political choice of the Athenian citizens themselves. Critics of the democracy viewed with grave misgivings the resting of all property rights in the last instance on the continuing political choice of the less wealthy members of the community. Just the same misgivings were forcibly expressed whenever the demand for democratization resurfaced in subsequent centuries: in the Putney Debates within the Parliamentary armies at the end of the English

Civil War, in revolutionary Paris, and in the debates in Britain leading up to the Great Reform Bill of 1832. It is not hard to see why.

In the long run, however, these more recent critics have proved no better prophets than their ancient predecessors were of the performance of Athenian democracy. In less strident terms, nevertheless, their argument remains a prominent theme in contemporary politics, pressed, for example, over recent decades by right-wing assailants of the spending patterns (and attendant fiscal exactions) of the American or British or Swedish legislatures. If the principal contribution of modern constitutional representative democracy has been to make both the modern state and the standard of democratic legitimacy compatible with the operating requirements of an international and domestic economic order founded on private ownership and market exchange—to reconcile the needs of capitalist production with the practical and ideological requirements of effective rule in the modern world—it is easy to exaggerate the completeness of this reconciliation. The most intractable interpreters of the modern state (Max Weber, Carl Schmitt) and the stoutest defenders of the unique merits of market exchange (Friedrich von Hayek) have all viewed the workings of representative democracy with acute suspicion.

These hesitations go back to the two greatest eighteenth-century Scottish theorists of the market as a system of natural liberty and uniquely decisive element in the progress of modern civilization. Neither David Hume nor Adam Smith was in any sense an advocate of democracy. Each insisted firmly on the practical indispensability of maintaining a framework of firm political authority and was perfectly at ease with the absolute monarchies of Europe's *ancien régime*. Smith himself emphasized brusquely that the main task of government was the defence of the rich against the poor (a task necessarily less dependably performed where it is the poor who choose who is to govern, let alone where the poor themselves, as in Athens, in large measure simply *are* the government). Hume explained, with meticulous care, that the structure of property rights on which a market economy fundamentally rests will inevitably and systematically clash with the natural workings of human sympathy, relentlessly allocating scarce goods to those who palpably neither deserve nor need them, and at the expense of those who emphatically do. Both Hume and Smith stressed imperturbably that the system of private property must be protected in its entirety and as a system, since its collective benefits over time required it to operate as such; and any distribution of these benefits at a particular time under the impress of concern for suffering and deprivation, short of real famine, would unevitably sooner or later threaten its capacity to generate those collective benefits, and so disrupt the natural progress of opulence. In contrast with Aristotle's and Plato's aristocratic critique of the distributive taste of democracy for assigning social, economic, and political goods without due regard for the massive inequalities in human merit, Hume and Smith defended the private property that emerged from the workings of market exchange against the most edifying of democratic impulses: the urge to redress the balance of suffering and enjoyment amongst fellow creatures.

Even today it is far from clear why representative democracy has had such striking success in providing that defence. But the answer plainly has much to do with a unique combination of appeal and viability. What has made it viable (its effective protection of a market economy) is scarcely the same as what has made it imaginatively appealing (its resting the legitimate power of the state on the regular free choices of its citizens). But after 1989 it has become clear that appeal and viability are more closely linked than one might expect. A somewhat laundered version of what has made it appealing (if the power of the state rests on the free choices of its citizens, it does so in a highly intermittent and elaborately mediated fashion) is still appealing enough to help greatly over time in consolidating its viability (in enabling it to protect the structure of capitalist property rights). A somewhat laundered version of what has made it viable (the fact that an essentially market economy is an overwhelmingly more effective mechanism for securing the progress of opulence in the long term than any alternative so far envisaged) has helped decisively to buffer it against the turbulence of modern history. It has done so, in the last instance, because of the comparative democratic credibility of the political thesis that an essentially market economy is a genuine collective good, as against the contention that any extant competitor really is a collective good. The starkness of this comparison at the level of popular perceptions across the world is extremely recent: a matter of the last dozen years rather than the last half-century. (Even now it plainly has some way to go within the Union of South Africa.) It would be hard to exaggerate its political importance.

But it would be easy to exaggerate the clarity of its political implications. The clear implications are all negative. In particular, it implies that there is no specifiable and categorical alternative to modern capitalism, with its own special and historically privileged political setting, and with a range of appeals that combines the charms of humanity and justice with either the directness of personal political agency of ancient democracy or the detached cognitive authority of modern science. (Still less both.)

Until 1989 the history of socialism had been the history of the presumption in some version or other that there is indeed such an alternative. Now that this presumption must be abandoned as a matter of historical right, it will be interesting to see which aspects of it (if any) can be resuscitated as a matter of responsible causal judgement.

The recent history of social democratic governments or parties does not at present suggest that much will be resuscitated at all durably. But that history has been strongly marked by the sheer scale and pace of the imaginative collapse in socialism's presumption of a privileged relation to modern social and economic life: its fond expectation that it would prove in due course to be the universal heir to the world made by capitalism— its residuary legatee. As the disadvantages of the policies pressed by its victorious opponents become more blatant, the imaginative balance will begin to tip again in the opposite direction. Even domestically, no one at present can rationally be wholly confident how far the political viability of the OECD countries since the Second World War (their capacity to protect the workings of an essentially market economy) has depended on the welfare systems which they have installed and the redistributive taxation which they have used to fund these. Still less can anyone be rationally confident that the international structure of trade liberalization which has fostered the growth of a world market since Bretton Woods will continue to be secured or extended by the political decisions of individual sovereign states or supranational political communities. The view that socialists had the least idea how to handle an international economic system more benignly and effectively than the political protectors of their capitalist competitors has proved to be a woeful delusion. But even the most stalwart advocates of the market economy have never supposed that a political framework yet existed that could be confidently expected in practice to ensure the unobstructed workings of a free market across the globe.

The set of political and economic choices that will best ensure the domestic economic flourishing of a particular community over time is a matter of extravagantly complicated and deeply unobvious causal judgement. The natural political dynamics of representative democracy, for as long as this persists, probably set some limits on how far and how long it is practicable for a given community to diverge from benign policies in precisely the same direction. But nothing about these dynamics suggests an intrinsic likelihood for it to converge on a happy outcome. The immediate human attractions and repulsions of any particular distributive arrangement are so much clearer and motivationally more compelling

than the necessarily nebulous judgements of overall economic consequence that they can scarcely fail to play a steadier and more decisive role
in determining political decisions. Political parties, professional politicians, even in some measure career bureaucrats, must answer to them,
and answer more promptly, whether they like it or not, than they can
afford to do to their own most sophisticated and best considered overall
causal judgement. Today, as Harold Wilson famously observed, a week is
a very long time in politics. But in the life rhythms of an economy, a
week is a mere twinkling of an eye.

The relationship between constitutional representative democracy and
capitalism is both intimate and deeply untransparent. The historical services which each has rendered to the other over the last two centuries
have been profound. But neither, in the end, can be wholly at ease with
the other: completely confident of its ultimate fidelity. The source of this
ultimate disharmony is not obscure. Each, clearly understood, is in
essence a system of free individual choice. But the choices in question are
located in wholly different fields, and there is no reason whatever why
the choices made in either field should ever dovetail neatly with those
made in the other. Political choice governs the content and enforcement
of public law. Its imaginative aim, however, fitfully attained, is the collective good of the set of human beings directly concerned. Economic
choice in a capitalist economy takes the form (however unobviously) of
individual decisions to sell and buy; and virtually everything may well
turn out to be for sale. Some goods of the greatest importance, of course,
are irretrievably public, as Adam Smith clearly recognized. They will
only be supplied if they are bought collectively (paid for out of taxes
imposed and enforced by public law). But no account of why a capitalist
economy can be trusted to work spontaneously for the long-term overall
advantage of its participants has ever succeeded in explaining why any
system of public decision-making can be trusted to identify and secure
the public goods required to enable it to work effectively. Nor has any
such account explained why the political defenders of that economy can
be relied upon not to pursue other apparent human goods which may (or
may not) impede its effective working quite dramatically.

Over the last two centuries, and especially since the end of the Second
World War, constitutional representative democracy has been extensively
tested out in a wide variety of settings. In some (the United States of
America in particular) its performance has been not merely remarkably
protracted but also in many respects humanly quite encouraging. In many
others, especially the poorer ex-colonies of Europe since 1945, its fate has

been brief and inglorious. It ought by now to be relatively easy to judge why it works effectively where it does do so, and why it fails badly in other settings or at other times. Yet it has proved remarkably difficult to reach clear and well-founded conclusions about this crude and increasingly urgent practical question. All that can be said with complete confidence is that it is easy to understand why economic failure and constitutional disruption often reinforce one another in a country once either has begun to occur, and why economic success and democratic constitutional continuity likewise help to foster one another where either proves protractedly available. With representative democracy, as with capitalist development, nothing succeeds quite like success, and nothing fails as comprehensively as failure. This is hardly a cheering thought for the populations of East and Central Europe or the erstwhile Soviet Union, still less for those of Africa.

We have travelled a long way from the Athenian hillside where the people met in assembly week after week to decide what the *polis* would do. How much has modern democracy really to do with that glittering but very distant picture? Some contrasts are very harsh. No sovereign citizen-body in the modern world is a real political agent, choosing and acting for itself with the directness and efficacy of the Athenian *demos*. No sovereign citizen-body in the modern world protects itself abroad and at home with its own arms. Modern states, as Max Weber explained, have pressing reasons to disarm the populations over which they rule. Some (the United States of America, Yugoslavia, the Lebanon) may do so, for one reason or another, far less thoroughly than others. But in place of a citizenry in arms defending themselves as and when they see the need to do so, all modern states provide such physical security as they furnish for their subjects through distinct and specialized agencies—civil police force, standing army, with their ramifying modern supplements—and choose for themselves, and often with scant attention to the views of their subjects, how and when to use these instruments for the purpose. It is never the people today who decide when war is going to be made. In these and many other ways constitutional representative democracy accepts the modern state without noticeable inhibition, offering itself as the most civilized and politically just format which can be superimposed upon the intractable reality of that state.

Athenian democracy, as we have seen, was an improvised practical response to a highly immediate political problem in a very different world. It could scarcely have been further, either in purpose or in content, from a plausible proposal for how to organize modern states in a capitalist world economy, still less for how to reorganize modern political and economic life in its entirety in a way that ceased to privilege the current owners of capital. No practical component of ancient democracy has survived intact into the world in which we now live. (Even *isegoria*, the equal entitlement to speak freely in public affairs, has been more effectively justified and protected in this century as an aspect of Constant's modern liberty, the entitlement to live as one pleases, than as a clear prerequisite for the political functioning of the modern state.) A cynical view of the history of democracy would see in the term's verbal triumph a mere mirage, a comprehensive and potentially hazardous condition of mass delusion. A cynical view is probably less misleading than a sentimental view. But that does not make it true. What does it leave out? It is clear that what has survived from the experience of ancient democracy is not simply a word, but also a diffuse and urgent hope: the hope that human life in the settings in which it takes place may come to be more a matter of committed personal choice and less a matter of enforced compliance with impersonal and external (and unwelcome) demands. Both the diffuseness and the urgency of that hope have their perils. In combination, those perils have often been deadly. It is impossible (and perhaps also pointless) to try to assess the rationality of that hope at all precisely except in relation to very specific questions. But its emotional urgency and intrinsic haziness make it very easy to understand why human judgement in face of it, today as much as ever before, should collapse so insistently into the greater imaginative relaxation of cynicism or sentimentality.

In either of these two last moods, it is all too easy to take the measure of modern democracy: a coarsely effective (if perhaps on balance practically beneficial) fraud, a brutally aborted Elysium, without effective power to defend itself outside the idle dream-life of modern populations (and especially of their idlest of all dreamers, the temporary or permanent denizens of universities). But neither view captures both the power and the elusiveness of the idea they claim to diagnose. To see both the power and the elusiveness together we need to turn our minds back to the citizens of Athens as they lived out their public life together year after year. For anyone who played at all a prominent part in that life, Athenian politics, as Constant underlined, was extraordinarily dangerous. Defeat could come at any time and on any issue. It could mean exile, ruin, or even death. Political prominence, though, has had its rewards and penalties in every human society. For the ordinary Athenian citizens, political life was normally far less hazardous; and to them it gave a unique historical role, one which identified, and with only minor elements of fiction, the acts of the *polis* of which they were citizens with their very own acts.

This was the opportunity which Constant insisted that the movement of modern history had removed for ever. As a claim about the domestic politics of modern states within a world economy (and still more about the politics of reproducing a world economy) it is plain that Constant's assessment was right. He was not right because modern citizen bodies could not choose far more often than they do (by an interminable cascade of televisual referenda or other such expedients), or even because they would speedily regret doing so, if the opportunity were duly provided. He was right because nothing in principle can or could be done to enable modern citizens to know about, or choose coherently in relation to, the vast bulk of the factors which shape, constrain, or endanger their lives. (It is quite unclear, in fact, that even the most skilfully designed and devoted of modern governments—or, for that matter, of modern multinational corporations or transnational welfare agencies—can organize themselves to be capable of doing anything of the kind.) Understanding the world in which we live requires an extravagantly complicated division of cognitive labour—perhaps a more complicated division than human beings are politically capable of creating or sustaining, and certainly one far more complicated and trustworthy than they have yet contrived to create. When Hobbes first sketched out the idea of the modern state he presented its core as a necessary alienation of coercive power and entitlement to judge from each of its individual subjects. But in the modern world economy it is even more important to see in the modern state an equally necessary alienation of cognitive responsibility: to see the state, in Émile Durkheim's metaphor, as society's brain. It is relatively easy to transfer both coercive power and entitlement to judge for oneself, but perhaps simply impossible to transfer cognitive capacity: the power of understanding what is really going on. Modern states at present are palpably in no condition to take up these awesome cognitive responsibilities. It is not an accident that the most devastating blow to twentieth-century socialist hopes of protecting the poor against the would-be rich came from the open failure of the state to elicit, grasp, and act upon the endless deluge of accurate information which it needed to master to be able to provide that protection. It has taken a grisly three-quarters of a century to revive a degree of real plausibility in Macaulay's early nineteenth-century Whig confidence that the rich are, in a subtle way, a sort of public good: that protecting them against the anger and resentment of the poor might be as much in the latter's interests as protecting the poor against the direct oppression of the rich has always so evidently been.

But the most punctiliously constitutional of representative democracies which confines its energies to protecting the rich against the poor is not merely a somewhat lacklustre political goal. It is also a singularly implausible claimant to monopolize modern political legitimacy. There have been even more implausible claimants to monopolize that legitimacy; and no doubt at intervals there will continue to be so. (Human beings are sometimes beyond shame.) But it is hard to imagine that another candidate of equal implausibility will in future win, even momentarily, in this respect the degree of imaginative dominance that constitutional representative democracy at present enjoys.

It is clear enough how it came to win this eminence—the brusque juxtaposition, whilst the Communist regimes of Eastern Europe crumbled in the course of 1989, of, as Timothy Garton Ash put it (1990: 136), 'a set of ideas whose time had come' with 'a set of ideas whose time had gone'. As always in such juxtapositions, the sudden and devastating clarity, the sheer historical incontestability, of the judgement rested not on what was affirmed but on what was so definitively rejected. We shall not see self-professed Communist parties ruling unchallenged over European capitals again, not in our own lifetimes, nor in anyone else's.

Constitutional representative democracies do have some real claim to political legitimacy. They can, whilst they last, provide with some success the three major services we have already noted: the physical security, and in some degree the personal liberty, of their own subjects; a measure of real responsibility of governors to governed; and at least partial protection for the successful operation of an essentially capitalist economy. But we should remember the historical experiences which gave birth to their now decisively vanquished antagonist, and which committed so many hundreds of millions of human beings over vast areas of the world, in some cases for several generations, to the epic folly, and the at times almost unimaginable horror, of the states and economies which it built. We should remember, too, that many over those decades in other lands, often men and women of good faith and sometimes of very high intelligence and real (if partial) political insight, saw these great and terrible experiences as in part a model for the constitutional representative democracies in which they themselves lived. (No human being ever has comprehensive political insight.)

Under adverse conditions in the past representative democracies have often proved quite easy to overthrow. This is unlikely to cease to be the case. If one considers each instance of overthrow as a single unit, it must still be true today that more constitutional representative democracies have failed to survive the political and economic challenges which faced them than have lived through without interruption to the present day. No regime can provide the services of which it is capable, unless it can protect itself in some way against its enemies: unless it has the capacity to survive. The disappearance of one particularly dramatic alternative will not render representative democracy invulnerable as a state form. It will do nothing durable to elide the notably unattractive features which made so many for so long deeply convinced that representative democracy, as a state form tenaciously committed to the defence of a capitalist economy, was deservedly fated to disappear. Nor will it by itself improve the capacity of representative democracies to deal with the immense range of practical problems, domestic and international, which now confront each of them. Above all, it will do nothing to lay to rest the haunting promise which still hovers over the determinedly ordinary everyday political business of ancient Athens, if only for the male citizen body itself—the promise that, in the life which human beings live together, the balance between arbitrary external constraint and reasonable personal choice can be shifted decisively toward the latter.

At the height of its present triumph, three great questions still confront representative democracy as a state form with unique claims to legitimate political authority. One, plainly, is a question about economic causality: about how modern economies really work and what constraints their workings really place on how governments can hope to act effectively. How rigorously and narrowly, how relentlessly, does any modern government have to choose between protecting the rich against the poor and contributing more directly to improving the living conditions and the economic and cultural opportunities open to the poor? How often and for how long, for example, do modern populations have to accept millions of disemployed and neglected fellow citizens as the price for higher living standards for their own children or grandchildren? How far must modern governments confine themselves to fostering the market as a pseudo-egalitarian arena in which families may deploy their cumulative comparative advantage? How far instead can they set themselves to try to make the economic opportunities open to every one of their citizens at adulthood genuinely equal to one another, without massively impairing that market's capacity to augment wealth? Was Maynard Keynes's hope of taming the business cycle and civilizing the market economy just a product of intellectual confusion? Were the decades of post-war success which seemed to vindicate that hope, and which did so much to consolidate the popular legitimacy of representative democracies in the West, in fact a fortuitous outcome of something completely different and an episode, in retrospect, of collective economic and political delusion? If they were, it is certainly reasonable to expect representative democracies in the future to continue, at intervals, either to elect governments, or to succumb to regimes, committed to class revenge and the more direct service of the poor. (When Greek democrats advocated the abolition of debts or the redistribution of land, they did not on the whole do so because they expected these to enhance the overall productivity of their economy.) This first question is very much one for professional economists. It would be helpful for them to learn to answer it more clearly and convincingly than at present they seem able to do.

The second question, by contrast, is one for every citizen of a democracy. But it is a singularly difficult question, and we do not as yet have any coherent idea of how to answer it with the slightest authority. How exactly should we see the relation between science or knowledge and the claims of different human beings to be equipped to rule, or even to decide between the merits of different possible rulers? This is a question which has been largely stricken from the public record of modern democratic life, though it surfaces recurrently in the musings of social scientists. What the *demos* of modern representative democracies in fact does, as Schumpeter memorably explained, is to choose between relatively organized teams of candidates to govern. One of the criticisms pressed by ancient enemies of democracy was that democratic rule was morally untrustworthy, a claim that can necessarily be levelled with some plausibility against any actual system of human rule. But a second, vehemently pressed by Plato in particular, was that it inevitably reflected the rule of the unknowing over the knowing. As even Aristotle had the grace to point out, most human beings in fact know quite a lot that is relevant to the question of how best to rule. But it is frivolous to neglect the force of Plato's criticism. It cannot in itself be a merit of any system for co-ordinating human action that it routinely implements the decisions of those who have not the blindest idea of what they are doing. Schumpeter's analysis (1950: 250–302) meets this charge by bluntly pointing out that representative democracy places massively effective barriers between the feckless decisions of individual citizens and the consequential choices of those whom they select to rule. This scarcely consolidates the pretension that its ruling decisions derive their authority from free popular choices. But it also does rather little to suggest that it must be well equipped to meet Plato's charge.

Since the challenges which face political authority today are so extravagantly complicated, and since the difficulty of meeting them effectively is correspondingly acute, it is evident enough that every human society now needs an instrument for assessing accurately how these challenges may best be met. To see the modern state as society's brain is to assign to it the task of performing this assessment far too crisply and narrowly. But this in no way diminishes the human urgency of effective cognitive co-ordination in carrying out the assessment; and it does nothing to enhance the claims of any version of democratic choice to provide such co-ordination with much dependability. The task for which democracy was initially devised, and for which it has very palpable advantages, was the avoidance of direct subjugation. It was emphatically not the steady genesis of valid understanding of an extravagantly complicated and tautly interconnected world-wide interaction.

Here, the human societies of today and tomorrow really do need to look back to the world of the *polis*, and to do so in a more chastened and realistic fashion. As we confront the momentous threat of a world rendered humanly uninhabitable by the unintended consequences of developing the powers of our own species, our need for accurate and systematic understanding of what we are really doing is more acute than it has ever been before in human history. Unless we can learn to meet that challenge, the species itself will come to an end. Democracy, a political system of citizen self-rule, offers in itself no recipe whatever for grasping the scope of that challenge and no plausible means, accordingly, for meeting it effectively. The question of how to defend the ozone layer, for example, is not one that can be answered by any system for summing human choices or preferences.

But that does not mean that it is a question to which the Greek experience of democracy is simply irrelevant. There were the closest ties, as Geoffrey Lloyd has long explained, between that experience and some of the most distinctive and humanly consequential features of Greek thinking: between democratic life and Greek cognitive style, the style that gave rise in classical Greece to the cumulative critical development of so many different branches of analytical thought. It may well be true, as Martin Bernal has argued, that the Greeks drew many of their most valuable intellectual resources from other Near Eastern and Mediterranean peoples. But they put them together in a quite new way; and what enabled them to do so was not some obscure and idiosyncratic biological superiority but the distinctive political character of the societies in which they lived. Between the political and social institutions of the *polis*, with

its citizens ruling and being ruled by turns, and the self-critical and ana-
lytically precise techniques of much of Greek thinking, there was a clear
elective affinity. Both rested in the last instance on practices of public discussion, of the open giving (and taking) of reasons as grounds for conclusions. Despite the regular appeals of esoteric knowledge for groups of
Greek thinkers, and the clear persistence of aristocratic political conde-
scension in even the most stalwartly democratic Greek *polis*, the Greeks
learnt how to develop mathematics, logic, philosophy, and several of the
natural sciences as structures of publicly responsible belief, just as they
learnt how to develop democratic rule as a structure of publicly responsible authority. For all the permanent mutual suspicion and the intermit-
tently focused mutual animosity of philosophical or scientific enquiry and
democratic authority, both were rooted in the same collective social
experience.

Most modern philosophers or social theorists who still suppose it possible to cast clear light on the technical efficacy of natural science in pre-
dicting and controlling the external world still attribute that potency in
the end to the degree to which the sciences contrive to remain structures
of publicly responsible belief rather than of closed coercive power. No
modern thinker has yet seen how to judge that degree in a wholly con-
vincing fashion, although the German social theorist Jürgen Habermas
has lavished more public effort on the attempt to do so than any of his
contemporaries and perhaps made more headway in it than anyone else
has so far done. What is certain is that we are no closer to seeing a clear
and harmonious relation between scientific validity and democratic
acceptability than the Greeks were. Amongst the Greeks the lack of clarity in this relation was a source of offence to a small number of fastidious
male intellectuals. But for us it has become a burning political issue, and
one on which the ultimate fate of all our descendants may well prove to
hang.

The third great question confronting representative democracy as a
state form is easy enough to state but far harder to answer. How far is it
sane to hope that representative democracy can ever realize for all its
vastly expanded citizen-body the ferociously demanding value which
Greek democrats claimed for their own far narrower *demos*: the goal of
living in freedom together? There are many grounds for pessimism. The
history of twentieth-century states suggests strongly that however effusive
the assertion of equality of status amongst modern citizens, the structure
of the state itself will always ensure a drastic alienation of power from virtually all of them. The history of twentieth-century economies, almost as

clearly if rather more recently, also strongly suggests that the same asser-
tions of equality of status will continue in the future to be combined with
immense inequalities of economic enjoyment, not merely between the
populations of different countries across the world but also within every
country the great bulk of whose inhabitants do not fester in the most
abject poverty.

The equality of status itself (of political and civil rights across a citizen-
body) is not a trivial matter. For Hume and Adam Smith, one of the
greatest virtues of the new commercial society was its softening of the
harsh, direct subordination characteristic of the predominantly rural society of earlier centuries: its erosion of intimate personal dependence as the
main organizing principle of human society. For socialist critics of commercial society, the wage contract, and the private ownership of the
means of production which forced that contract upon a propertyless
labour force of legally free agents, still frustrated this promise of genuine
independence for all. But once the private possession of the means of
production had been taken back, this last barrier would be removed for
ever. From then on, adult men and women could live freely together
without personal dependence upon one another, or alien authority lord-
ing it over their lives. This vision was never very clear; but what it lacked
in definition it more than made up for in power. What has to be abandoned in it now is certainly not the hope that the grotesque contrasts
between squalor and luxuriance in our societies can be narrowed to the
advantage of those who now have to suffer the former. Whether this can
be done or not will be a matter of political skill and determination as well
as analytical ingenuity and force. But what must be accepted, as Hume
and Smith made clear, is that participation in modern economic life
involves an alienation of personal control over the use of our own powers, if not necessarily to existing owners or managerial hierarchies, at least
to an immensely complicated system of production and exchange which
we will never fully understand and which none of us can sanely hope to
subject to our own will.

Set over against the direct and incessant self-rule of the citizens of
Athens, there are many ways in which we can never hope to rule ourselves again. We can never make ourselves at a national (or supranational
or global) level, as Kleisthenes made the Athenian *demos*, into a single
coherent collective agent, choosing sovereignly for ourselves over any
matter that any of us can convincingly argue requires such a choice.
What we can hope to do, however, is to defend and extend over time
the powers to choose for ourselves, individually and locally, how we will

263

act and make our own lives, and defend, too, the political framework which has best secured this opportunity over the last two and a half centuries. Athenian democracy, after Kleisthenes, did not merely defend Athens as a political community of free citizens ruling themselves; it also exemplified that community prominently and persistently in its most ordinary and day-to-day activities. The demand to be recognized as citizens over the last three centuries and more is not best understood any longer as a demand to rule (a demand which is now necessarily forlorn). Rather, it should be understood as a demand for the opportunity to make power in our adult lives always ultimately answerable to those over whom it is exercised: a demand for the practical political means to replace subjugation by authority, and to do so wherever we find ourselves subject to the former. (Why should we accept these often lamentable arrangements? What claims can they possibly have to our compliance: let alone our loyalty?) There are no clear limits to this quest: no definite, if as yet unsighted, outcome.

None of us has any idea how far it can or will go. But even today, amidst the rubble of socialism's vast transformative promises, we can be sure that this quest will take our descendants very far away from the political and social common sense of the world we now inhabit: from its sense of how power must be distributed and where authority can hope to lie. This endless and elusive process of calling power to account, of making it effectively answerable to its human objects, echoes the historical reality of Athenian democracy quite directly, and in two distinct ways. The first is as a continuous recreation of the capacity to act together, in the forging of new collective agents in an endless variety of human settings. Here, in effect, modern democrats aspire to play the role of Kleisthenes within the setting of their own lives, if to do so, necessarily, on a less comprehensive, and a palpably far from sovereign, scale. The second is in the reconstitution of community, of shared hope (or fear), meaning, and purpose, which these fresh agents can alone make possible. It is easy to describe such reconstitution sentimentally: to impute a virtue, purity, and innocence to new communities which no old community of human beings has ever displayed. (Few less pure and innocent than the Athenian *demos*, at work at the task of ruling and being ruled by turns.) Analysts of modern capitalist economies often stress how urgently these need to reinvent economic agency all the time, and do so in the face of the strong organizational tendencies throughout every modern economy to construct monopoly, extract unearned rents, and protect comforting routines. But we have a far less clear and vivid sense of the permanent need to reinvent political and social agency throughout the world in which we now live.

The often painful history of the demand for citizen equality has been a somewhat baffled expression of both the insistence and the elusiveness of that need. For the present, we can see it most dramatically in the varieties of contemporary feminism. The judgement that the relations between men and women over most of the known history of the species have been purposefully organized by and for the former at the expense of the latter is a bit flat and ingenuous. (All women are agents too.) But it also has a large and intractable core of manifest truth. Because of the scale, intimacy, and obscurity of this huge historical bloc of human experience, no one can have a clear sense of what the relations between men and women would be like if every trace of subjugation were somehow to be expunged from them. The challenge which this recognition poses to men and women today is acutely disconcerting; but it is also of the keenest interest. Except in the idlest of senses, it is not well seen as a challenge to democracy—in the sense that it might have a permanent, superior but undemocratic answer. But it is certainly a challenge for democracy: above all to its capacity for nurturing social imagination. More especially, it is a challenge to judge what forms of community across gender are at present possible, and what forms of collective agency can reasonably be expected to prove benign. We can hear it clearly in the words of the American feminist Catherine MacKinnon:

My issue is what our identifications are, what our loyalties are, who our community is, to whom we are accountable. If it seems as if this is not very concrete, I think it is because we have no idea of what women as women would have to say. I'm evoking for women a role that we have yet to make, in the name of a voice that, unsilenced, might say something that has never been heard. (MacKinnon 1987: 77)

Its careful aesthetic resonance locates this firmly within the modern academy. But it carries the voice of democracy across the ages: the demand to speak for oneself, to be heard, and to make what is said effective in the texture of lives lived together. That voice has never gone unchallenged, and it has often been very thoroughly suppressed. But two and a half millennia after Kleisthenes it is clearer than it used to be just how hard it is to keep it suppressed. The democratic hope is that, for as long as there continue to be human beings, it will never again be silenced.

Fear is just as democratic (and just as important) an emotion as hope. Athenian democracy began in fear: as a response to perceived danger. It also ended in fear, as the speeches of Demosthenes vividly bring home: the eminently realistic fear of alien conquest. In the interim, however, what it gave was a long and enduring lesson in reasonable hope. The power of representative democracy as a state form today has come largely from very practical and unexhilarating achievements. But the power of democracy as an idea is far less closely tied to these achievements. It is also distinctly less harmonious either with representative democracy as a state form or with much (perhaps most) of the reality of contemporary societies in the West, or Far East, or anywhere else. Many interpreters of Kleisthenes' somewhat inadvertent legacy equate it firmly with one or other of these two great shaping forces: either, to put it unsympathetically, with ideology or with utopia. But the way we should see it is as an incessant and turbulent encounter between the two. Perhaps not a journey without end, but certainly a journey to an unknown destination.

REFERENCES

Aristotle (1977), *The Politics*, trans. H. Rackham (London).

Ball, Terence (1988), *Transforming Political Discourse* (Oxford).

Constant, Benjamin (1988), *Political Writings*, ed. and trans. Biancamaria Fontana (Cambridge).

Garton Ash, Timothy (1990), *We the People* (London).

Hansen, Mogens Herman (1991), *The Athenian Democracy in the Age of Demosthenes* (Oxford).

Herodotus (1982) *History*, vol. iii, trans. A. D. Godley (London).

MacKinnon, Catherine (1987), *Feminism Unmodified* (Cambridge, Mass.).

Manville, Philip Brook (1990), *The Origins of Citizenship in Ancient Athens* (Princeton, NJ).

Plato (1987), *The Republic*, vol. 2, trans. Paul Shorey (London).

Schumpeter, Joseph (1950), *Capitalism, Socialism and Democracy* (London).

Skinner, Quentin (1989), 'The State', in Terence Ball, James Farr, and Russell Hanson (eds.), *Political Innovation and Conceptual Change* (Cambridge).

Further Reading

CHAPTER 1   Democratic Institutions in Ancient Greece

Far and away the best account (full, fair-minded, elegantly readable, and up-to-date) of the Athenian democracy is M. H. Hansen, *The Athenian Democracy in the Age of Demosthenes* (Oxford, 1991). This cites earlier work, including Hansen's own numerous contributions, which have transformed the subject. Of these the most accessible is *The Athenian Assembly in the Age of Demosthenes* (Oxford, 1987), a companion volume to the above.

For accounts of the development of Athenian democracy embedded in general narratives of Greek history see the following volumes of the second (actually completely new) edition of the multi-author *Cambridge Ancient History*, iii. 3 (1982); iv (1988); v (1992); vi (1993).

The most important ancient source is the *Athenian Constitution* ascribed to Aristotle. This was discovered, on papyrus, only a century ago. It is the subject of a full-length commentary by P. J. Rhodes (Oxford, 1981), a masterpiece of ancient historical scholarship. Rhodes has done an excellent abridged version, with translation, in the Penguin Classics series (Harmondsworth, Middx., 1984).

CHAPTER 2   Ancient Greek Political Theory and Democracy

For a more expansive and detailed account of the evolution of political theory as a response to issues raised by democracy, see Cynthia Farrar, *The Origins of Democratic Thinking* (Cambridge, 1988).

For illuminating general discussions of the meaning of politics to the Athenians, see Hannah Arendt, *The Human Condition* (Chicago, 1958); Alasdair MacIntyre, *After Virtue* (South Bend, Ind., 1981); and Christian Meier, *The Greek Discovery of Politics* (Cambridge, Mass., 1990).

Useful and penetrating interpretations of the ideas of particular theorists discussed here include G. B. Kerferd (ed.), *The Sophists and their Legacy* (Wiesbaden, 1981); Gregory Vlastos, *Socrates: Ironist and Moral Philosopher* (Cambridge, 1991); C. D. C. Reeve, *Philosopher-Kings* (Princeton, NJ, 1989); Jonathan Lear, *Aristotle: The Desire to Understand* (Cambridge, 1988). R. G. Mulgan, *Aristotle's Political Theory* (Oxford, 1977) is a good introduction to this topic.

CHAPTER 3   Greek Democracy, Philosophy, and Science

M. I. Finley, *Democracy Ancient and Modern* (London, 1975).

M. I. Finley, *Politics in the Ancient World* (Cambridge, 1983).

M. H. Hansen, *The Athenian Democracy in the Age of Demosthenes* (Oxford, 1991).

G. E. R. Lloyd, *Magic, Reason and Experience* (Cambridge, 1979).

—— *Demystifying Mentalities* (Cambridge, 1990).

N. Loraux, *The Invention of Athens*, tr. A. Sheridan (Cambridge, Mass., 1986).

M. Ostwald, *Nomos and the Beginnings of the Athenian Democracy* (Oxford, 1969).

J.-P. Vernant, *The Origins of Greek Thought*, tr. J. Lloyd (London, 1982).

—— *Myth and Thought among the Greeks*, tr. J. Lloyd (London, 1983).

P. Vidal-Naquet, *The Black Hunter: Forms of Thought and Forms of Society in the Greek World*, tr. A. Szegedy Maszak (Baltimore, 1986).

CHAPTER 4   The Italian City-Republics

Daniel Waley, *The Italian City-Republics*, 3rd edn. (London, 1988) provides the best general introduction. For further details see J. K. Hyde, *Society and Politics in Medieval Italy* (London, 1973) and J. Larner, *Italy in the Age of Dante and Petrarch, 1216–1380* (London, 1980).

A number of individual cities have been excellently studied. See, for example, J. K. Hyde, *Padua in the Age of Dante* (Manchester, 1966); David Herlihy, *Pisa in the Early Renaissance* (New Haven, Conn., 1958); William Bowsky, *A Medieval Italian Commune: Siena under the Nine, 1287–1355* (Berkeley, Calif., 1981).

For the most up-to-date survey of the intellectual setting of Italian civic life, see Charles Schmitt and Quentin Skinner (eds.), *The Cambridge History of Renaissance Philosophy* (Cambridge, 1988). On the evolution of Renaissance humanism, the essays collected in P. O. Kristeller, *Renaissance Thought*, 2 vols. (New York, 1961–5) are indispensable. For an outline of the political ideas associated with the rise of the communes, see Quentin Skinner, *The Foundations of Modern Political Thought*, i. *The Renaissance* (Cambridge, 1978). The later development of Florentine 'civic humanism' is classically surveyed in Hans Baron, *The Crisis of the Early Italian Renaissance* (revised edn., Princeton, NJ, 1966). For a very useful anthology of texts, see Benjamin G. Kohl and Ronald G. Witt (eds.), *The Earthly Republic: Italian Humanists on Government and Society* (Manchester, 1978).

On the ideology of the early communes, especially as reflected in the visual arts, see H. Wieruszowski, 'Art and the Commune in the Time of Dante', *Speculum*, 19 (1944); Nicolai Rubinstein, 'Political Ideas in Sienese Art', *Journal of the Warburg and Courtauld Institutes*, 21 (1958); and Quentin Skinner, 'Ambrogio Lorenzetti: The Artist as Political Philosopher', *Proceedings of the British Academy*, 72 (1986).

On Marsilius of Padua and the theory of communal government see Jeannine Quillet, *La Philosophie politique de Marsile de Padoue* (Paris, 1970); and Marino Damiata, *Plenitudo potestatis e Universitas civium in Marsilio da Padova* (Florence, 1983). The best study of the civic context of Marsilius' thought remains Nicolai Rubinstein, 'Marsilius of Padua and Italian Political Thought of his Time', in

John Hale, Roger Highfield, and Beryl Smalley (eds.), *Europe in the Later Middle Ages* (London, 1965).

On the republicanism of Machiavelli and his contemporaries see the important discussion in Part II of J. G. A. Pocock, *The Machiavellian Moment* (Princeton, NJ, 1975). See also Gisela Bock, Quentin Skinner, and Maurizio Viroli (eds.), *Machiavelli and Republicanism* (Cambridge, 1990). Gennaro Sasso, *Niccolò Machiavelli: Storia nel suo pensiero politico*, new edn. (Bologna, 1980) contains a full analysis of the *Discorsi*. For a brief outline, stressing Machiavelli's theory of free government, see Quentin Skinner, *Machiavelli*, revised edn. (Oxford, 1985).

CHAPTER 5   The Levellers

One book on Civil War radicalism stands out above all others: Christopher Hill's *The World Turned Upside Down*, 2nd edn. (Harmondsworth, Middx., 1975). Specifically on the Levellers, a valuable short introduction with selected texts is G. E. Aylmer, *The Levellers in the English Revolution* (London, 1975). The best narrative is that of H. N. Brailsford, *The Levellers and the English Revolution*. Key texts are to be found in W. Haller and G. Davies (eds.), *The Leveller Tracts* (reprint Gloucester, Mass., 1964); and in A. S. P. Woodhouse (ed.), *Puritanism and Liberty*, 2nd edn. (London, 1974).

The most vexed question in the literature is that of whether the Levellers were democrats. For the case against, C. B. Macpherson, *The Political Theory of Possessive Individualism* (Oxford, 1962). The best of the replies is K. Thomas, 'The Levellers and the Franchise', in G. E. Aylmer (ed.), *The Interregnum* (London, 1972).

On the relationship between the Levellers and the army, the best authority is now Austin Woolrych, *Soldiers and Statesmen* (Oxford, 1987). On their relationship to the sects, Murray Tolmie, *The Triumph of the Saints* (Cambridge, 1977).

In order to assess the novelty of the Levellers' views, one can usefully start with Brian Tierney, *Religion, Law and the Growth of Constitutional Thought, 1150–1650* (Cambridge, 1982); followed by Quentin Skinner, 'The Origins of the Calvinist Theory of Revolution', in B. Malament (ed.), *After the Reformation* (Philadelphia, 1980); and D. Wootton, 'From Rebellion to Revolution', *English Historical Review*, 105 (1990), 654–69.

There is little of value on the significance of the transition from manuscript to print for political theory: on the subject as a whole, Elizabeth Eisenstein, *The Printing Revolution in Early Modern Europe* (Cambridge, 1983).

Finally, my greatest debt in writing this essay has been to the work of Stephen Greenblatt. I particularly recommend 'Murdering Peasants', in his *Learning to Curse* (New York, 1990), which serves to remind one with a start what an exceptional event the Putney Debates were.

CHAPTER 6   Democracy and the American Revolution

To place the emergence of democracy in the American Revolution in the context of the eighteenth-century Atlantic world, see R. R. Palmer's two volumes, *The Age of the Democratic Revolution: A Political History of Europe and America, 1760–1800* (Princeton, NJ, 1959, 1964). Excellent starting points for understanding the political theory of the American Revolution are Richard Buel, Jun., 'Democracy and the American Revolution: A Frame of Reference', *William and Mary Quarterly*, 3rd ser., 21 (1964), 165–90; and Bernard Bailyn, *The Ideological Origins of the American Revolution* (Cambridge, Mass., 1967). See also Gordon S. Wood, *The Creation of the American Republic, 1776–1787* (Chapel Hill, NC, 1969); and Wood, *The Radicalism of the American Revolution* (New York, 1992), from which this chapter is derived. J. R. Pole, *Political Representation in England and the Origins of the American Republic* (London, 1966), compares English and American developments. Garry Wills, *Inventing America: Jefferson's Declaration of Independence* (New York, 1978); and his *Explaining America: The Federalist* (New York, 1981), present exciting but sometimes perverse readings of two crucial documents. Morton White, *The Philosophy of the American Revolution* (New York, 1978); and his *Philosophy, The Federalist, and the Constitution* (New York, 1987), treat the same two documents but formally and philosophically. Robert E. Shalhope, 'Toward a Republican Synthesis: The Emergence of an Understanding of Republicanism in American Historiography', *William and Mary Quarterly*, 3rd ser., 29 (1972), 49–80; and his 'Republicanism and Early American Historiography', ibid. 39 (1982), 334–56, demonstrate the importance of republicanism to American culture. Michael Lienesch, *New Order of the Ages: Time, the Constitution, and the Making of Modern America* (Princeton, NJ, 1988); Thomas L. Pangle, *The Spirit of Modern Republicanism: The Moral Vision of the American Founders and the Philosophy of Locke* (Chicago, 1988); and Jennifer Nedelsky, *Private Property and the Limits of American Constitutionalism: The Madisonian Framework and its Legacy* (Chicago, 1990), relate Lockean liberalism to republicanism at the time of the founding.

CHAPTER 7   Democracy and the French Revolution

Amongst the contemporary sources which highlight the political impact and implications of the revolution, see: Edmund Burke, *Reflections on the Revolution in France*, ed. Conor Cruise O'Brien (Harmondsworth, Middx., 1969); Emmanuel-Joseph Sièyes, *What is the Third Estate?*, ed. S. E. Finer, tr. M. Blondel (London, 1963); Benjamin Constant, *Political Writings*, ed. Biancamaria Fontana (Cambridge, 1988); see also the anthology edited by William Church, *The Influence of the Enlightenment on the French Revolution* (Lexington, Mass., and London, 1974). Of the many classic general histories of the subject the political aspects are probably more prominent in Jules Michelet, *History of the French Revolution*, tr. C. Cocks, ed. G. Wright (Chicago, 1967) and Alphonse Aulard,

The French Revolution: A Political History, 1789–1804, tr. Bernard Miall, 4 vols. (London, 1910); amongst the recent ones see D. M. G. Sutherland, *France 1789–1815: Revolution and Counter-Revolution* (London, 1985); and William Doyle, *The Oxford History of the French Revolution* (Oxford, 1989), both of which include a good bibliography of English texts. On the origins and social interpretations of the revolution see William Doyle, *The Origins of the French Revolution*, 2nd rev. edn. (Oxford, 1988); the collection of classic studies edited by Ralph W. Greenlaw, *The Social Origins of the French Revolution* (Lexington, Mass., and London, 1975); Alfred Cobban, *The Social Interpretation of the French Revolution* (Cambridge, 1964); Patrice Higonnet, *Class, Ideology and the Rights of Nobles during the French Revolution* (Oxford, 1981). On popular protest and the sansculottes see: George Rudé, *The Crowd in the French Revolution* (Oxford, 1959); Georges Lefebvre, *The Great Fear of 1789: Rural Panic in Revolutionary France*, tr. J. White, introd. by G. Rudé (London, 1973); Albert Soboul, *The Parisian Sansculottes and the French Revolution, 1793–1794* (Oxford, 1964); Richard Cobb, *The Police and the People: French Popular Protest, 1789–1820* (Oxford, 1970). On the origins of political terrorism: Norman Hampson, *Prelude to Terror: The Constituent Assembly and the Failure of Consensus, 1789–1791* (Oxford, 1988). The best recent contributions to the study of terror are in fact local studies on its impact on different provinces, like Colin Lucas, *The Structure of Terror: the Example of Javogues and the Loire* (Oxford, 1973); for the more general aspects see Noel O'Sullivan (ed.), *Terrorism, Ideology and Revolution: The Origins of Modern Political Violence* (Brighton, 1985); George Armstrong Kelly, *Victims, Authority and Terror* (Chapel Hill, NC, 1982). On the Jacobins see the two volumes published thus far of a large-scale study of the Jacobin Clubs: Michael L. Kennedy, *The Jacobin Clubs and the French Revolution*, i. *The First Years*, and ii. *The Middle Years* (Princeton, NJ, 1981 and 1988); Ferenć Feher's theoretical study *The Frozen Revolution: An Essay on Jacobinism* (Cambridge, 1987) is an interesting assessment in the light of the socialist experience of Eastern Europe. On 1789, the theory of revolution and socialism see Albert Soboul, 'Some Problems of the Revolutionary State, 1789–1796', *Past and Present*, 65 (1974), 52–74; François Furet, *Interpreting the French Revolution* (Cambridge, 1981); Theda Skocpol, *States and Social Revolutions: A Comparative Analysis of France, Russia and China* (Cambridge, 1979); John Dunn, 'Revolution', in *Interpreting Political Responsibility* (Cambridge and Princeton, NJ, 1990), 85–99; cf. also R. B. Rose, *Gracchus Babeuf: The First Revolutionary Communist* (London, 1978). On the military experience see Richard Cobb, *The Revolutionary Armies*, tr. Marianne Elliott (New Haven, Conn., 1987). For a recent economic reading of the revolution see Florin Aftalion, *The French Revolution: An Economic Interpretation* (Cambridge, 1990). Finally, a helpful recent survey of political themes can be found in Colin Lucas (ed.), *Rewriting the French Revolution* (Oxford, 1991).

CHAPTER 8 Democracy since the French Revolution

Almost all political history of the nineteenth and twentieth centuries will bear on the problem of democracy. But the theme is most likely to be treated in histories of political ideas, of parties, and revolutions, and sometimes in discussions of the welfare state. Of the works of political theory, the interested reader must consult, in the first instance, James Madison's *Federalist Papers* (1787); John Stuart Mill's *On Liberty* (1859) and *Considerations on Representative Government* (1861); and Alexis de Tocqueville's *Democracy in America* (1835), *The Old Regime and the French Revolution* (1856), and finally his *Recollections* (1859). (The standard French texts are included in the ongoing *Œuvres, papiers, et correspondances*—Paris, 1951–). In the United States, reformist writers and statesmen devoted concerted effort to reformulating the tasks of democracy in an age of encroaching interest groups at the turn of the twentieth century. The reader can sample the speeches of Woodrow Wilson included in *The New Freedom* (New York, 1913), or the more statist 'New Nationalism' of Theodore Roosevelt in *Works* (New York, 1926); also Herbert Croly, *Progressive Democracy* (New York, 1914), and the contemporary analysis in A. Lawrence Lowell, *Public Opinion and Popular Government* (New York, 1913). Writers of the 1930s and 1940s usually approached democracy by analysing the authoritarian movements that then seemed so powerfully in contention. For the mid-twentieth-century emphasis on welfare-state democracy by British theorists, see T. H. Marshall, *Citizenship and Social Class* (Cambridge, 1950); and also in a reformist spirit: Anthony Crosland, *The Future of Socialism* (London, 1956). Renewing the debate on the connections between democracy and capitalism, see Charles Lindblom, *Politics and Markets* (New York, 1977); as well as the other works by Lindblom and Robert A. Dahl, Jun., cited in the References.

Some of the recent intellectual and political biographies that thoughtfully explore the relationship between liberalism and democracy or democracy and socialism include: Stephen Holmes, *Benjamin Constant and the Making of Modern Liberalism* (New Haven, Conn., 1984); Stefan Collini, *Liberalism and Sociology: L. T. Hobhouse and Political Argument in England, 1880–1914* (Cambridge, 1979); Pierre Rosanvallon, *Le moment Guizot* (Paris, 1985); Pierre Sorlin, *Waldeck-Rousseau* (Paris, 1966); Harvey Goldberg, *The Life of Jean Jaurès* (Madison, Wisc., 1962); Peter Gay, *The Dilemma of Democratic Socialism: Eduard Bernstein's Challenge to Marx* (New York, 1952); Ronald Steel, *Walter Lippman and the American Century* (Boston, 1980). For a recent survey of Socialist Party development, see Albert S. Lindemann, *A History of European Socialism* (New Haven, Conn., 1983); while the intellectual implications are often brilliantly analysed in the works of George Lichtheim, *Marxism: An Historical and Critical Study*, revised edn. (New York, 1970); and Leszek Kolakowski, *Main Currents of Marxism*, 3 vols. (Oxford, 1981).

On political parties and governmental institutions, see Richard Hofstadter, *The Idea of a Party System* (Berkeley and Los Angeles, 1969); the classic treatment by François Goguel, *La politique des partis sous la IIIᵉ République* (Paris, 1953); Robert A. Dahl, Jun. (ed.), *Political Oppositions in Western Democracies* (New Haven, Conn., 1966); Michael Fogarty, *Christian Democracy in Western Europe, 1820-1953* (London, 1957); and Jean-Marie Mayeur, *Des parties catholiques à la démocratie chrétienne: XIX et XX siècles* (Paris, 1980); and most recently, Angelo Panebianco, *Political Parties: Organization and Power* (Cambridge, 1988), which will orient the reader in the literature and questions concerning European party development. For transformations of parties and the emergence of social movements after the 1960s, see Claus Offe, 'New Social Movements', and Suzanne Berger, 'Religious Transformation and the Future of Politics', in Charles S. Maier (ed.), *Changing Boundaries of the Political: Essays on the Evolving Balance between the State and Society, Public and Private in Europe* (Cambridge, 1987). Democracy threatened to become 'overloaded' and states 'unruly' in Michel Crozier *et al.*, *The Crisis of Democracy* (New York, 1975). More recently democracy has appeared irresistible and emancipatory. See Philippe C. Schmitter, Guillermo O'Donnell, and Laurence Whitehead, *Transitions from Authoritarian Rule*, 4 vols. (Baltimore, 1986).

Just as the emphasis on civil rights in the 1950s and 1960s helped to enlarge US concepts of democracy, so the emphasis on human rights in Communist countries has reinvigorated recent discussions. See Václav Havel, *The Power of the Powerless: Citizens against the State in Eastern Europe* (Armonk, NY, 1985); and, to cite just one of the many recent works concerning the democratic movements in Eastern Europe: Roman Laba, *The Roots of Solidarity* (Princeton, NJ, 1990).

CHAPTER 9　The Marxist-Leninist Detour

Karl Popper's two volumes on *The Open Society and its Enemies* (London, 1945) remains the most comprehensive assault on the anti-democratic and illiberal implication of élitist theory and historical prophecy in Western political thought. A more concise statement of his position is set out in his *Poverty of Historicism* (London, 1957). In similar vein J. L. Talmon's *Origins of Totalitarian Democracy* (London, 1952), explores the simultaneous emergence during the French Revolution of rival liberal and totalitarian conceptions of democracy. Most influential of all (perhaps because it was shorter and less theoretical/historical) has been F. A. Hayek's *Road to Serfdom* (London, 1944). A whole literature on 'totalitarianism' subsequently grew up to which the most prominent contributors were Hannah Arendt, Zbigniew Brzezinski, Leszek Kolakowski, Herbert Marcuse, and Leonard Schapiro.

The more concrete historical setting in which the Bolsheviks established their monopoly of power in the Soviet Union is explored in Schapiro's *Origin of the Communist Autocracy* (New York, 1965), whilst the Communist impoverishment of politics as a discourse is pursued in A. J. Polan's highly original study *Lenin and the End of Politics* (London, 1984); the more authentically Russian roots of Lenin's authoritarianism are traced in C. S. Ingerflom's *Le Citoyen impossible*

(Paris, 1988). The 'Budapest School' of Agnes Heller, Ferenc Feher, and György Markus have produced, from a neo-Marxist standpoint, perhaps the most pene-trating accounts of the authoritarianism of Soviet society, summarized in their joint book *Dictatorship over Needs* (Oxford, 1983). Alexander Zinoviev's *The Reality of Communism* (London, 1985) and Roy A. Medvedev's *On Socialist Democracy* (New York, 1975), are both incisive accounts by Soviet dissidents of the narrow limits of democracy within the Soviet system. The reductionist rela-tivism of the orthodox Soviet view is recited in Arthur Kiss, *Marxism and Democracy* (Budapest, 1982).

The relationship of Marxism to Leninism and the implicit problem of whether Marx was, in some way, 'responsible' for what occurred in the Soviet Union has long been debated, most notably by John Plamenatz in his *German Marxism and Russian Communism* (London, 1954) and more recently by David Lovell in *From Marx to Lenin* (Cambridge, 1984). The present author's *Lenin's Political Thought*, 2 vols. (London, 1982) finds more authentic Marxism in Lenin than either of these texts allows.

CHAPTER 10   Democracy in India

There is a rich vein of historical writing on India, and this provides the essential starting-point for understanding its modern politics. The period between the eighteenth and mid-nineteenth century is excellently covered in C. A. Bayly's *Indian Society and the Making of the British Empire* (Cambridge, 1988); for the sub-sequent period, there is much useful if rather blandly presented detail in J. Brown, *Modern India: The Origins of an Asian Democracy* (Oxford, 1985). A fas-cinating consideration of the intellectual sources of British policy towards India is E. Stokes, *The English Utilitarians and India* (Oxford, 1959). On agrarian politics and their historical significance for nationalism, E. Stokes, *The Peasant and the Raj* (Cambridge, 1978), sets a very high standard; and for interpretations that high-light the insurrectionary character of the Indian peasantry, see the work pub-lished in *Subaltern Studies*, i–vi (Delhi, 1982–), edited by R. Guha. There is a vast and disputatious literature on the emergence of Indian nationalism and the role of the Congress Party: A. Seal's study of the urban social bases of nationalist support, *The Emergence of Indian Nationalism* (Cambridge, 1971), was aimed against nationalist pieties which predominated in the 1950s and 1960s; other use-ful essays are contained in C. Baker, G. Johnson, and A. Seal (eds.), *Power, Profit and Politics: Essays on Imperialism, Nationalism and Change in Twentieth-Century India* (Cambridge, 1981); in P. Brass and F. Robinson (eds.), *The Indian National Congress and Indian Society, 1885–1985* (Delhi, 1987); and in R. Sisson and S. Wolpert (eds.), *Congress and Indian Nationalism: The Pre-Independence Phase* (Berkeley, Calif., 1988). Intellectual responses to foreign rule are treated very interestingly in A. Nandy, *The Intimate Enemy: Loss and Recovery of Self under Colonialism* (Delhi, 1984); and in P. Chatterjee, *Nationalist Thought and the Colonial World: A Derivative Discourse* (Delhi, 1986). For first-hand accounts by

political leaders who played decisive roles in the creation of modern Indian poli-
tics, see Mahatma Gandhi, *Moral and Political Writings*, 3 vols., ed. R. Iyer
(Oxford, 1986–7); and J. Nehru, *Autobiography* (London, 1936). Also helpful is
S. Gopal, *Jawaharlal Nehru: A Biography*, abridged edn. (Delhi, 1989).

Until recently, the only worthwhile general interpretation of India's politics
was R. Kothari's *Politics in India* (Delhi, 1970), and it remains a useful starting-
point. But in the past few years a number of more synoptic works have
appeared: for the best of these, see P. Brass, *The Politics of India since Independence*
(Cambridge, 1990); A. Kohli, *Democracy and Discontent: India's Growing Crisis of
Governability* (Cambridge, 1990); and the articles in A. Kohli (ed.), *India's
Democracy* (Princeton, NJ, 1988). Even more useful as guides to understanding
India's politics are those accounts which attend to its economics: for a study
which draws heavily on American models of political pluralism, see L. Rudolph
and S. Rudolph, *In Pursuit of Lakshmi: The Political Economy of the Indian State*
(Chicago, 1987); and for a Marxist view, see A. Vanaik, *The Painful Transition:
Bourgeois Democracy in India* (London, 1990). Best of all (and essential for the years
it covers) is still F. Frankel, *India's Political Economy, 1947–1977: The Gradual
Revolution* (Princeton, NJ, 1978). For elegance and sharpness of argument,
P. Bardhan, *The Political Economy of Development in India* (Delhi, 1984), is
unmatched.

G. Austin, *The Indian Constitution: Cornerstone of a Nation* (Oxford, 1966), is
good on the drafting of the Constitution, and on the principles of the legal system it established. For the later vicissitudes of India's legal system, U. Baxi, *The
Indian Supreme Court and Politics* (Lucknow, 1980), has some trenchant observa-
tions. On political culture in India, A. Nandy, *At the Edge of Psychology* (Delhi,
1980), is rich in suggestions. On the role of caste in Indian politics, see
R. Kothari (ed.), *Caste in Politics* (Delhi, 1971); a major and invaluable recent
collection on the connections between caste, class, and political action, sensitive
to regional variations, is F. Frankel and M. S. Rao (eds.), *Dominance and State
Power in Modern India: Decline of a Social Order*, 2 vols. (Delhi, 1989). The initial
secular commitment of the Indian state is well treated in D. E. Smith, *India as a
Secular State* (Princeton, NJ, 1963). On the background to the recent emergence
of religious nationalism, B. Graham's *Hindu Nationalism and Indian Politics: The
Origins and Development of the Bharatiya Jana Sangh* (Cambridge, 1990), is useful.
Finally, a provocative and illuminating general account of how India has been
represented in the intellectual discourse of the West is R. Inden, *Imagining India*
(Oxford, 1990).

CHAPTER 11   Feminism and Democracy

Readers who are interested in the position of women in the writings of the
'great dead' philosophers should look at Susan Moller Okin, *Women in Western
Political Thought* (London, 1979); and at Diana Coole, *Women in Political Theory:
From Ancient Misogyny to Contemporary Feminism* (Brighton, 1988).

The most important historical texts advocating enfranchisement for women are: John Stuart Mill, *The Subjection of Women*; and Harriet Taylor, *The Enfranchisement of Women*. *Subjection of Women* was first published in 1869 and *Enfranchisement of Women* in 1851. They are now available in a single volume from Virago (London, 1983).

Dale Spender's *Feminist Theorists* (London, 1983) is a useful collection of articles on feminist writers of the past three centuries. The book includes essays on Mary Wollstonecraft, Emma Goldman, Christabel Pankhurst, and Simone de Beauvoir as well as other, less well-known feminists. *Engendering Democracy* by Anne Phillips (Cambridge, 1991) is the most recent, and most stimulating, contribution to the British debate on women and democracy. It includes a very accessible account of the modern debate in Europe and America, and is highly recommended for its clarity and vigour.

There is a huge volume of modern American writing on this topic. One of the most stimulating and provocative books is Iris Marion Young, *Justice and the Politics of Difference* (Princeton, NJ, 1990), which argues for the affirmation of group difference and includes the controversial proposal that in some cases groups should have power of veto over policies which affect them directly.

CHAPTER 12   1989 in Eastern Europe

Tim Garton Ash, *The Uses of Adversity* (Harmondsworth, Middx., 1989).
—— *We the People: Revolution of '89 Witnessed in Warsaw, Budapest, Berlin and Prague* (Harmondsworth, Middx., 1990).
Misha Glenny, *The Rebirth of History: Eastern Europe in the Age of Democracy* (Harmondsworth, Middx., 1990).
Mark Frankland, *Patriots' Revolution: Reports on the Liberation of East Europe* (London, 1990).

CHAPTER 13   Conclusion

For the contrast between ancient and modern democracy, see John Dunn, *Western Political Theory in the Face of the Future* (Cambridge, 1979), ch. 1. The best single description of the practical character of Athenian democracy is now Mogens Hansen, *The Athenian Democracy in the Age of Demosthenes* (Oxford, 1991). For the shaping of Athens as a political community, see Philip B. Manville, *The Origins of Citizenship in Ancient Athens* (Princeton, NJ, 1990). For interpretation of Greek understandings of politics, see especially Moses Finley's incisive *Politics in the Ancient World* (Cambridge, 1983); Christian Meier, *The Greek Discovery of Politics* (Cambridge, Mass., 1990); Josiah Ober, *Mass and Elite in Democratic Athens* (Princeton, NJ, 1989); and Cynthia Farrar, *The Origins of Democratic Thinking* (Cambridge, 1988). The most immediately instructive sources are still the *Histories* of Herodotus and Thucydides and the very different verdicts of Aristotle's *Politics* and Plato's *Republic*. The most moving expression of the meaning of Athenian citizenship for Athens' most extraordinary 'ordinary' citizen is in Plato's dialogue the *Crito*. For Benjamin Constant's decisive contrast between ancient and modern politics, see his *Political Writings*, ed. Biancamaria Fontana (Cambridge, 1988); and her *Benjamin Constant and the Post-Revolutionary Mind* (New Haven, Conn., 1991).

For dispute over the degree of democracy in Roman politics, see Finley (1983); Fergus Millar, 'The Political Character of the Roman Republic', *Journal of Roman Studies*, 74 (1984), 1–19; and 'Politics, Persuasion and the People before the Social War', ibid. 76 (1986), 1–11; P. A. Brunt, *The Fall of the Roman Republic* (Oxford, 1988), ch. 9; and especially J. A. North's excellent 'Democratic Politics in Republican Rome', *Past and Present*, 126 (Feb. 1990), 3–21.

For the eighteenth-century decay of pre-modern republics see Franco Venturi, *Utopia and Reform in the Enlightenment* (Cambridge, 1971). For the formation of the idea of the modern constitutional representative democracy, see Gordon Wood's classic *The Creation of the American Republic 1776–1787* (Chapel Hill, NC, 1969), for the American case; and Biancamaria Fontana (ed.), *The Invention of the Modern Republic* (Cambridge, forthcoming). A particularly illuminating discussion of the difficulties of combining constitutional democracy with state agency is Stephen Skowronek's *Building a New American State* (Cambridge, 1982). For the shaping of the modern idea of the state, see Quentin Skinner, 'The State', in Terence Ball, James Farr, and Russell Hanson (eds.), *Political Innovation and Conceptual Change* (Cambridge, 1989), 90–131. For the political and social vision of Hume and Smith, see Istvan Hont and Michael Ignatieff (eds.), *Wealth and Virtue* (Cambridge, 1983). Durkheim's conception of the cognitive role of the state is set out in his *Professional Ethics and Civic Morals* (London, 1958).

The impact on modern political authority of ever-tightening incorporation into a global economy is discussed in John Dunn (ed.), *The Economic Limits to Modern Politics* (Cambridge, 1990). The significance of Keynes's attempt to re-establish political control over (and responsibility for) economic life can be considered by comparing Peter Clarke, *The Keynesian Revolution in the Making, 1924–1936* (Oxford, 1988) with Peter A. Hall (ed.), *The Political Power of Economic Ideas: Keynesianism across Nations* (Princeton, NJ, 1989).

For especially striking discussions of the social and political roots of Greek thinking and of the historical reach of aspects of that thinking, see Geoffrey Lloyd, *Magic, Reason and Experience* (Cambridge, 1979); and Bernard Williams, 'Philosophy', in M. I. Finley (ed.), *The Legacy of Greece: A New Appraisal* (Oxford, 1981), 202–55. The issue of the residual significance and scope of the cognitive authority of the natural sciences is one of the most pervasive and bemusing aspects of contemporary thinking. An interesting (if beleaguered) attempt to apply some of Habermas's conclusions about it to important issues in modern politics is John Dryzek's *Discursive Democracy* (Cambridge, 1990). One of the most sceptical interpreters of that significance, Richard Rorty, applies his own approach to the issues raised by recent North American feminism in

'Feminism and Pragmatism', *Michigan Quarterly Review*, 6: 2 (Spring 1991), 231–58. Joseph Schumpeter, *Capitalism, Socialism and Democracy* (London, 1950), remains the most powerful interpretation of the workings of modern democratic institutions. The historical circumstances in which a variety of societies in the twentieth century set out on the Marxist-Leninist detour are assessed in John Dunn, *Modern Revolutions*, 2nd edn. (Cambridge, 1989). The clearest perspective on the causes of the collapse of socialist planning is W. Brus and K. Laski, *From Marx to the Market* (Oxford, 1988). Timothy Garton Ash, *We the People* (London, 1990) gives a wonderfully vivid picture of the collapse of Communism in Eastern Europe. Adam Przeworski, *Democracy and the Market* (Cambridge, 1991) is the most penetrating analysis of the political mechanisms and implications of the collapse.

For differing views of the reasonable range of democratic hope today see Roberto Mangabeira Unger, *Politics*, 3 vols. (Cambridge, 1987); Robert Dahl, *Democracy and its Critics* (New Haven, Conn., 1989); and John Dunn, *Interpreting Political Responsibility* (Cambridge and Princeton, NJ, 1990).

Index

Index compiled by Frank Pert